TECHNIQUES OF SOCIAL INFLUENCE

Every day we are asked to fulfil others' requests, and we make regular requests of others too, seeking compliance with our desires, commands and suggestions. This accessible text provides a uniquely in-depth overview of the different social influence techniques people use in order to improve the chances of their requests being fulfilled. It both describes each of the techniques in question and explores the research behind them, considering questions such as: How do we know that they work? Under what conditions are they more or less likely to be effective? How might individuals successfully resist attempts by others to influence them?

The book groups social influence techniques according to a common characteristic: for instance, early chapters describe "sequential" techniques, and techniques involving egotistic mechanisms, such as using the name of one's interlocutor. Later chapters present techniques based on gestures and facial movements, and others based on the use of specific words, re-examining on the way whether "please" really is a magic word. In every case, author Dariusz Dolinski discusses the existing experimental studies exploring their effectiveness, and how that effectiveness is enhanced or reduced under certain conditions. The book draws on historical material as well as the most up-to-date research, and unpicks the methodological and theoretical controversies involved.

The ideal introduction for psychology graduates and undergraduates studying social influence and persuasion, *Techniques of Social Influence* will also appeal to scholars and students in neighbouring disciplines, as well as interested marketing professionals and practitioners in related fields.

Dariusz Dolinski is Professor at the University of Social Sciences and Humanities, Wrocław Faculty in Poland, editor of the *Polish Psychological Bulletin*, president of the Polish Association of Social Psychology and past president of the Committee for Psychology of the Polish Academy of Sciences.

TECHNIQUES OF SOCIAL INFLUENCE

The psychology of gaining compliance

Dariusz Dolinski

Routledge
Taylor & Francis Group

LONDON AND NEW YORK

First published 2016
by Routledge
27 Church Road, Hove, East Sussex BN3 2FA

and by Routledge
711 Third Avenue, New York, NY 10017

Routledge is an imprint of the Taylor & Francis Group, an informa business

British Library Cataloguing in Publication Data
A catalogue record for this book is available from the British Library

Library of Congress Cataloging in Publication Data
Dolinski, Dariusz.
Techniques of social influence : the psychology of gaining compliance /
Dariusz Dolinski. — 1st Edition.
pages cm
Includes bibliographical references and index.
1. Social influence. I. Title.
HM1176.D65 2015
302'.13—dc23
2015004167

ISBN: 978-1-138-81517-9 (hbk)
ISBN: 978-1-138-81519-3 (pbk)
ISBN: 978-1-315-74687-6 (ebk)

Typeset in Bembo
by Swales & Willis Ltd, Exeter, Devon, UK
Printed in Great Britain by Ashford Colour Press Ltd.

CONTENTS

ILLUSTRATIONS

Figures

Tables

1

INTRODUCTION

As a rule, the introduction is where the author explains to the reader what the book is about. Before I do that, however, I will take the liberty of a brief digression of a personal nature. Whenever I'm at some sort of gathering and find I am acquainted only with the host, my interactions with other guests go off "without a hitch". I'm not a particularly shy person, so it's rather easy for me to get to know others and to talk to them about more or less serious subjects. Problems begin when they ask me what I do for a living. My answer – that I am a psychologist – provokes a feeling of unease in my interlocutors. "So you must be observing us and analyzing," I hear. "What do you think about us?" My answer, that I'm not observing or analyzing anybody but, just like everybody else, having a beer, chatting about Almodóvar's latest film, Kundera's books, recent sports events or political happenings, isn't taken at face value by others. It gets worse when the conversation turns to questions like "So what is it you do exactly? Do you put people through psycho-therapy, or devise intelligence tests?" I respond that I'm not a therapist and that I've never created any intelligence test, and nothing would indicate that I ever will. I explain that for many years I have been engaged in the study of social influence techniques. When I give a few examples by way of explanation, opinions about me are uniformly devastating: I am a guy who sits in a lab and dreams up schemes for effectively manipulating people.

As it is, psychologists concerned with social influence techniques usually aren't thinking up new tricks. Our approach to the subject is just the opposite. The metaphor of *full-cycle social psychology,* applied by Robert Cialdini (1980), would seem to be a good illustration of this. The *full cycle* is a construction under which a social influence technique emerges in social life, and after it is "discovered", investigated and described by scientists, it winds up back in that "real life". So, a psychologist interested in these techniques observes the tricks applied by individuals whose professions or social roles involve them exerting influence on others.

He thus watches the behaviour of a waiter with an interest in his client leaving a generous tip, a car salesman focused on getting people to buy automobiles from him, door-to-door salespeople determined to leave a set of knives in someone's home and walk out with a fat wallet. Also of interest to the psychologist may be those working for charitable causes who are skilled in acquiring donations from sponsors, as well as politicians who quickly gain in popularity, which translates into votes from constituents. Of equal interest may also be observing a married couple in which one partner is able to convince the other to agree to far-reaching concessions.

Every social psychologist has a wealth of opportunities to observe practitioners of social influence techniques. I live and work in Wrocław, a city located in the centre of Europe – and more precisely in south-west Poland – with around 700,000 inhabitants. Yesterday I got out of my car, which I had parked around 200 metres from the Market Square, where I had arranged to meet up with a friend. While exiting my car I was approached by a man showing me where I could find a place to park, waving at me while I helplessly drove along the kerb in search of a free spot. I hadn't even got out of the car when he offered me "a deal" on some car air fresheners. Why not? He was polite and pleasant, he had helped me and he also had one of my favourite scents, vanilla. A moment after this transaction and after I had closed my car door, a young boy who seemed around 12 years old ran up to me, bringing a bucket and an offer to wash my car. I might have taken him up on it if it weren't for the fact that the water in his bucket looked even dirtier than the exterior of my vehicle. Besides that, I was probably feeling a bit 'had' by the air freshener salesman, whose offer wasn't really that cheap, so I decided I wouldn't just agree to everything people offered me. I set out briskly for the Market Square. Along the way I passed by two sellers of a newspaper I usually read (I wasn't enticed, as I had already bought a copy earlier), one seller of another newspaper (I didn't buy it because I don't care for its politics) and one vagrant (I didn't give him a cent). I did, however, take three flyers (two from language schools and one from a glassworks), which I immediately placed in the bin. I always take flyers. I know that some people, usually youngsters, are paid by the hour, but others are paid for the number of flyers they give out. I think this is a rather thankless and poorly paid job. Taking a flyer and throwing it into a bin, which is usually nearby, doesn't cost me a thing. So I usually let people press flyers into my open hand, then maybe I take a look at them or not and throw them away immediately. On the way to the Market Square I was additionally tempted by storefronts promising incredible thrills inside, and a bank tried to talk me into taking out an unbelievably attractive loan. Before I had made it to City Hall, I walked by a man who resembled Lenin and was standing on a fruit box holding a giant red flag in his hand. At his feet lay a prominently displayed hat for tossing money into, and it contained 10- and 20-zloty banknotes. Obviously, the idea was to prevent someone from thinking that they could just toss in some loose change. Not even for a moment did I consider throwing anything in there. Next, I encountered a man dressed up in a suit and tie who tried to press a business card into my hand while explaining the virtues of a central vacuum system, and a painting salesman encouraging me to pick up an image of a beautiful deer in rutting season, saying that I could get it at steep discount while helping young artists at the same time. In both cases, I managed to not break my stride and avoided closer interaction.

The car fragrance salesman, the owner of a bucket with water, the panhandler, the Lenin lookalike, the newspaper salesmen and the deer painting peddler . . . in most of these cases, the people involved applied some more or less refined social influence technique. These techniques – as the aforementioned "sample of events" demonstrates – are relentlessly used by practitioners of social influence. I assume that you, the reader, have had experiences similar to mine, even if you live in another part of the globe. Regardless of their geographic location, practitioners of social influence all want one and the same – they want us to order and purchase various things from them, to give money for their causes, to fill in the surveys, questionnaires and other forms they put in our faces, to leave them generous tips and to undertake all sorts of obligations. We succumb to such pressure – sometimes subtle, sometimes less so – dozens or even hundreds of times a day. Quite often, as Daniel Howard indicates (1995), practitioners of social influence apply techniques consisting of connecting various methods into a chain, which makes it even more difficult to defend oneself from undesired social influence. Why do social influence techniques work? Why do they work even when we are perfectly aware that someone is attempting to influence us? Contrary to appearances, these are very difficult questions.

The basic question a psychologist who has succeeded in sniffing out some particular trick applied by practitioners of social influence must pose concerns the actual effectiveness of the technique. For example, does the way a shoe salesman usually "can't find" a pair of shoes in the right size for the customer, but then manages to locate "the last pair" after a few minutes, really increase the chances that the customer will buy those shoes? Perhaps he would be equally inclined to buy them if the salesman took them out straight away? How to determine this? There is no better means than a carefully planned and meticulously performed experiment, or even better – a series of experiments. If the results of such empirical studies in fact reveal the effectiveness of the trick under analysis, then one of science's most important questions must follow: "Why?" Why is a given technique a successful instrument of social influence? Here, the investigator primarily makes use of his knowledge about the mechanisms governing people's reactions. Over the last few decades, psychology has made significant strides in this area.

However, many things remain uncertain, unclear and opaque. This is why there may be several potential mechanisms underlying the effectiveness of a particular social influence technique. The following series of experiments is thus aimed at determining which of them is in fact responsible for a particular trick's effectiveness. Uncovering the mechanism thus also leads to the generation of knowledge about factors that can enhance, sometimes significantly, the effectiveness of the studied behaviour. The precisely verified and described technique now becomes an element of psychological knowledge. As such, it is also often propagated during all sorts of training sessions, university classes or seminars. It is also sometimes the case that a description of the technique can be found in books, such as this one. As a consequence, the technique can become an instrument of social influence for those who learn of it thanks to this manuscript. In this way, the circle of social psychology described by Robert Cialdini is complete. It has closed. The technique was born in real social life and has returned to it.

The great majority of psychological influences described in this book have travelled a similar path: from practice, through detailed empirical and theoretical analysis, to practice. It is no different with the techniques that my collaborators and I have studied for many years. We thus stake no claim to being the authors of most of these tricks. They are not our inventions. They are the creations of anonymous practitioners of social influence over thousands of years, individuals who derive all sorts of benefits, not only material, from their effectiveness. To obtain a full picture, it is necessary to say that, at times (although rarely), psychologists think up social influence techniques, or somewhat accidentally uncover them in the course of conducting empirical research.

In this book I also describe the results of various experiments by a host of social psychologists conducting research around the world. My primary objective is to introduce the reader to the current state of knowledge in the area of social influence techniques. At the same time, however, I devote significant space to research conducted by myself and my co-experimenters. I do this not because I feel our experiments are more interesting or more important than others; the possibility of offering a detailed presentation of one's own research and thoughts is simply a natural privilege enjoyed by every author. I have decided to take advantage of it.

In works dedicated to social influence, various means of organizing the presented material have been adopted. The author of one of the most popular psychological books, Robert Cialdini (2001), states that six main laws or principles of social influence can be distinguished. They are the principles of reciprocation, commitment and consistency, social proof, liking, authority and scarcity. Cialdini dedicates successive chapters of his best-selling monograph *Influence: Science and practice* to them. This approach allows him to provide a good structure to the presented material. There is no doubt in my mind that the aforementioned principles are of particular significance, and they allow for an excellent explanation of various phenomena belonging to the area of social influence. The approach consisting in an argument constructed on six rules of social influence does, however, have certain flaws. First and foremost, it should be acknowledged that all techniques of social influence (or at least the majority of them) can be counted as one of these rules. Cialdini himself is of this opinion, but this is not so obvious to many other researchers. The framework of the aforementioned six basic rules is a poor fit for such techniques as those associated with emotions experienced by people, techniques based on the sudden induction of incogitance or those making use of egotistical mechanisms.

It is also worth noting that Cialdini uses descriptions of various tricks and techniques as specific illustrations of the rules he himself has differentiated, rendering the book coherent and believable. The problem is, among researchers there is no consensus as to the psychological basis for the effectiveness of particular means of exerting influence on people. In the relevant literature we may observe vigorous debate over the psychological mechanisms that underpin the effectiveness of assorted social influence techniques. Thus it is often possible to take issue with Cialdini's "classification" of particular techniques.

In this book, the problem of organizing the content is resolved in a different manner. Pride of place is given to descriptions of particular social influence techniques and empirical studies testing their effectiveness. In addition, competing interpretations of techniques and research results under discussion are presented, and it is my hope that they will assist readers in coming to their own conclusions on the accuracy of each of them.

It is thus time to enumerate the subjects to be addressed in the individual chapters of this book. You are presently reading the first of them; it is an introduction to the subject of social influence and to the content of this manuscript. Chapter 2 examines what are referred to as sequential social influence techniques. They all consist in the main request being preceded by a different one. Depending on the particular technique, the secondary request can be harder or easier to fulfil than the one that follows it. The subject's contact with the initial request — meaning whether he fulfils it, attempts to fulfil it or rejects it — influences the probability that he will want to fulfil the next one. Research on the effectiveness of sequential techniques and the search for mechanisms underlying them have a long and rich tradition in the science of psychology, which is why I have devoted many pages to describing them.

The remaining chapters are shorter. This is not because I feel the techniques presented in them are uninteresting, but rather because there is far less empirical research concerning them. The third chapter contains a presentation of techniques associated with people's need to satisfy their ego and for self-presentation. Individuals undertake all sorts of activities throughout their lives in order to maintain self-esteem and to make a positive impression on others. These motivations can, in some cases, result in them being more inclined to act on requests, suggestions and orders addressed to them. Some social influence techniques are thus grounded in just these human needs.

Chapter 4 focuses on the content and form of messages directed at an individual on whom social pressure is being applied. Here I attempt to demonstrate the complex role words play in processes of social influence. A specific phrase or an individual word appearing in a particular moment of a social interaction can significantly affect the reaction of an individual to whom we turn with a request or suggestion. The thesis that interpersonal interactions are of a dynamic nature is a truism. That this dynamic can find itself under the control of the individual forming the request, and thus take the form of a social influence technique, is itself not a truism.

The fifth chapter describes just those techniques in which something out of the ordinary occurs when one person asks another for something. Chapter 6 contains descriptions of successful influence techniques based on emotional mechanisms. Here we can observe just how significant readiness to fulfil a request is on the influence of affective states experienced by the addressee of said request.

The seventh chapter – "A few more issues and final remarks" – as the term would suggest, closes out the book. Alongside a summary, I grant myself the liberty of presenting some of my reflections and doubts. I also consider the possibility of using psychological knowledge in practice and others of an ethical character, of particular importance concerning the exertion of influence on others. That should suffice to describe what you, dear Reader, will find in this book.

There is one more thing that requires clarification, something that with all certainty concerns social influence but is not in this work. In the book I focus almost exclusively on techniques designed to induce people to behave in a particular manner. However, I neither present nor analyze techniques for influencing cognitive attitudes. It must be stated clearly that such an approach under which the researcher is primarily interested in observable behaviours is not, at present, the dominant one in psychology. Quite the opposite, we may even say that it is "unfashionable". As jokingly stated in the title of an article by Roy Baumeister, Kathleen Vohs and David Funder (2007), contemporary psychology has become "a science of self-reports and finger movements". Since the 1970s there has been a steady decline of interest on the part of psychologists in non-verbal human behaviour. While writing their article, Baumeister and his colleagues opened up the then newest edition (January 2006) of the *Journal of Personality and Social Psychology*, one of the most influential psychological journals. And what did they find? The articles contain descriptions of individuals' judgements and opinions. The contemporary researcher no longer follows in the footsteps of his predecessors, introspective types who listened to what subjects had to say; he rather asks them to press the appropriate button on a keyboard. The psychologist thus studies behaviours . . . consisting of pecking at a keyboard, he explores . . . finger movements! "We have to break up!" cries out Robert Cialdini – the leading researcher on altruism and social influence – in the title of his 2009 article. He observes that psychology is focusing more and more on explaining behaviours, while ignoring the actual causes of those behaviours. It is hardly an exaggeration to say that social psychology, in its drive to explain, has lost sight of just what is to be explained. In some places psychologists have got themselves into such a quagmire that they are only explaining processes of explanation.

The book which you hold in your hands is thus a continuation of Cialdini's appeal "We have to break up!" It focuses on the reality of human behaviour, and not on their judgements, opinions or verbal declarations of particular behaviours. While this is an unfashionable approach, I follow it in the firm conviction that it is a proper one. Experiments studying real human behaviours are difficult to conduct, time-consuming and labour intensive. It is far easier to just ask subjects to imagine themselves in a situation and say how they would behave . . . simpler, quicker, easier . . . but doubts of a fundamental nature arise: do we, in this manner, get closer to the truth of human behaviour, or do we get further from that truth?

One of the most important experiments in the history of social psychology was conducted by Stanley Milgram (1974). Milgram demonstrated that in certain conditions the majority of participants in an experiment, ostensibly concerning the effect of punishment on learning, can be induced into shocking another participant with 450 volts of electricity. However, if we were to ask people how they would behave in the same circumstances, hardly anyone would be able to imagine themselves in the role of a person zapping another with such a horrendous amount of electricity. Things are similar in the case of investigations of social influence techniques. In Chapter 5 I describe research concerning the role of touch. As it occurs, when an individual is asked to do some favour, such as signing a petition, the chances that this request will be fulfilled are greater when we gently grasp this person by the arm or forearm. I told my students to imagine a stranger asking them to sign a petition, and then asked them whether the fact that this stranger were delicately touching their arm at the same time would influence the probability that they would agree to do so. They responded that it would obviously have an influence! But . . . they were convinced that the touch of a stranger would result in their refusal to fulfil the request! There are countless examples demonstrating that investigations of real human behaviours generate an entirely different picture than research on imagined own reactions.

Thus, in this book I consistently describe research concerning real social behaviours, and not work concerning verbal declarations about such behaviours. What is more, a clear majority of experiments presented within are field studies in which people are studied in their natural environment (in parks, libraries, restaurants, at universities or in their own homes) and not in a psychological laboratory. Furthermore, in the majority of these experiments, the subjects were unaware that they were interacting with psychologists conducting scientific research; they did not know that they were participating in an experiment. These facts give us the right to be confident in the veracity of the results, and that they demonstrate how people really behave in various situations and what conditions their reactions.

As the author, I obviously bear full responsibility for the content presented in this book. However, I would like its readers to be aware that it would not have come about without my friends, colleagues and collaborators – and also my students – with whom I had countless opportunities to conduct scientific discussions, debates and polemics, and from whom I have learned so much. I deeply wish to thank them sincerely for their comments, which have helped me to avoid assorted errors, vagueness and inaccuracies. I would also like to thank Matthew La Fontaine for his strong language support. I'm truly grateful to Routledge and their staff for their cooperation and lending their hand at all stages of producing of the book. Thanks are due, as well, to Christopher Carpenter, Michael Hogg and one anonymous reviewer for their insightful comments on an earlier version of parts of the text and to Robert Cialdini and Nicolas Gueguen who expressed opinions about the final version of this book. I acknowledge the Ministry of Science and Higher Education, whose grants (N N106 327339 and BST WROC/2013/A/02) helped make this book possible.

Last but not least, I would also like to thank everyone who has decided to read this book. For them (and for myself) I hope the time sacrificed reading it will prove well spent.

2

SEQUENTIAL TECHNIQUES OF SOCIAL INFLUENCE

"Honey, are we finally going to paint the walls in the hallway?" a wife asks her husband. "Yes, we talked about that already," the husband replies. "Maybe we can remodel the bathroom too, since there's already going to be such a mess, let's just do it all together?!"

This sort of conversation is an example of what are referred to as sequential techniques of social influence. The wife starts discussing remodelling the bathroom only after she has been assured by her husband that the walls in the hallway will get painted. Sequential techniques are based in the assumption that we can boost the potential of another person's acceding to our request, succumbing to urging, taking advantage of a proposal or carrying out a demand by presenting a different request (suggestion, proposal, command) first. Particular techniques assume that the initial request will be fulfilled (at least with a verbal declaration, as in the example given at the beginning of the chapter), will be rejected or will simply be impossible to be fulfilled. Our presentation of sequential techniques of social influence will begin with the first type of situation.

Foot-in-the-door

Proverbs highlighting people's tendency to escalate their demands are seemingly present in nearly every culture. In the USA and United Kingdom people say "give them an inch, they'll take a mile"; Germans and Poles – while speaking different languages – jointly declare that "give someone a finger, they'll take your whole hand". Both Hungarians and Spanish speakers are in agreement that "if you give someone your hand, they'll take the entire arm". The essential idea in all of these expressions is the same: if someone convinces us to cede a bit of ground, the chances increase that we will take a much larger step back. To look at it from a different perspective: if we want someone to agree to fulfil a difficult request, we should first ask him to fulfil a clearly simpler one.

If we look at these issues from the perspective of social influence techniques and their efficacy, is it really the case that if someone has reason to believe a direct request will go unfulfilled, the chances of it succeeding can be enhanced by first lodging a less serious request? The first to attempt at answering this question were American psychologists Jonathan Freedman and Scott Fraser (1966). Their research constitutes what were likely history's first experiments exploring social influence techniques.

The participants in Freedman and Fraser's experiments (1966) were housewives; they were contacted by telephone and asked to allow a few men to enter their homes. They were told that the men were members of a consumer's organization and their task was to enumerate and classify all the household products. It turned out that only around 22% of those asked gave their consent. The researchers treated this group as the control group. The experimental group was comprised of other housewives, who were also called by phone but to whom a much simpler request was submitted: they were asked to answer a few questions about the kinds of soaps they used. The vast majority of women agreed and responded to all of the questions given. A few days later, the experimenters called those women again and asked them to allow a few men to visit them so they could enumerate and classify the household products. It turned out that in this case the women were more inclined to let the unfamiliar men into their home than were people in control conditions. In these circumstances, consent to a visit from the unknown men was given by 53% of respondents. Why was this so? One answer stands out: the women who had previously answered questions about their consumer behaviours felt their telephone interlocutor was someone they were familiar with (or at least represented a company they already knew). It is commonly known that people are more likely to fulfil the requests of people (and likely institutions) they are familiar with than of those they are not. The results obtained by the study should not strike us as unusual, all the more so considering that it involved participants letting someone into their home, where the element of trust would seem to be crucial. We hasten to mention, however, that Freedman and Fraser were testing a hypothesis assuming that the key to acquiring consent to the fulfilment of a difficult request is to first convince people to perform an easier task. Thus we are faced with a dilemma: does the greater percentage of women in the experimental cohort consenting to allowing a group of unknown men into their homes result from the fact that the women previously fulfilled some request, or rather because they consider those men to constitute acquaintances, at least to a certain degree? Freedman and Fraser foresaw this ambiguity, and therefore brought two more groups into their experiment's structure.

In the first of them, the women were asked to give a brief interview. After agreeing, they were then told that, in fact, only initial registration was being conducted, and that the interview would be held at a later time. In the case of the second group, the experimenter only informed the study participants that a special organization had been formed that investigated consumers' behaviours, and he explained that he wanted the women to be aware of that fact. When the women from those two groups were again contacted by telephone a few days later and asked if they would agree to host a group of men who would enumerate and classify all the household products in their home, this request was not fulfilled with significantly greater frequency than in the case of the control group (consent was given by around 33% and 28% of women, respectively). We can thus observe that the factor increasing pliancy in the face of a serious, difficult request is previous submission to a similar, clearly easier request; the mere earlier contact with an individual who then formulated a serious request was not enough to generate increased compliance. Freedman and Fraser thus proved in this experiment that the trick "first a small request, then a big one – the real one" is an effective social influence technique. They also proposed the name *foot-in-the-door* for this technique. The name would seem to reflect the essence of that technique: in order to enter someone's home (to get a lot), it is first necessary to get the owner's permission to put your foot in the door (to get a little).

In order to determine whether the results of the study under discussion were fully reliable, and also to find answers to a range of other questions, the authors conducted another experiment. This time, they started with the assumption that it would be relatively difficult to convince the owners of homes located along the roadside to give their consent to the installation of large billboards in their yards displaying messages to drivers asking them to drive carefully. Indeed, who would like to have a giant billboard in their yard, blocking their houses? As it turned out, individuals selected at random were quite resistant to the idea; fewer than 17% of those questioned gave their consent. In the remaining four study groups, 2 weeks before the request to install a billboard was formulated, they were asked for their agreement to do something far easier. Participants were asked either to put up a small sign or to sign a petition, and the issue was either safe driving or keeping California beautiful. It can easily be observed that in the case of two of the groups, the first (initial) and the second (main) request addressed the same issue – improving road safety. In the case of the remaining two groups, the first request concerned a different issue (keeping California beautiful) from the second (road safety). Regardless, in two groups we encountered a similarity in the actions required of study participants – both cases involved expressing consent to the installation of visual propaganda (a sticker in the case of the initial request, and a billboard in the case of the target request). In the other two conditions, there was a discrepancy in the character of the two tasks given to participants (first to sign a petition, then to consent to placing visual propaganda on their property).

Freedman and Fraser were of course interested in seeing which experimental groups would give their consent to placing a billboard in their front yards with greater frequency than the control groups. The results of this experiment can be reviewed in Table 2.1.

As we can see, in the first group (similar themes, similar nature of tasks), consent to putting up a billboard was given by over two-thirds of those asked. In the remaining three groups, the percentage of participants agreeing to fulfil the target request was lower, yet even this was clearly higher than in the control group.

The results of this experiment indicate that the "foot-in-the-door" technique is at its most effective when both requests are similar in content (in this case, both of them concern road traffic safety) and involve similar activity (expressing consent to

TABLE 2.1 Percentage of subjects complying with the large request in Freedman and Fraser (1966) experiment

Issues	Task			
	Similar	N	Different	N
Similar	76.0	25	47.8	23
Different	47.6	21	47.4	19
One-Contact 16.7 (N = 24)				

Source: *Journal of Personality and Social Psychology*, 1966, vol. 4, p. 201
Copyright 1966 by the American Psychological Association, Inc.

the presence of visual propaganda). On the other hand, however, it is not necessary for any of the aforementioned similarities to be strong in order for the technique to succeed (i.e. in order for the addressee's fulfilment of the target request to be more likely than in conditions in which the request is made directly). Increased compliance was observed even in situations when both requests concerned different issues and required different actions. It is worth emphasizing that the aforementioned dissimilarity is not total. Indeed, both requests concern some sort of engagement on behalf of the common good.

What is the psychological mechanism that results in people who fulfilled an easier introductory request then being more inclined to fulfil a significantly more serious one? Before we try to answer this question, let us consider two details in the experimental procedure applied by Freedman and Fraser. First, one fact that stands out is that the initial request (sign a petition or put on a sticker) and the target request (install a billboard) were formulated by entirely different people. What is important and should be emphasized is that the person who requested consent to install a billboard behaved as though he had nothing in common with the person who had made the introductory request. Second, it should be noted that 2 weeks passed between the initial and the second request. The first of these facts indicates that the "foot-in-the-door" technique does not owe its effectiveness to any interpersonal mechanisms (e.g. the establishment of a bond between the person formulating the request and the person to whom it is addressed, nor any particular obligation resulting from such an interaction that would induce the addressee of the request to fulfil further ones). The second of the aforementioned facts, however, suggests that the technique under discussion here is not based on any sort of short-term mechanism. With these issues in mind, Freedman and Fraser took on the assumption that an individual who agrees without being placed under pressure (threats, blackmail, offer of financial reward, etc.) to fulfil the first request will then begin to view himself as "the kind of person who does this sort of thing, who agrees to requests made by strangers, who takes action on things he believes in, who cooperates with good causes" (Freedman & Fraser, 1966, p. 201). The authors posit the presence of a principle that was later elaborated in full by Daryl Bem (1967, 1972) and is presently referred to as *self-perception theory*.

If you ask a man whether his wife likes soap operas, he might respond "I think so, after all, she does watch them all the time". But what if we pose the same question to the wife? If she said, "I think I do, after all, I watch them every day", then it could be said her process of deduction about her own TV preferences is exactly the same as her husband's. In Bem's opinion, this would be nothing unusual. The answers to questions about what leads to one's own reactions, decisions and choices are generally located in the external world (someone induced us to do something, someone forced us, someone offered a large reward, someone did a favour for us previously). However, in the absence of such factors, or when they are not very convincing as explanations for our own reactions, we come to the conclusion that the root causes lie within – in our own attitudes, convictions and inclinations. The woman in our example, wondering whether she likes soap operas, first considers whether it's because her friend forces her to watch them, or maybe because she only watches them because she has just one TV station, or maybe because a research company pays her to. If it turns out that this "review of the circumstances" fails to indicate any external factors influencing her choice to watch soap operas, she will then search for the answers inside herself. She thus comes to the conclusion that she likes this form of entertainment. Let us observe that not only does Bem assume the process of deduction about one's own preferences or attitudes takes a course analogical to that of deduction about the preferences of others, but he also turns the association between our attitudes and actions upside-down. It is commonly known that our attitudes lead us to engage in some behaviours and to refrain from others. If I like books, I read them. If I like exotic animals, I go to the zoo. If I'm happy I laugh, and if I'm sad I cry; Bem does not call this association into question, but he does ask: how can I know that I like books and exotic animals? Because I read a lot, and I spend my free time at the zoo. How do I know that I am happy or sad? Because I laugh out loud, or I feel tears streaming down my cheeks. Of course, Bem does not declare that thinking about the causes of one's own behaviours is the sole source of knowledge about self. Sometimes, however, we have no other foundations for coming to conclusions about our own preferences and attitudes.

Possibly the most suggestive evidence in support of Bem's theory is an experiment conducted by Fritz Strack, Leonard Martin and Sabine Stepper (1988). The experimenters asked a portion of their study's participants to assess some jokey cartoons. Another group assessed the same jokes while holding a pencil between their teeth. Still another group assessed the jokes with a pencil between their lips and with their teeth closed. What was the result? The jokes seemed the funniest to those who held the pencil between their teeth, and the least funny to those who held it using their lips (Strack et al., 1988). Thus it was the loosening or tightening of the facial muscles associated with expressing joy and amusement, or disgust and distaste, lead to us concluding that we find something more or less humorous! I know that a joke is funny because I feel the activity of my zygomatic muscle extending from the base of my ear to the corner of my mouth. I know that it irritates me and seems stupid because I can perceive the activity of other facial muscles.

The theory of self-perception is most often referred to in the literature as the psychological underpinning for the effectiveness of the "foot-in-the-door" technique. Someone who accedes to the first, initial request begins to question why he has done so. Not finding any sensible external explanation (nobody has blackmailed him, nobody has offered him serious money for doing so), he arrives at the conclusion that his own preferences and convictions must be at the heart of the decision. Put differently, he comes to the conclusion that he possesses attitudes and convictions that are consistent with that decision. Owing to the process of self-perception he becomes a psychologically somewhat different person, a person who now defines or expresses himself in a slightly different fashion. The next, more serious request is now in line with this new self-image, thus it comes as no surprise that the chances he will agree to it increase.

Several decades have passed since the publication of the experiments by Freedman and Fraser described above. In that time, many experiments demonstrating the effectiveness of the "foot-in-the-door" technique have been conducted, encompassing quite a few areas of life. For example, it can be used to boost the chances of receiving large donations to charitable causes. This has been explored in several experiments, with direct practical implications. Patricia Pliner, Heather Hart, Joanne Kohl and Dory Saari (1974) did this in conjunction with a campaign in support of the fight against cancer. One day they handed out stickers with messages about caring for those afflicted by cancer to randomly selected residents of a small town, and asked them to display the stickers on their clothes. Not once did someone refuse. The next day, donations for the fight against cancer were collected among residents of the same town. It turned out that those who had previously agreed to sport the stickers were more generous than others. Joseph Schwarzwald, Aharon Bizman and Moshe Raz (1983) asked randomly selected individuals to sign a petition to authorities concerning funding for a disabled persons' social club. Almost everyone approached agreed to give their support. Two weeks later, people were asked to donate money. In this case as well it turned out that people who had previously been asked to do a small favour were more likely to reach for their wallets.

Peter Reingen (1978) decided to examine whether the positive effect of the foot-in-the-door technique could be achieved in the framework of single interactions. He asked students on a university campus to make a charitable donation. It turned out that he was much more effective when the participants were first asked to answer a few questions in a survey concerning the organization (engaged in the fight against heart disease) on whose behalf the money was being collected. Similar positive effects were noted by Morton Goldman (1986) while conducting a campaign for the municipal zoo, by Robert Bell and Matthew Cholerton (1994) as they collected funds for educational campaigns to raise awareness about AIDS and ways of avoiding the disease, and by Sebastien Meineri and Nicolas Gueguen (2014) encouraging people to get involved in protecting the natural environment.

Jacob Hornik and Tamar Zaig (1991) demonstrated that the technique under discussion can prove very helpful in conditions involving a telephone survey with questions about issues that respondents are not particularly keen on discussing (e.g. income, sexual education for children, watching pornographic films, etc.). The portion of respondents refusing to answer questions in such surveys is generally high, which leads to the study sample losing its representative character. Hornik and Zaig show that a double-digit increase in the readiness of respondents to answer such questions can be attained if they are first asked personal but less invasive questions.

The foot-in-the-door technique is exploited extensively in totalitarian political systems. New regimes rarely require extremely immoral acts from their subjects at the beginning, but rather step up their demands over time, escalating the expectations and requirements addressed to them (Gilbert, 1981).

Meta-analyses aimed at determining the conditions necessary for the foot-in-the-door technique to be effective show that it is successful both when the first and the second request are formulated by the same individual and when two different people are involved in the process (Fern, Monroe & Avila, 1986). The length of time between requests and the difficulty of the initial request are relatively inconsequential (Beaman, Cole, Preston, Klentz & Steblay, 1983; Dillard, Hunter & Burgoon 1984; Fern et al., 1986). It also turned out that the foot-in-the-door effect can be achieved even without the queried individual fulfilling an initial request; it is enough that he attempts to do so in spite of adversity. In one such experiment, individuals walking along the pavement were approached (Dolinski, 2000). Participants were randomly assigned to one of two conditions: experimental and control. In the experimental conditions, a young man approached participants and asked for directions to Zubrzyckiego Street (in fact, the city in which the study was conducted has no such street). The normal response was to stop and think for a moment, then respond "I don't know", "I don't have any idea" or something similar. Next, after the participant had gone another 100 metres down the street, he was approached by a second experimenter, a young woman. She stood on the pavement with a large bag, pointed at the top floor of a multi-storey building and asked for a favour, saying that she wanted to visit her friend living on the fifth floor, but that she had an unusually heavy bag, which there was no good reason to carry up there. She then asked the participant to watch the bag for a few minutes. It turned out that while 34% of participants agreed in the control condition to watch the bag, 58% consented to do so in the experimental condition.

While there have already been a large number of experiments concerning the effectiveness of the foot-in-the-door technique, far fewer have addressed whether the mechanism of self-perception in fact lies at the heart of its success. As we shall see, this is a complex issue. Miron Zuckerman, Michele Lazzaro and Diane Waldgeir (1979) observed that, in accordance with Bem's theory, if the fulfilment of the first request is accompanied by the promise of a reward, the process of self-perception should be halted. Individuals often have a purely external explanation for their reactions. As a consequence, such conditions should not lead to increased readiness to carry out a second, more serious request. The authors called people randomly selected from the phone book and asked them to participate in a 5-minute discussion on pedestrian safety in the city. Half of the participants were offered a reward of $1.50 for their involvement, while in the case of the other half there was no mention of any reward at all. After two days another experimenter called study participants and asked them to give a 25-minute interview concerning the household products they used. The experimental design also included a control group whose cohort was asked straight away to participate in such an interview. It turned out that in the control group, 45% of participants agreed to carry out the request. Participants from the group that had given the 5-minute interview for no reward agreed with greater readiness (64.3%), while in the group that received an award for participation in the short interview only 33.3% of participants consented. Such results are entirely consistent with self-perception theory. The absence of external motivation (in this case, a reward) for fulfilling the first, relatively simple request induces people to think of themselves in categories such as "since I did THAT, then I am THAT KIND of person". However, monetary compensation for doing so leads to explaining one's own behaviour as "I did it because they paid me". This type of thinking, in turn, prevents the occurrence of the "since I did THAT, then I am THAT KIND of person" line of reasoning, and the individual is not inclined to do similar things in the future in the absence of some benefit. The link between offering a reward for fulfilling an initial request and decreased effectiveness of the foot-in-the-door technique is also confirmed by the results of various meta-analyses (e.g. Burger, 1999; Dillard et al., 1984).

It may be assumed that self-perception also does not appear in conditions involving the presence of an explanation other than non-monetary reward, which unequivocally explains the individual's compliance with the initial request. Taking this assumption as his starting point, Seymour Uranowitz (1975) asked women shopping in supermarkets to guard his shopping bag for a few minutes. He explained to a few of the participants that he needed to find a lost one-dollar bill, while he told others that he had lost his wallet and needed to look for it. After a few minutes he returned, declaring that he had found what had gone missing, and thanked the women for his help. After he walked away, a situation was staged in which the participant became a witness to a parcel falling out of the bag of another experimenter. It turned out that for the condition in which a weak justification for guarding the bag belonging to the man who went to look for something was offered (i.e. when he went to look for a one-dollar bill), as many as 80% of participants informed the second experimenter that something had fallen out of his bag. However, when the justification for fulfilling the initial request was an obvious one (i.e. when the man went in search of a wallet), this number dropped to 45%. In the control conditions, when the reactions of women who had not been asked to guard the bag were tested, 35% of them informed the experimenter that something had fallen out of his bag. Thus, the patterns of results from other experiments involving conditions modifying the effectiveness of the foot-in-the-door technique also coincided with the assumptions underlying self-perception (e.g. DeJong & Musilli, 1982; Dolinski, 2012; Gamian-Wilk & Dolinski, 2015; Wagener & Laird, 1980). Self-perception as the mechanism underlying the effectiveness of the foot-in-the-door technique would also seem to be indicated by the results of a meta-analysis conducted by William DeJong (1979).

However, not all of the empirical data gathered over the years by psychologists from around the world provides verification that this particular mechanism under-lies the effectiveness of the technique being reviewed here. Beaman et al. (1983), undertaking a meta-analysis of an even greater number of studies than did DeJong, claim that the conclusions of those studies are not as definitive as initially thought. At the same time, the psychological literature is seeing an increasing number of theoretical interpretations differing from self-perception intended to explain why fulfilling a simple request makes an individual more likely to then carry out a more serious later request. We shall review them one by one, starting with the model proposed by Robert Rittle (1981), who draws attention to the possibility that after fulfilling an easier initial request, an individual perhaps does not begin to perceive himself in any particular associated categories (e.g. I am a person who helps others, I am a person who fulfils the requests of others), but rather his attitude to the idea itself of helping other people is what changes. Helping other people is nearly always associated with some cost, and to a certain degree with risk. Indeed, it could turn out that someone doesn't wish us to intervene and exhibits disapproval or even aggression. It may also occur that a social milieu demonstrates some sort of hostility towards an individual trying to help. Rittle thus suggests that fulfilling the easier request is linked with positive emotional experiences. The person who has been given help is generally nice, usually smiles and says thank you. This leads to a change in the attitude of the individual towards the very act of providing assistance. He then begins to perceive altruistic activities as a general human obligation, and it also seems relatively unlikely to him that something bad would happen to an individual offering help.

In one of his experiments Rittle received a certain confirmation of his ideas. Participants were invited to a psychological laboratory. In the waiting room of the laboratory, some of them encountered a helpless child struggling with a vending machine offering sweets and beverages. In the large majority of cases the partici-pants spontaneously made an effort to help the child. (The few times they did not do so, the child asked them directly for help. Nobody refused). Next, they proceeded to the laboratory, where they were first asked to fill in a questionnaire. It measured, among other things, their convictions regarding their own altruistic tendencies and attitudes concerning helping others. It turned out that the differ-ence in their assessments of own levels of altruism between the experimental group (helping the child) and the control group (not encountering the child) was not great, and even statistically insignificant. Participants from the experimental group, however, were demonstrably less convinced than those from the control group that an individual helping a stranger could experience problems.

Rittle goes on to suggest that this pattern of results contradicts the theory of self-perception, and rather confirms his proposed interpretation. Many researchers dispute this conclusion. The primary charge is that Rittle's experiment does not match the situation assumed in the foot-in-the-door procedure. In his experi-ments, most people spontaneously provide help to a child, while foot-in-the-door (at least in its classic form) requires the individual to be asked to fulfil some initial request. Also important is that self-perception can concern not only one's own altruism, but also many other things – such as one's own submissiveness, support for "good causes" or engagement in "good deeds".

Particularly sceptical of the conclusion arrived at by Rittle are Nancy Eisenberg, Robert Cialdini, Heather McCreath and Rita Shell (1987). These authors relied on earlier psychological studies demonstrating that children under the age of 7 do not possess sufficient cognitive resources to draw inferences from their own behaviours, and then use them as the foundation for formulating predictions as to their own reactions. For example, they are not capable of such thoughts as "since I helped someone before, I will also probably help someone in the future if I'm in a similar situation". It is this absence of such cognitive capacities that leads to children behaving inconsistently in successive similar situations.

Eisenberg and her collaborators therefore assumed that if the foot-in-the-door technique is based on the mechanism of self-perception and the need to exhibit consistency in behaviour, then it should not be effective on children under 7 years of age. The experimenters invited people from three age groups to participate in their experiments: the first group was composed of 5- and 6-year-old children, the second of 7- and 8-year-olds, and the third of 10- and 11-year olds. In each of the groups, studies were conducted in control conditions (directly addressing the target request to the children) and in experimental conditions (first lodging a small initial request). In the experimental conditions, children were given six coupons that they could exchange for toys, and were then asked if they would give back one of them to benefit poor children who had no toys at all. One or two days later the children were given a choice – they could either play with fun toys or they could engage in the much less enjoyable activity of sorting pieces of coloured paper into four single-colour stacks for sick children in hospital. The control conditions involved only the second situation: a choice between playing and sorting the coloured paper. The youngest children displayed no difference between the control and experi-mental conditions. In both cases, they were uniform in rarely agreeing to sort the paper. A difference approaching statistical significance did appear with the 7- and 8-year-old cohort, and a clear, statistically significant difference came out in the case of the 10- and 11-year-old children. While this effect is entirely in line with the authors' expectations, I do not agree that it is proof of the inaccuracy of Rittle's suggestion. Indeed, doubts arise whether children 7 years and younger are capable of changing their attitudes and convictions concerning assisting others under the influence of some incidental experience. If this is not the case, then it could be argued that the results attained by Eisenberg et al. (1987) are consistent with the interpretation offered by Rittle.

The aforementioned studies were aimed at indirectly testing theories that state the self-perception mechanism is what underlies the effectiveness of the foot-in-the-door technique. We should, however, observe that this can also be tested directly, by measuring changes in what participants believe about themselves (they should transform following the fulfilment of a simple request), and then examine whether a change in beliefs is accompanied by an increased propensity to carry out a subsequent request. Taking this very assumption as his point of departure, James Dillard (1990) asked study participants for help in addressing envelopes to be used in correspondence for an organization engaged in environmental protection efforts. After a certain time – a period of 1 to 3 weeks – another experimenter asked a number of the same participants to complete a specially constructed scale regarding their attitudes towards environmental protection. Other participants were asked to do something difficult. The request involved sacrificing several hours on the construction of a hiking trail. A control group of participants to whom no initial request was addressed was also asked to either fill in the scale or to join in the construction of the hiking trail. It turned out that those who had previously agreed to help with the envelopes displayed a more positive attitude towards the need to protect the environment than participants from the control group. In addition, agreement to work on the construction of a hiking trail was more frequent among those who had been subjected to the foot-in-the-door procedure than among those to whom the request had been addressed directly. Such results are consistent with the hypothesis that assumes the foundation of the effectiveness of the foot-in-the-door technique is the act of self-perception. Dillard's studies do, however, display a certain weakness. Asking different groups of people to fill in an attitude scale and to carry out a serious request does not facilitate an investigation of the causal links between an attitude transformed as a result of fulfilling an initial request and later compliance with the real request. To put it more simply, in this case we have no evidence that the individuals whose attitudes undergo change are then inclined to fulfil a subsequent request.

Donald Gorassini and James Olson (1995), operating differently than Dillard, decided to measure self-assessment and inclination to fulfil a subsequent request in the same group of individuals. They observed that if the self-perception interpretation is correct, then individuals who carry out the easier initial request should begin to perceive themselves differently than those from the control group, and those differences should be reflected in later varying levels of compliance of participants from both groups towards a serious request. Carrying out a series of experiments, Gorassini and Olson (1995) first asked participants to help them for 5–10 minutes in preparing a psychological experiment, and then to complete a specially designed survey. This survey measured such items as self-assessment of participants' tendency towards altruistic behaviour. The same survey was also filled in by members of the control group. After that, the target request was addressed to all of the participants, in accordance with which they were asked for their consent to participate in a time-consuming psychological experiment. The results turned out to be quite problematic for the theory that the foundation of the technique under analysis here is self-perception. While there was a difference between the experimental and control groups in respect of self-assessment of tendencies towards altruism and a greater propensity of compliance with the target request in the experimental group than the control group, those phenomena affected different people. In other words, those who had begun to view themselves as altruists after fulfilling the initial request were not subsequently more likely to accede to another request than were participants from the control group. However, those who did not begin to perceive themselves as altruists after fulfilling the first request were inclined to sacrifice their time to participate in a psychological experiment.

Gorassini and Olson conclude that three primary elements must be taken into account when considering the mechanisms underlying the effectiveness of the foot-in-the-door technique. First, compliance with the initial request must activate an attitude already held by the individual that will correspond most closely with the content of the next request. Second, the target request must be formulated in a manner that the entity acceding to it behaves in a manner consistent with the aforementioned attitude. Third, when fulfilling the initial request, the individual should be in a position to see the association between that attitude and his own reactions, which will make it clear to him that rejection of a subsequent request would be inconsistent with his accepted values. This interpretation is somewhat similar to that offered a while back by Mary Harris (1972), which holds that fulfilment of the first request leads to an enhanced feeling of social responsibility. The norm demanding that people help each other and extend a hand to those in need of aid comes into sharper focus, and by the same token exerts a greater influence on future behaviour.

A different view of the mechanism underlying the foot-in-the-door technique is taken by William Crano and John Sivacek (1982). They assume that the fulfilment of an initial request may be associated with the receipt of rewards with a social dimension. An example of such a reward is an expression of gratitude from an individual receiving help, or a pleasant smile. These types of occurrences boost the likelihood that individuals will behave in a similar manner in the future. The authors' interpretation seems interesting and suggestive. I would also add that one particular reward could be the simple fact of satisfaction experienced by the person who has helped another.

Yet another theory is advanced by James Cantrill and David Seibold (1986). They state that when an individual makes the decision to comply or not to comply with a request, that the difficulty of the request is evaluated in relation to the amount of the effort that would need to be made, the amount of time to be sacrificed, or the amount of money to be spent. All of these estimates, while rather objectified, do not generally provide a definite answer to the question about whether the request is an easy one to fulfil or not. For example, is it a simple matter to watch someone's bag for 5 minutes, or a difficult one? At times it is definitely easy, while at others hard. What determines our judgement in these matters? In Cantrill and Seibold's opinion, people subjected to the effects of the foot-in-the-door technique estimate the difficulty of the target request based on information about the difficulty of a request that is at least somewhat similar in nature and which they have fulfilled in the recent past (that is, the initial request in the sequence). Because there was no great expense in performing the first request, there are grounds to assume that the second one will not prove problematic. The so-called assimilation effect is at work, manifesting itself in overestimation of the similarity of difficulty levels exhibited by the two requests. Those from the control group are deprived of this point of reference, which can lead to difficulties in estimating the difficulty involved in requests directed to them, in turn making refusal to fulfil them seem a rational step.

While the authors' idea is quite interesting, it does have some weak points. First and foremost, it seems unlikely that, assuming a relatively long period of time between two requests (initial and main) and their formulation by different individuals, an individual would spontaneously recall information concerning the difficulty involved in fulfilling the first request and compare it with information about the task at hand. In addition, according to the proposal of Cantrill and Seibold, the individual's contact with the first request rather than consent to its fulfilment is the key issue. Merely the appearance of the initial request provides a convenient frame of reference for estimating the difficulty of the next one. If this is the case, we could expect that the consent of the individual to fulfil the initial request is not a necessary condition for the effectiveness of the foot-in-the-door technique. However, research results indicate that individuals who refuse to fulfil the initial request nearly always refuse to go along with a subsequent one. Existing research results also fail to confirm the key assumption in this model of a linear association between the difficulty of the first request and the effectiveness of foot-in-the-door (see e.g. Beaman et al., 1983; DeJong, 1979). Finally, the authors themselves failed to empirically demonstrate the accuracy of their model.

It would thus seem that, in spite of a wealth of theoretical approaches, the first one remains the best – that offered by Freedman and Fraser (1966) assuming the occurrence of an act of self-perception following the fulfilment of the initial request. That said, there remains a fundamental problem associated with this particular interpretation. In most of the studies recording the foot-in-the-door effect, the pause between the issuing of the first and the second request lasted several days (Beaman et al., 1983; Dillard et al., 1984; Fern et al., 1986). Let us recall that in Freedman and Fraser's original study (1966, exp. 2) this period lasted as long as 2 weeks. It would seem that in explaining their research results with the mechanism of self-perception, the authors accept the unspoken assumption that an individual fulfils the initial request, comes to the conclusion that she is an altruist, and then hears no other requests for favours over the following several days. Suddenly, a serious request is issued by the experimenter, and the individual agrees to it. This line of reasoning would assume that a given participant is shoved into a freezer after performing the first request, then is taken out a split second before the experimenter decides to state the second (final) request. In the real world, there is no such freezer. Participants live their normal lives, hearing dozens of requests every day from different people. They agree to some of them, while to others they do not (Dolinski, 2009). So why should the reaction to the initial request from an experimenter be more important than favours later asked for by other people? Let us imagine that someone agrees in the morning to a request from an experimenter to fill in a short survey, but in the afternoon ignores the plea of an Internet user asking for the completion of a survey that is to serve as the basis for a master's thesis. Why should a reaction to the request of the experimenter induce self-perception and lead the individual to the conclusion "I am altruistic", but the reaction to the Internet user's request would not lead to the thought that "I am not altruistic"? Additionally, if study participants engaged in self-perception after every request, whether fulfilled or not, their perception of themselves in respect of altruism or submissiveness would be ridiculously unstable. Every instance of agreement should boost one's conviction as to one's own altruism or submissiveness, while every refusal should lead to a drop in the strength of those beliefs. Meanwhile, studies indicate that people exhibit rather stable beliefs about themselves (Campbell, 1990; Goldman, 2006).

In this context it is worth remarking that this criticism does not apply to an interpretation very similar to that based on self-perception while remaining distinct. Specifically, I am referring to Robert Cialdini (2001), who invokes the human need for consistency. In this case, an individual considering whether to fulfil a difficult request may take into consideration past behaviours in similar situations. If he acceded, he should now behave consistently. This interpretation has found confirmation in experiments concerning personality indicators and susceptibility to the application of the foot-in-the-door technique, in which participants first completed a specially designed preference for consistency scale (PFC) measuring the individualized need for consistent behaviour in situations occurring sequentially (Cialdini, Trost & Newsom, 1995). Next, some participants were asked to agree to an easy request. They were asked by telephone if they would be willing to spend 60 seconds answering three questions about TV programmes. After receiving the consent of the participant, the three questions were posed, and then the target request was issued. It concerned agreeing to fill in a special questionnaire comprising 50 items. Participants in the control group were asked immediately to respond to the experimenter's questions. It turned out that the foot-in-the-door effect was only noted among participants who had received high scores on the PFC scale. Among those characterized by a reduced need for consistency, this effect was not observed. Such participants from the experimental group also expressed their consent to complete the questionnaire with the same infrequency as those from the control group (see Table 2.2).

In respect of my rather strong criticism of the assumption that the mechanism underlying the effectiveness of the foot-in-the-door technique is self-perception,

TABLE 2.2 Percentage of compliance with the large request in Cialdini et al. (1995) experiment

Preference for consistency	Foot-in-the-door	Control
Low	68 (45/66)	71 (49/69)
High	66 (33/50)	50 (27/54)

Source: *Journal of Personality and Social Psychology*, 1995, vol. 69, p. 323
Copyright 1995 by the American Psychological Association, Inc.

I hasten to add that my reservations concern only the classic dependency as expressed in the literature, meaning the sequence of "fulfilment of the first request – act of self-perception – appearance of the second request". However, it could be assumed that this mechanism is slightly different. It would seem to me that we could assume with a great degree of probability that the performance of easy, relatively frequent requests is generally automatic. When asked for directions to the train station, we stop and point in the right direction; asked for the time, we pull out our phone and provide an answer. It is taken as self-evident that we will fulfil such requests, and they do not lead to questions such as "Why did I behave in that manner?" Why, indeed, should I stop and think about the reasons I agreed to answer some questions over the phone, or what caused me to complete a questionnaire when asked to do so by some psychologist doing a study? (I've already done it, why wouldn't I?). However, if a similar but more difficult second request is made, I neither accede to it nor reject it out of hand. Now I begin to think about whether I should fulfil it. While analyzing the problem, I can recall that not long ago I agreed to carry out what was indeed an easier but still similar request. If I also recall the circumstances surrounding that event without observing external factors that would lead me to carry out the request (nobody forced me, nobody paid me, etc.), then I might come to the conclusion that I am "the kind of person who does those things". So, while the act of self-perception in the classic model of foot-in-the-door occurs after the initial request is fulfilled, in the theoretical proposition made above, it only occurs at the moment a clearly more difficult request is made (Dolinski, 2009).

Four walls and repeating "yes"

Door-to-door salesmen around the world apply a technique of some similarity to do foot-in-the-door. Frequently, before they try to sell their potential customer something, they ask a few questions. Such questions are designed to ensure that the vast majority of people answer them in a predictable manner. Immediately after, the salesman pitches them some product or service. Refusal to take the salesman up on his offer would contradict the answers given to those questions. We can imagine that a salesman would ask us something like "Is it worth living a healthy lifestyle?", "Does the body need vitamins?", "Isn't it worth feeling confident that our body has enough of the nutrients it needs to function properly?", and then after the third "yes" he offers us "an amazing multivitamin supplement with added zinc and magnesium". Robert Cialdini and Brad Sagarin (2005), who were likely the first to describe this type of sales strategy in scholarly literature, named it the "four walls technique". A team of French researchers interested in social influence decided to examine the effectiveness of such strategies empirically (Gueguen, Joule, Courbet, Halimi-Falkowicz & Marchand, 2013).

A young woman approached men walking alone on the pavement who, unaware of the fact, became participants in the study. In the control conditions the participant was invited to participate in a survey study for which they would need to answer 45 questions on people's food habits. The questions were to be answered at home, and apart from the survey participants also received a stamped addressed envelope for returning the completed survey to the researcher. In the experimental conditions, before asking the participant to take the survey home, complete it and post it back, he was asked if he would agree to answer eight simple "yes or no" questions about odd jobs in the home (the participant thus likely expected that the interaction would not take long). In half of the cases the questions were designed in order to ensure that nearly every one would be answered in the affirmative (e.g. "Have you ever assembled a storage unit?"), while in the other cases they were crafted in order to generate a series of negative responses (e.g. "Have you ever installed a solar water-heater?"). After answering the eight questions, the men were asked to participate in a survey study, thus making the same request as the men in the control conditions.

It turned out that 30% of participants from the control group agreed to participate in the time-consuming survey; in conditions where participants first carried out an initial request and responded "no" several times this number jumped to 60%, while when they answered "yes" eight times, over 83% of men agreed to the subsequent request. The differences between each of the three conditions were statistically significant. The experiment's authors concluded that a scenario involving the initial fulfilment of an easy request and negative answers to eight simple questions followed by participation in a time-consuming survey study could be considered a demonstration of the effectiveness of the "foot-in-the-door" technique, which you, dear Reader, read about in the previous section of this book. However, the greater readiness to fulfil the final request in conditions where the participant had first given several "yes" responses, compared to circumstances in which he said "no", was an illustration of the four walls technique's effectiveness. While the technique itself seems interesting, and the experiment described here would attest to its efficacy, some doubts do arise (as they usually do at the outset of investigations into a particular psychological phenomenon). Let us try to present them here.

First, we have no idea why the authors presented only the percentages of individuals who agreed to complete a long survey concerning food habits in their homes. If the participants were directly handed such questionnaires, together with stamped envelopes, it was also possible to easily determine what percentage of people in particular groups actually did fulfil the request to participate in the time-consuming survey. Second, while it is true that the proportion of individuals in the group that responded in the negative and then fulfilled the target request was greater than in the control group, the actual consequences of multiple repetitions of the word "no" remain unclear. Unfortunately the experimental design did not contain a group in which the questions would require a different response than "yes" or "no". It is easy to imagine a question like "How often do you eat fruit?", "What time do you usually go to sleep?" or "Do you prefer to wear a sweater or a blazer?" If it turned out that in those conditions there was also an increase in the tendency to fulfil a subsequent, more difficult request compared to the control group, it would be worth engaging in more in-depth analysis. Differences in compliance among participants in three experimental groups could be examined: in a group that used the word "yes" several times in a row, in a group that said "no" with equal frequency", and in a group that fulfilled the initial request and agreed to answer a few questions but without answering "yes" or "no". This would help us establish whether multiple uses of the word "no" reduces the effectiveness of a classic social influence technique (foot-in-the-door) or whether it is of no significance from that perspective.

However, the most important issue remains that of the psychological mechanism underlying the technique being discussed here. Let us observe that if we return to the practices of clever door-to-door salesmen, we can imagine an effective marketer who first leads his interlocutor to answer "no" to some questions, but then inclines him to purchase a given product. We can imagine such questions as "Is it worth needlessly risking your health?", "Should you ignore symptoms of the common cold?" or "Would you like to gain 10 pounds over the next 2 years?", and after hearing the answer "no", the salesman then offers a supplement designed to protect people from these problems. What would seem to be the key element in the behaviour of door-to-door salesmen is not so much getting their interlocutor to say "yes", but rather to guide them into the trap of commitment and consistency. Indeed, the interlocutor should behave consistently with his or her previous verbal declaration. However, it should not matter whether an answer of "yes" was given to a question about whether we should take care of our health, or "no" to a question about whether it is worth thoughtlessly endangering our health. In both cases, the proper course of action is to purchase the vitamin supplement. The situation created by Gueguen, Joule, Courbert and their collaborators (2013) in their experiment is entirely different. There is no association between the content of the introductory questions (concerning e.g. a storage unit or solar water-heater) and the request to complete a long questionnaire at home about food habits. The commitment and consistency trap here concerns the very fact of consenting to participate in a time-consuming survey study after previously participating in a short survey study. It is thus limited to the foot-in-the-door effect. This mechanism does not, however, explain why people who have repeated the word "yes" several times in a row are particularly inclined to fulfil a subsequent and more difficult request. We are therefore dealing with a slightly different technique than four walls. How can we explain the effectiveness of a strategy designed to induce another person to repeatedly respond "yes"?

The results noted in the experiment by Gueguen, Joule, Courbert et al. (2013) can be explained by reference to the mechanism of activation of selected mental representations and patterns of action (Higgins, 1996). Multiple repetitions of the word "yes" lead to an increased likelihood that the response to successive questions or another request or proposal will be the same. It should be observed, however, that accepting this interpretation leads to the conclusion that the effectiveness of this technique, aimed at inducing an individual to repeat the answer "yes" multiple times, should be limited to situations in which the target request appears immediately afterwards. The technique should then be unsuccessful in conditions when the target request surfaces after a certain time (e.g. on the next day). Separate empirical studies would be needed to determine whether this really is the case.

While researchers are just beginning to explore the "four walls" and "repeating yes" techniques, the next sequential technique of social influence to be presented here has already been the subject of empirical study.

Door-in-the-face

A group of social psychologists researching social influence techniques – Richard Miller, Clive Seligman, Nathan Clark and Malcolm Bush (1976) – presented readers of one of their articles with a story from the popular comic strip "Blondie". Because this story is an excellent illustration of the essence of the door-in-the-face technique, I will repeat it here. The action begins with Blondie returning home. The situation differs from the everyday in that she comes back in a new hat, new shoes and new dress. She asks her husband Dagwood if he likes what he sees. His response is to ask how much they cost. After hearing the answer, he becomes enraged and demands that Blondie return the new items. The woman begins crying and asks him to let her at least keep the hat, which she is particularly fond of. Dagwood magnanimously agrees, but emphasizes that he doesn't want to hear of any other purchases. The story concludes with a scene in which Blondie congratulates herself on getting her husband to agree to her buying an expensive hat, and Dagwood is pleased that he managed to recover the majority of the money spent by his beloved but spendthrift wife.

The door-in-the-face technique is based on the assumption that if we want to induce an individual to fulfil a rather difficult request, we should begin by presenting an even more difficult one. This request will almost certainly be rejected by its addressee. However, the chances grow that he will agree to fulfil a request easier than the one which he has just refused. The first psychological experiments addressing this technique were conducted by Robert Cialdini and a group of his collaborators (Cialdini et al., 1975). In one of them, the experimenter introduced himself as an employee of an institution that assisted juvenile offenders, and asked the study participant to lend a hand. The control group's participants were asked to go on a two-hour trip to the zoo with a group of young people who had experienced trouble with the law. Just under 17% of participants agreed to do this. In the experimental group, the first request was a very difficult one: to assume the role of a counsellor and advisor for juvenile offenders. This would require 2 hours a week of involvement over a period of 2 years. Participants refused to carry out this request. However, when a one-off form of activity was then proposed (taking juvenile offenders to the zoo), 50% of participants gave their consent. The experimental design also contained a group that was asked to engage in the process of resocializing underage offenders; participants were given the choice of two forms of involvement: 2 years of regular consultations or taking a group of "difficult youngsters" to the zoo. In this case as well, the first alternative was universally rejected, while one in four participants agreed to act as a chaperone at the zoo (see: Table 2.3).

TABLE 2.3 Percentage of subjects complying with the smaller request in Cialdini et al. (1975) experiment

Treatment	% Compliance
Rejection-moderation condition	50.0
Exposure control	25.0
Smaller request only control	16.7

Source: *Journal of Personality and Social Psychology*, 1975, vol. 69, p. 209.
Copyright 1975 by the American Psychological Association, Inc.

In considering the mechanism that underlies the effectiveness of the door-in-the-face technique the authors take into consideration the contrast effect and the norm of mutual reciprocity. The contrast effect (Kenrick & Gutierres, 1980) can be illustrated by something experienced by one of my colleagues. He owned an apartment that he wanted to sell. I wouldn't say it was particularly attractive. It was located on the top floor of an old, tall tenement house without an elevator. The layout of the apartment was also not the nicest. Hallways took up more space than the rooms did. However, the owner of a real estate agency assured my colleague that he was sitting on a treasure worth a fortune. He appraised the property at a very high price, and guaranteed that he should be able to sell it quickly. My colleague was delighted, and he expected to quickly come into a tidy sum of money. Soon thereafter, crowds of people came to see the apartment. They looked around, shook their heads and walked away. However – in the agent's opinion – there was no reason to worry. "If they don't buy it, someone else will," was what he said to steady the nerves of my colleague. But nobody came to buy the apartment. By chance, the owner of the unfortunate apartment ran into a woman who had come to see the apartment the previous day. "The thing is . . . you wanted so much money for such a little cage. Right after we left, the agent took me to a bigger, cheaper apartment in a good neighbourhood. I liked it so much that I bought it on the spot." As my colleague belatedly came to understand, the agent was only using his apartment to evoke the contrast effect. After a potential client had looked over his apartment, viewing one whose price seemed to be realistically calculated made an excellent impression on him.

Continuing our exploration of topics related to social influence, it is worth mentioning studies by Sotohiro Kojima (1994). This psychologist asked people about their subjective feelings associated with the acquisition of various consumer goods. Participants spoke of the joy they felt when purchasing new furniture or photographic equipment, but they also emphasized the discomfort associated with the necessity of paying for those products. Kojima observed that this discomfort was reduced among those who had recently purchased homes compared to those who had not. Considering that the groups were no different in terms of financial status, it could be supposed that the aforementioned contrast effect was at play. When people have recently spent a lot of money on something, then another object that costs a fraction of that sum feels inexpensive to them. However, without this frame of reference the same item seems expensive. Kojima generated similar results in other studies. For example, he demonstrated that sales staff in electronics stores were very adept at convincing customers to pick up some little gadget in the course of a high-value transaction.

In respect of the experiment by Cialdini et al., (1975) under discussion here, the contrast effect consists in the request to take difficult youngsters on a trip to the zoo seeming easy (or even very easy) when compared to the extremely difficult request to become a mentor to underage offenders. We should also observe that the contrast effect is present in the third group, which was presented with the choice between the two aforementioned activities, and the proportion of people who decided to take the youngsters to the zoo was in this case half that of the group in which the sequence of extremely difficult – relatively easy request was applied. Thus, while the contrast effect may play a certain role, Cialdini et al. perceive the primary psychological mechanism underlying the effectiveness of the door-in-the-face technique in the norm of mutual reciprocity.

This norm is a particular version of the broader and more general rule of reciprocity. According to this rule, individuals are obliged to compensate others for goods received from them (Uehara, 1995). This is a principle that organizes the lives of individuals, social groups and entire societies. It facilitates the establishment of social bonds, trust and lasting coalitions. Alvin Gouldner (1960) even feels that the norm of reciprocity is the "starting mechanism" of societies, without which the establishment of any lasting group life would be impossible.

In the case of the door-in-the-face technique the norm of mutual reciprocity is materialized when someone makes a difficult request, is refused, and then reduces his expectations towards the partner in the interaction, making a particular type of concession. The partner in the interaction is now obliged under the principle of symmetrical reciprocity to make a concession himself, which may come in the form of fulfilling the second, easier request addressed to him.

Support for an interpretation involving the norm of reciprocity can be found in results that indicate the door-in-the-face technique loses its effectiveness when the second, easier request is formulated by a different individual than the one who submitted the first, extremely difficult one (see e.g. Dillard et al., 1984; Feeley, Anker & Aloe, 2012). In essence, we cannot speak in this case of perceiving a concession from the partner in the interaction, and what follows is that the norm of mutual concessions is absent. By the same token, there is no motivation to accede to a subsequent request. However, the assumption that the norm of mutual reciprocity is at the heart of the effectiveness of the technique being analyzed here is not consistent with results indicating that such effectiveness is associated with the length of time separating the lodging of the two requests. Arnie Cann, Steven Sherman and Roy Elkes (1975) called up study participants, introduced themselves as employees of an organization promoting road traffic safety, and asked their interlocutor to join in a campaign being planned by their organization. The request involved standing for 2 hours on the pavement and counting the cars passing by on the street. The overwhelming majority of people refused to agree to this obviously excessive request. A second request was then issued. The participant was asked to distribute among friends and acquaintances 15 brochures that the road traffic safety organization would send via post. Depending on the experimental conditions, this request was formulated either immediately after the participant gave notice of refusal to stand and count cars, or during a follow-up phone call made after 7–10 days had elapsed. In the control group, who were asked immediately for their consent to receive the brochures and distribute them to their friends, 62% of participants agreed. In the group to which the aforementioned request was made immediately following refusal to carry out the very difficult request, this number was much higher and amounted to nearly 90%. However, in the group which experienced a delay between the two requests, the percentage of those agreeing to the easier one was even lower (albeit statistically insignificantly) than in the control conditions: half of the participants agreed to hand out the brochure.

Results from meta-analyses paint a similar picture. Dillard et al., (1984) demonstrated that the longer the break between the two requests, the less effective the technique becomes. Thomas Feeley, Ashley Anker and Ariel Aloe (2012) determined that in experiments during which the final request appeared more than one day after the rejection by the participant of the initial request, compliance rates did not exceed those in the control conditions.

Meanwhile, in real-life situations people adhere to the reciprocity principle even after a very long time has passed. We send Christmas cards to those who sent them to us last year, we loan money to friends who loaned us a large sum of cash ten years ago, etc. Why, then, does the door-in-the-face technique stop being effective on the very next day? There is yet another result that proves troublesome for the assumption that the effectiveness of this technique is grounded in the norm of reciprocity. Indeed, it may be assumed that the intensity of the obligation felt by an individual to fulfil an easier request should correlate with the extent of the concession made by the individual who first made a difficult request, followed by the easier one. However, it turns out that the extent of the concession is not associated with the effectiveness of the technique (Fern et al., 1986; O'Keefe & Hale, 1998).

Daniel O'Keefe and Marianne Figge (1997) hold that the interpretation set forth by Cialdini et al. is fundamentally incorrect, and propose their own alternative. They state that the mechanism explaining the effectiveness of the door-in-the-face technique is the feeling of guilt. Refusing the first request leads to this feeling, because the individual knows that while it would be difficult to do, it is socially desirable. Acceding to the easier request helps to minimize the unpleasant feeling of guilt. Taking this perspective, it becomes clear why the technique is less effective when requests are made by people representing commercial interests as opposed to conditions in which they are advanced by charitable organizations (Dillard et al., 1984; Fern et al., 1986). Refusing to purchase a vacuum cleaner does not lead to a feeling of guilt, and thus there is no subsequent agreement to buy a less expensive hair dryer. The extent of the concession also plays no role here, for it is correlated neither with the intensity of the feeling of guilt nor the potential to successfully reduce it.

In turn, results attesting to a negative correlation between the extent of the delay separating the two requests and the efficacy of the door-in-the-face technique, problematic for an interpretation grounded in the principle of reciprocity, become relatively easy to explain from the perspective of the feeling of guilt. The emotion dies down over time, thus rendering the technique increasingly less effective.

The authors also draw attention to two limitations on the effectiveness of the door-in-the-face technique that result from their model. This technique should prove unsuccessful in conditions in which refusal to fulfil the first request does not evoke a feeling of guilt, as well as when the fulfilment of a subsequent request cannot serve to reduce the feeling of guilt. O'Keefe and Figge have not conducted studies to confirm the accuracy of these assumptions (or at least they have not published them), but they have tried to demonstrate, through a review of the subject literature, that the results of studies conducted in the past are more consistent with their interpretation than with the one advanced by Cialdini and his collaborators. Indirect support for their ideas is also provided by the research of Lohyd Terrier and Robert Joule (2008). They demonstrated that if the individual making the requests clearly demonstrated an understanding of the fact that the other person would refuse to agree to the first of them, saying something like "Of course, I quite understand that you may not be able to accept", the technique is less effective than in conditions when that statement is not made. It could be thought that such an expression of understanding leads to a reduction in the intensity of the guilt felt by the addressee of the request, and thus that person experiences reduced motivation to actively deal with the guilt by acceding to the subsequent, easier request.

O'Keefe and Figge (1997) do not, however, stop to consider an effect that is not consistent with their own proposal. Studies on the door-in-the-face mechanism primarily feature situations involving a brief interaction with a stranger. The feeling of guilt in these situations could be limited not only by doing something positive for him, but also by fulfilling a similar request made by another person. Meanwhile, as the results of meta-analyses demonstrate definitively (Feeley et al., 2012), the technique ceases to be effective.

The norm of mutual concessions and the appearance of negative emotions stemming from a feeling of guilt are not the only potential sources of the effectiveness of the door-in-the-face technique. Mark Pendleton and Daniel Batson (1979) draw attention to the role potentially played by mechanisms associated with self-presentation. Rejection of the initial request may lead an individual to feel concerned that this will be taken badly by his partner in the interaction, as well as by any potential witnesses. This concern induces compliance with the subsequent easier request. Such an interpretation would be linked with the expectation that the dimension of the initial request would be the decisive factor in the conviction of the request's addressee that his interlocutor could have a poor opinion of him. The likelihood that an obviously difficult request will lead to such a feeling is smaller than the likelihood that it will appear after the rejection of a modestly difficult one. Indeed, the rejection of a more difficult request is easier to understand and socially justifiable. Pendleton and Batson (1979) received data consistent with this assumption; however, Robert Reeves, Gary Baker, Jeffrey Boyd and Robert Cialdini (1991) did not succeed in replicating that result in their research.

Yet another theoretical proposition is offered by Tusing and Dillard (2000). They assume that individuals do not worry so much about what others think of them, but just the opposite: they begin to focus on their own internal standards. Rejection of the first request leads them to begin thinking that it is socially responsible to help people who deserve it. Activation of this mental scheme makes it easier to submit to a new request. While there is not yet empirical research providing direct evidence of this model's accuracy, there is some indirect support for it in the results of meta-analyses (Feeley et al., 2012).

Matthew Abrahams and Robert Bell (1994) have also conducted some interesting research aimed at identifying the mechanism responsible for the effectiveness of the technique under analysis here. In their experiments they differentiated the dimensions of the initial request, the level of expectation on the part of the addressee that there would be future interaction with the individual formulating the request, and also that person's emphasis on the fact that withdrawing the initial request is a concession.

Each participant was invited to a psychological laboratory. In the waiting room they encountered another person who was in fact a confederate of the experimenter. The experimenter soon arrived and informed the pair that they would soon be participating in a study (conditions of expected interaction), or that they would soon be separated (conditions of absence of expected interaction), after which they were then left alone while the experimenter (supposedly) went to prepare the laboratory equipment. The experimenter's confederate confided to the participant that he was involved in a campaign to assist AIDS victims and to raise awareness in society of how to avoid the disease. He also said that a march of solidarity with those afflicted by the illness was being organized, and asked the participant if he would be willing to devote 30 hours (very high level of difficulty of the initial request) or, in other conditions, 10 hours (moderate level of difficulty of the initial request) to the organization. When the participant refused, the confederate responded either that it would be equally helpful if he agreed to sponsor the march and donate some money, or suggested that volunteers were needed more now than ever before. However, if the participant could not afford to get involved personally, it would at least be good if he agreed to sponsor the march. The assumption was that the second case would involve an emphasis on the concession and a reduction of expectations towards the participant.

The authors assumed that differentiation of the individual experimental factors would enable them to identify the mechanism responsible for the effectiveness of the door-in-the-face technique. If it turned out that the factor of emphasizing the concession made to the addressee was significant, this would indicate that the rule of reciprocity plays a role. If it was the dimensions of the initial request that turned out to be significant, this would be explained rather by the contrast effect. If, however, the significant factor was to prove the expectation of a future interaction with the partner, this would point to self-presentation (an interpretation grounded in the feeling of guilt was not taken into consideration).

Unfortunately, the study's results were not definitive, but the effectiveness of the door-in-the-face technique was very high (66.4% compliance in experimental conditions compared to only 25.9% compliance in the control conditions, which involved the proposal to sponsor the march being issued to the participant directly). The recorded results were the least consistent with the contrast effect, as the dimensions of the initial request did not lead to differentiation in the compliance of participants. The other two factors, however, led to differences in the behaviour of participants only in specific circumstances that are beyond the scope of the questions being discussed here.

While the experiment described above, as well as other studies, have failed to produce unequivocal results, it is my belief that the hypothetical mechanisms discussed so far are not exclusive of one another in any way. We cannot exclude the possibility that they frequently combine to induce compliance, while in particular situations one of those mechanisms (not necessarily the same one) plays the lead role. It can also not be excluded that this is precisely why the door-in-the face technique proves effective in very different areas of social life. For example, it has been demonstrated that the technique can be effectively employed for conducting a charitable collection drive in both face-to-face situations (Reingen, 1978) and over the Internet (Gueguen, 2003), for convincing people to participate in opinion polling (Mowen & Cialdini, 1980), in seminars addressing the subject of racism (Rodafinos, Vucevic & Sideridis, 2005), and even for convincing people with greater frequency to purchase home-made cheese (Ebster & Neumayr, 2008).

From one perspective, research conducted by Magdalena Paska (2002) is particularly interesting. It explores the issue of whether this technique can prove effective in conditions under which requests concern behaviours that violate ethical norms. Paska asked drivers getting out of their cars in a supermarket car park to participate in a campaign for the elimination of separate parking places for disabled individuals. In the control conditions participants were asked to sign a petition in which customers were demanding that store management take action to remove the parking spaces. It turned out that 37.5% of people approached agreed to sign the petition (as an aside, it is worth musing over that alarmingly high number). In the experimental conditions, participants were first asked to help in gathering signatures. They were asked to approach drivers in the same manner as the researcher, asking them to place their signatures on the petition. None of those who were asked gave their consent. Immediately after hearing the refusal, the experimenter submitted an easier request – to sign the petition. Only 12.5% of participants agreed. It thus turns out that the "door-in-the-face" technique leads to a clear decline in people's inclination to perform the unethical act they are being encouraged to do! Paska received similar results in a second experiment during which students were first (unsuccessfully) encouraged to participate in a protest against providing support for the homeless from public funds, and then asked to sign a petition on the matter. None of the students agreed to sign the petition, yet in the control group – where students were simply given the petition to sign – one third of those approached agreed to do so. Analogical patterns of results were attained in both studies: opposite patterns to those in situations in which people were encouraged to engage in ethical or ethically-neutral behaviour. This would seem to demonstrate the very interesting potential for practical application of the door-in-the-face technique in circumstances where people display a tendency to exceed moral boundaries.

Foot-in-the-face

As we know, in the case of the foot-in-the-door technique discussed at the beginning of this chapter, an easier request is first issued assuming its fulfilment will increase the chances that the individual will later fulfil the more difficult, target request. With regard to the sequential technique discussed in the preceding section (door-in-the-face), the procedure is reversed: first, a clearly difficult request is formulated with the assumption that its rejection will make the individual more inclined to carry out an easier one. From a certain perspective we could say that an increase in the chance that a moderately difficult request will be fulfilled can be generated either by starting with an easier request, or with a clearly more difficult one. The foot-in-the-door and door-in-the-face techniques are thus symmetrical to one another.

The question may arise of what will happen if we apply a sequence involving two requests of the same level of difficulty. This question was asked by Cialdini et al. (1975) during research on the door-in-the-face technique. Their starting point was the assumption that we may not exclude the possibility of the technique relying not on the second request being easier than the first, but rather on the simple renewal of the request by its initiator. This repetition is a social signature indicating that the person making the request is in real need of help, and this may constitute the key mechanism in achieving compliance from people subjected to this technique. Thus, the experimenters created a situation in one of their experiments involving a sequence of two requests with analogical levels of difficulty. Participants were first asked to accompany a group of youngsters in danger of falling into a life of crime on a two-hour trip to a museum. Regardless of their agreement or lack thereof, they were then asked if they would be willing to go on a two-hour walk with the same youths to the zoo. It turned out that 8 of 24 people agreed to the museum trip, and 7 of that 8 agreed in turn to go to the zoo. From among the 16 who refused to go to the museum, only 1 agreed to take the youths to the zoo. Thus it can be said that in general participants behaved consistently (save for two cases) – if they agreed to the first request, they agreed to the second, while if they refused the first they also refused the second. The compliance rate of 33.3% with the target request (to go to the zoo) was analogical to the control group, which was directly issued with the proposal to go to the zoo. The researchers thus received information leading them to believe that the concession of the one making the request is key to the door-in-the-face technique. The mere repetition of the request (urging) is not sufficient.

It should be kept in mind that Cialdini et al. applied a sequence of requests that was adequate in respect of their research objectives. They thus took care to ensure that the addressee of the request had no doubt that the two requests were of equal difficulty, and similar to each other. In both cases the request involved caring for a group of young people in danger of succumbing to the temptation of a life of crime. In both cases it was necessary to devote 2 hours to the youngsters. Finally, in both cases the trip was to take place on a Saturday. One may, however, wonder what would happen if we applied a sequence of two requests whose respective levels of difficulty are difficult for the addressee to compare. It is obvious that devoting 2 hours to an activity is a greater sacrifice than 1 hour to the same activity, and equally it is less of a burden than devoting 4 hours. How much of a loss is 2 hours spent on some activity when compared to, for example:

- completing a long questionnaire when we are not in a position to estimate how much time it will take us?
- making a donation equivalent to our hourly wage?
- spending 2 hours on an entirely different activity?

It would seem that doubts could arise in all three of these examples. So, what will happen if an individual is asked to carry out in sequence two requests which, while exhibiting entirely different characters, are performed by a similar proportion of people in control conditions (thus fulfilling the criteria applied in the relevant literature on social influence to state that they are of similar difficulty)?

It is obvious that in respect of the first request in the sequence, the addressee has two options: to carry it out or to refuse. Let us observe that if he accedes to the first request, then in accordance with the foot-in-the-door principle, he should be more inclined to fulfil the next request. This should be all the more likely if the second request is not in some way obviously more difficult than its predecessor. The majority of participants in the aforementioned experiment conducted by Cialdini and collaborators behaved in just this manner: of those who agreed to go to the museum, a significant majority also agreed to go to the zoo. What would happen, however, in the case of an individual refusing to carry out the first request? In the experiment by Cialdini et al., when such conditions were observed nearly everyone refused to carry out the subsequent request. That said, I believe that in conditions in which the second request was to involve an entirely different type of activity, we could encounter different results. The mere fact of the second request being clearly different itself constitutes a real alternative. The addressee of the request sees that he has been presented with a choice. This, in turn, may activate the rule of reciprocity in the same manner as a concession in the classic door-in-the-face technique. In addition, it would seem that in real-life social situations, when someone formulates a request or a proposal that is then turned down, this is followed by a more beneficial proposal or a request that should be easier to carry out.

We may assume that this individual has encountered similar situations on multiple occasions in the past. Thus, in conditions that render it difficult to accurately assess the objective difficulty of the two requests, the addressee may be inclined to interpret the second of them as easier than the first. Such a situation would be analogical to the door-in-the-face technique.

We can then imagine a technique whose essence consists in the successive presentation of two requests that are clearly different in form or content, but are very similar in respect of their objective levels of difficulty (measured by the percentage of people who fulfil such requests spontaneously, i.e. in control conditions). Regardless of what decision the addressee takes in respect of the first request, he will be pressured by psychological forces inclining him to fulfil a subsequent request. If he accedes to the first one, he sets off down the path of foot-in-the-door. Rejection of the first request places him on the path of door-in-the-face. Because this technique is a synthesis of the two techniques mentioned above, it could best be given the name foot-in-the-face (Dolinski, 2011).

One of the experiments dedicated to the foot-in-the-face technique was preceded by a series of pilot tests intended to identify two requests of average difficulty level, while at the same time being as similar in difficulty to each other as possible. It turned out that roughly half of the students approached agreed to complete a survey that the experimenter explained would serve as the empirical foundation of a master's thesis prepared by a blind student, and that it would take around 30 minutes to complete. A similar proportion of students agreed to a request to record a dictation of five pages from a psychology textbook, also allegedly for a blind student.

The design of an experiment testing the foot-in-the-face technique should, naturally, facilitate a comparison of compliance in the group to whom the request of average difficulty is submitted as the second request (that is, after the participant either carries out or rejects an initial request) with conditions in which the same request is issued immediately. The decision as to which of the two requests (completing a survey or dictating a few pages for a recording) should come first and second would of necessity be arbitrary. Instead, I operated under the assumption that a more appropriate design would involve the first condition beginning with the request to complete a survey followed by the request to record material for a blind student, while the second condition would reverse this order. The experimental design can be presented like this:

CONDITION 1: Request A, then, regardless of participant's reaction, Request B
CONDITION 2: Request B, then, regardless of participant's reaction, Request A

with A denoting the request to complete the survey and B denoting the request to dictate a recording of a few pages. It should be noted that this condition also allows for the omission of classic control groups. A test of the effectiveness of the foot-in-the-face technique could be based on comparing compliance with request B in condition 1 (in this case considered the experimental condition) to compliance with the same request (B) in condition 2 (in this case considered the control condition), along with a comparison of compliance with request A in condition 2 (experimental condition) and compliance with the same request (A) in condition 1 (control condition). In other words, the design is a comparison of compliance with the request that comes second in the sequence and compliance with the very same request when issued directly.

One more factor was added to the experimental design – the amount of time between the first and the second request. The assumption of Alice Tybout, Brian Sternthal and Bobby Calder (1983) concerning the classic foot-in-the-door and door-in-the-face sequential techniques is that an individual considering acceding to the second request can take two types of information into account. First: how he himself behaved in a similar situation in the past; and second: how the person issuing the second request behaves. The assumption under which this model operates is that people wish to view themselves as consistent and coherent. Thus, when the addressee ascertains that he has fulfilled the first request, this should make him more inclined to comply with the second. In turn, declaring that he rejected the first one should provide motivation to reject the subsequent one. In relation to the role of information about the behaviour of the other person in the interaction, the model's authors assume that if the addressee becomes aware of an escalation of the demand being made of him, he will refuse to fulfil the first request. However, if the addressee can observe that his partner in the interaction is scaling back his expectations, he will be more inclined to agree to the second request. We are therefore dealing with a situation where, in the case of foot-in-the-door, the addressee is influenced by information about himself to carry out the second request ("I agreed to a similar request before"), but information about the behaviour of his partner in the interaction leads him in the opposite direction ("he's stepping up his demands"). The opposite occurs in the event of door-in-the-face. Information about himself ("earlier I refused") leads the addressee to say "no", while information about the manner in which the person lodging the request is reacting ("he's lowered his expectations of me") push him towards complying with the second request. The model's authors assume that the key determinant in both techniques is the information that the addressee of the requests focuses on. The foot-in-the-door technique should prove particularly effective when the addressee concentrates on information of the first type (i.e. about himself) while ignoring information of the second type (i.e. about the behaviours of his partner in the interaction). Door-in-the-face, in turn, would prove to be an especially effective technique in precisely the opposite conditions. What does this have to do with the amount of time separating the requests? The authors' belief is that in the case of foot-in-the-door, the addressee's concentration on the second type of information can be made to wane when a particular amount of time lapses between the fulfilment of the initial request and the submission of the second one. This de-emphasizes the fact that the demands made of the addressee are escalating. With regard to the door-in-the-face technique, it would be more beneficial for the second request to come immediately after the first, as this serves to emphasize the concessions made by the partner in the interaction.

The experiment used the requests selected in the aforementioned pilot study. The individual carrying out the study visited students in dormitories and explained that he wanted to help his blind friend, himself a student as well. In half of the cases the participant was asked to complete a survey that was supposed to be an important element of the blind student's master's thesis, while the other half of participants heard a different request. It was explained to them that a blind student used recorded course material in order to study, and they were asked to dictate five pages of a textbook into a recorder. If the participant agreed to carry out the initial request, he was given the survey or (in the other conditions) a textbook and tape recorder. Those who refused to carry out the first request were politely thanked. In conditions involving the absence of a delay between the requests, the second request was made at a moment when the experimenter arrived to take the completed survey or textbook and tape recorder or directly after the participant declared his refusal to fulfil the first request. When there was a delay, the second request was issued after two days had elapsed.

The foot-in-the-face technique turned out to be effective. The request to help out the blind student was carried out by 58% of participants when it came as the second in the sequence, while 48.8% of them agreed in conditions when it was formulated directly. While these differences do meet the threshold for statistical significance, it would be a stretch to say that a difference of less than 9% was exceptional. The picture changes when we take into additional consideration the factor of time elapsing between the requests. Compliance with the second request reached a level of 66.8% if we take into account only conditions in which either compliance with the first request was followed by a two-day wait before the second request was issued, or if the first request was turned down then the second

TABLE 2.4 Decision tree of people who agreed to fulfil the second request in each condition in Dolinski (2011) experiment

	First request: Record or questionnaire	Second request: Questionnaire or record, respectively
Without delay		
	Yes = 98	Yes = 59
		No = 39
	No = 102	Yes = 59
		No = 43
2-3 days' interval		
	Yes = 97	Yes = 74
		No = 23
	No = 103	Yes = 40
		No = 63

Source: *Journal of Applied Social Psychology*, 2011, vol. 41, p. 1531.

came immediately thereafter (Dolinski, 2011). The results of this experiment are presented in Table 2.4.

A practitioner of social influence making use of the foot-in-the-face technique should thus observe the following rules: prepare two requests exhibiting similar levels of difficulty. If the person you are approaching agrees to the first then give him some time and do not rush with the second, but rather wait a few days. However, if he refuses the first one, issue the second one right away.

Dump-and-chase

As we have seen, the foot-in-the door technique consists of this sequence: easier introductory request – more difficult target request. The door-in-the face technique reverses the sequence as difficult request – easier (main) request. In turn, the foot-in-the-face technique allows for the use of two requests displaying similar difficulty levels, but different enough in content that it is difficult to view them as such. We also hasten to remind that Cialdini and his collaborators (Cialdini et al., 1975) demonstrated that if two requests appearing in sequence are obviously similar in content and difficulty, compliance with the second request is no greater than with the same request given to the control group (that is, in conditions where it is the only request lodged). It would therefore seem obvious that a technique based on a repetition of exactly the same request following its rejection ought to be ineffective.

Franklin Boster and his collaborators, however, argue that in such situations the matter is not entirely clear (Boster et al., 2009). They observe that refusal to accede to a request can take one of two forms: rebuff or obstacle. Rebuff is an open and unequivocal refusal, without explanation or justification. Obstacle is something different – the addressee of the request explains why he refuses to carry out the request. By doing so he opens the door to the possibility of convincing him that the grounds for refusal that he presents are not, in fact, important or may not even exist at all; it also creates the possibility of explaining why it is worth agreeing to the request. In other words, from the point of view of the person formulating a request, refusal in the form of an "obstacle" is far better than a "rebuff". What to do if a rebuff is encountered? Boster et al. propose a social influence technique that rests on the assumption that in such cases it becomes necessary to effect a "transformation of the target's rebuff into an obstacle" (Boster et al., 2009, p. 220). When we hear "no", we should just ask "why not?" If we receive an explanation, we can then begin questioning its sense, present arguments to the contrary and . . . even repeat our presentation of the same request many times over. The key to success is obstinacy. The authors also provide a name for the technique, which they label "dump-and-chase".

The experimenters decided to test the technique in conditions under which they asked passers-by to guard their bicycle for around 10 minutes. If the participant refused and gave a reason, an attempt was made to convince him that there was no good reason why he couldn't watch over the bicycle. If he refused without giving a reason, first the experimenters attempted to draw the reason out of him, and then to convince him that it wasn't a serious problem. The researchers compared the effectiveness of this with the application of the door-in-the-face technique (the participant was first asked to guard the bicycle for 20 minutes, and upon refusing was told that watching it for 10 minutes would be enough). The experimental design also included conditions in which the request was accompanied by a (superficial) justification for submitting the request (the person making the request said "will you watch my bike for me until I return because I cannot watch it?"). The authors of the study report that their technique was more effective than door-in-the-face. In the dump-and-chase conditions 60% of those approached agreed to watch the bicycle for 10 minutes, while with door-in-the face this was only 20%. The authors do not, however, examine the reasons why the door-in-the-face technique proved utterly ineffective in their experiment. This can easily be explained by the specifics of the study: if someone asks us to watch a bicycle for 20 minutes, but after hearing our refusal proceeds to assure us that 10 minutes is long enough, we might reasonably fear that the person making the request won't return after 10 minutes. The individual guarding the bicycle is then placed in a very uncomfortable situation regardless of how he chooses to behave. If he waits, he wastes time, but if he leaves, he faces the feeling that he has let down someone who entrusted him with property. As it turned out, the percentage of those agreeing to watch the bicycle in the door-in-the-face conditions was even lower (20%) than in the conditions in which the dump-and-chase technique was just beginning to be applied, meaning the request was simply formulated and addressed (40%). However, if we compare this indicator with the success of the dump-and-chase technique, it does not turn out to be effective. However, the authors themselves admit their technique may not be more effective than presenting the request with a superficial justification. In a second experiment the authors expanded the experimental design using foot-in-the-door conditions, as well as changing the nature of the requests. While in the first experiment the person making the request was clearly acting in his own interests (having his own bicycle guarded), this time the experimenters presented themselves as members of the "In Your Face Theater Troupe" and explained that they were attempting to combine education with entertainment in order to increase awareness of sexuality issues that may affect students. They stood on the pavement, handed out brochures with information about the group's activities, and tried to discern whether passers-by were interested in them. In the dump-and-chase conditions, participants were asked to perform a similar role at any chosen time the following week. In the door-in-the-face conditions, the initial request involved doing it in another city where the group was scheduled to perform, and then, after they refused, they were told that it would also be helpful to be active in the town in which they had been approached. In the foot-in-the-door conditions, participants were first asked to agree to wear a small sticker supporting the group, and then asked to distribute brochures to passers-by. The group in which the superficial justification was used heard the phrase "because it is essential that we have someone here" appended to the request. The dump-and-chase technique turned out only to be more effective than the request accompanied by a superficial justification. It was not proven to be more effective than the two classic sequential techniques. Unfortunately, the authors again failed to compare the percentages of those who ultimately agreed in dump-and-chase conditions with those who agreed to carry out the request at once (which could be treated as control conditions). This difference did not achieve statistical significance, which makes it difficult to label the technique a successful one. For the sake of accuracy, we must add that both experiments had very small sample sizes, which makes it hard to expect that the differences between groups would cross the threshold of statistical significance.

In spite of the absence of empirical evidence demonstrating the effectiveness of the technique under discussion here, it remains worthy of attention. However, there can be no doubt that proper studies conducted with larger groups of participants are necessary in order to answer questions about both the technique's effectiveness and, if it proves successful, the psychological mechanism underlying it. The most likely explanations for the (potential) effectiveness of this technique may be associated with the individual to whom the request is being addressed perceiving the persistence of the one making the request. This could lead to the conclusion that fulfilment of the request is of great importance to him. If this is the case, then a feeling of empathy towards the person making the request may arise, as well as a feeling of guilt from refusing to help someone in a difficult situation. (In Chapter 6 you will have the opportunity to read about experiments demonstrating that such emotions can induce compliance). It is, however, possible that another mechanism is at work, related to the cognitive and motivational sphere. If someone who is asked for something presents an obstacle, he implicitly states "if it weren't for certain reasons, I'd agree to the request". During the subsequent conversation, if it occurs that the problems preventing the request from being fulfilled are smoothed over or resolved, then the addressee may feel obliged to carry it out. It is also possible that the very conversation between the person formulating the request and the person to whom it is addressed is the key element (regardless of the substance of the conversation). Enmeshing one's interlocutor in a dialogue is a factor that markedly increases the chances he will agree to various requests, something that you will have occasion to read about in Chapter 4.

Low ball

Let us imagine that a shop display contains a pair of shoes and the information that they are on sale for a 40% discount. The offer is shockingly attractive. It's the beginning of the season, and the shoes are the height of fashion! An interested customer asks about the shoes, but it turns out that her particular size is out of stock. As she is heading, disappointed, to the exit, a pair of her desired shoes in just her size turns up! She tries them on and takes a look at herself in a large mirror. They're perfect! Her friends will all be jealous. They're a bit tight but they'll definitely loosen up (beautiful and fashionable shoes definitely loosen up; a tight squeeze would disqualify ugly shoes from consideration). The customer heads to the shop assistant, with a smile on her face. She asks for the shoes she was wearing when she arrived to be packed up, and she'll put the new ones on right away! The shop assistant, however, seems to be a bit troubled. He explains why he couldn't find the customer's size at first. Her shoes were on another shelf . . . and they aren't on sale. Will the customer who wished to have fashionable shoes for a song give in to temptation and purchase them at the regular price? If the answer is "yes", it means that the sales trick turned out to be successful.

Robert Cialdini, John Cacioppo, Rodney Bassett and John Miller (1978) observed similar behaviour among American car salesmen. They resort quite often to generating a client's interest with an exceptionally good offer, such as unusually low monthly instalments or an amazingly low price. When the customer, whose interest has been piqued by the outstanding opportunity, takes a test drive, asks about some technical details, warranty conditions and insurance, and then finally declares his desire to purchase the vehicle, the problems begin. It turns out, for example, that there are no more cars available on the outstanding instalment plan, and that the ones left on the lot are available under normal payment terms (it's the customer's own fault for taking too long to decide). If, however, the "once in a lifetime opportunity" consisted in a very low price, it turns out that "the higher-ups in corporate" won't agree to sell that particular car at a lower price because it's probably already reserved for another customer, or that the salesperson made a mistake and forgot to inform the customer that the price doesn't include some headers that regulations require to be installed (for an extra fee of course). One way or another, the situation is always the same: the factor that got the customer interested in the car and led him to decide to buy it (such as an instalment plan or a low price) has been removed. The conditions of the sale are now the standard ones, but the client is now aware that he is particularly fond of one particular car and wants to have it. He is therefore unlikely to withdraw from the transaction and will probably agree to purchase the car on worse terms than the ones initially offered to him.

The psychological mechanism underlying the effectiveness of this method, named the low-ball technique by Cialdini et al., is described by Charles Kiesler (1971) as the feeling of commitment. In Kiesler's model, if an individual engages in some behaviour assuming he has the freedom of choice to do so, and believes that he himself, without any external pressure, is working towards the pursuit of some goal, he then feels an obligation to continue. So even if the conditions involved in accomplishing a given aim are transformed, the individual feels obliged to continue the activities he has already begun and to reach the goals already set.

Cialdini and his collaborators decided to undertake empirical verification of the effectiveness of the strategy they had observed among car salesmen. University students were invited to take part in a psychological experiment. Participants in the control group were informed immediately that the experiment would begin at 7:00 am. Those from the experimental group were first asked if they would agree to take part in a psychological experiment, and then after they had agreed, they were told that the study would begin at 7:00 am. The students were then asked to reaffirm their readiness to participate in the experiment. Two measurements of the strategy's effectiveness were taken into consideration: a verbal declaration of participation in the experiment, and actual arrival at the laboratory at 7:00 in the morning. In the low-ball conditions, 56% of students declared their participation while only 31% did so in the control conditions. Comparisons of actual behaviours turned out to be even more suggestive. While 53% of those approached in the low-ball conditions turned up at the laboratory, only 24% from the control group did so.

Another study examined whether students living in dormitories would agree to put up posters from a charitable organization on the windows and doors of their rooms, assuming they themselves first had to go down to the dormitory's ground floor within the next hour. In the control conditions they were asked directly to do so, and 26% of the students agreed. In the low-ball conditions, participants were first asked if they would agree to display the posters in their rooms, and after receiving their agreement the experimenter dug through his bag and stated that he had just run out of posters. He went on to say that if the participant was still interested in hanging the posters up in his room, he could go downstairs within the next hour and take one. In these conditions, 60% of people agreed.

In the next experiment, the researchers offered students credit hours in exchange for participating in a psychological study. They were given a choice between two forms of activity, of which one (which we shall call B) was slightly more attractive than the other (which we shall call A). The researchers, however, stated that participation in study B was worth one credit hour, while volunteering for study A would net them 2 credit hours. Having received this information, the majority (81%) decided to participate in the activity that would give them 2 credit hours. At that moment, however, "a mistake was discovered", and it turned out that regardless of which study they chose to participate in, they would receive only one credit hour. In spite of this, when the participants were asked to make a final declaration, 61% of them indicated they would participate in study A. In the control conditions, the number of those volunteering for study A was reduced by nearly half (31%), and the vast majority selected task B. In another version of the experiment the participants were very strongly persuaded to select task A, allegedly worth 2 credit hours. When it then "occurred" that this activity was only worth one credit hour, only 41% elected not to change their original decision. Thus the low-ball technique requires that the addressee feels free to choose at the moment of selecting a given option. If, however, the choice is made under pressure from an external source, then the engagement of the addressee in a given activity is not strong enough to make him inclined to continue following the emergence of new circumstances that render that option less attractive.

One variation on the low-ball technique is known as 'the lure', described by a group of French researchers, Robert Joule, Fabienne Gouilloux and Florent Weber (1989). While in the case of the classic low-ball technique the addressee of the request retains the possibility of receiving what he wants in spite of a sudden change of circumstances increasing its cost (e.g. it happens to be necessary to get up at the break of dawn to participate in an experiment), in the case of the lure technique it "turns out" that the initial option becomes unavailable, and an alternative is proposed.

In their study, Joule et al., (1989) offered students the chance to participate in a psychological experiment. It was explained to the control group that the experiment would involve a test of memory, and volunteers were asked to sign up for one of two dates. In the experimental group, participants were invited to take part in an interesting experiment involving emotions, which would be described in greater detail after a short time. They were promised a sum of 30 francs (around $7 or £5) for their participation. When interested students arrived at the laboratory, they were told that due to some unspecified difficulties the experiment concerning emotions would not go ahead. However, they were offered the chance to take part in an empirical study for which they would, unfortunately, receive no financial benefit. It turned out that in those conditions, three times as many people decided to take part in the experiment concerning memory than in the control group.

The differences between the low-ball technique and the lure technique are just subtle enough that the literature fails to distinguish whether the changes concern the conditions involved in achieving something, or the thing that can be achieved. In this chapter, I treat the lure as a variation on the low-ball technique, presenting research on the two together. The relevant studies have shown, for example, that this type of influence can convince people to participate in time-consuming forms of protest against further tuition and fee increases, consisting of writing letters and postcards by hand to the Student Opinion Administration (Burger & Petty, 1981), to convince them to reduce the amount of tobacco they consume (Joule, 1987) or to lower the consumption of gas used in heating their homes (Pallak, Cook & Sullivan, 1980).

Jerry Burger and Richard Petty (1981) were interested in learning whether the low-ball technique would retain its effectiveness if the first and the second requests were made by different individuals. During their study they promised credit hours to students in exchange for participation in a psychological experiment. It then turned out that there would be no credit hours awarded, but the request to take part in the study was made again. In conditions in which both requests were formulated by the same experimenter, participants nearly always reaffirmed their desire to participate. However, when the request came from another researcher, the proportion of those willing to take part in the study was reduced by nearly threefold (see Table 2.5).

In another study carried out by the same authors, the experimenter knocked on doors in a dormitory and informed students that he was a representative of The National Multiple Sclerosis Society. He then asked the students to hang a poster from his organization on their doors. In some conditions the experimenter reached into his bag, gave the student a poster and left. In others, the experimenter also reached into his bag, but then put on an expression of surprise and stated that he had just given out the last one. He promised to deliver one promptly. After 10–15 minutes a representative of the organization again knocked at the student's door. In half of the cases it was the same individual who had visited previously, while in

TABLE 2.5 Percentages of subjects complying with initial and second requests in Burger and Petty (1981) experiment

Group	Initial Request		Second request	
	%	N	%	N
Same requester	65	13	55	11
Different requester	70	14	15	3
Control	—	—	20	4

Source: *Journal of Personality and Social Psychology*, 1981, vol. 40, p. 494.
Copyright 1981 by the American Psychological Association, Inc.

the other half it was a different person. This time, the participants who had earlier been given the posters were told that the association was looking for volunteers to work that evening, while those who had not received the posters were told that there were none left, but if they wished to demonstrate their support for the Society then it was a good day to do so, as in the evening volunteers would be needed for work. The experimental design also contained a group of participants who were asked directly to become volunteers. It turned out that the low-ball technique was only effective in conditions when the target request was made by the same person who had earlier run out of posters. The implication of the studies by Burger and Petty is that low ball is based rather on the obligation to make a concession to a specific person rather than to see a given commitment through. This conclusion is supported by the results of work by Konrad Maj (2002), who decided to examine how to explain to somebody that has given in to an attractive offer the fact that circumstances have changed and the offer is less beneficial than it was. In both real-life and experimental situations, the individual who must communicate this message offers an apology for the situation. If we concur with Burger and Petty that the foundation of the low-ball technique's success is the particular relationship established during the interaction between the initiator of the request and the addressee, then this pleasantry serves to maintain the relationship and leads to the addressee acceding to the request or offer in its final (less attractive) form. It would be easier for the addressee of the request to act in his own interest and refuse, if not for the person making the request being so polite and nice. In an experiment conducted by Maj (2002), students were given the opportunity to purchase special instructional materials helpful in studying for exams. This was done by an employee of an academic bookshop who appeared at the beginning of a class. In the control conditions, he said that the materials cost $20. The price given in the experimental conditions was $15. He then requested all those interested to place their names on a list. Participants from the experimental groups were again approached by the employee of the bookstore just before the end of the class and told that he had made a mistake. Sometimes he offered a sincere apology and explained that he had confused the price with that of materials intended for other students, while in other cases he simply stated that the price was different from the one initially given. In both situations, however, he gave participants the chance to cancel their purchase. In the control conditions, nearly 34% of participants purchased the instructional materials. In the low-ball conditions in which the shop assistant politely apologized for the mistake, 62.5% of them did so. However, when the low-ball technique was not accompanied by an apology, the percentage of those prepared to purchase the materials for $20 was even slightly lower (not quite 25%) than in the control group. Maj recorded similar results in a replication experiment. It would seem the results generated by Maj suggest that, contrary to what Cialdini et al. suggest, the individual who is the target of the low-ball technique does not feel the need to continue the action engaged in, but rather simply cannot break off the interaction with an individual treating him politely and respectfully. Indeed, if these elements emphasizing the interpersonal connection go missing, the technique becomes utterly ineffective.

Summary

Sequential techniques are based on a model in which the target request is preceded by a different one. Researchers have devoted the most attention to the foot-in-the-door technique. It consists in an easy request being made first, and then when the addressee of the request carries it out (or at least agrees to do so), a subsequent, more difficult request appears. While the literature generally assumes that the foundation of this technique's success is the mechanism of self-perception, not all study results provide confirmation. Four walls is a technique similar to foot-in-the-door, but the key element is for the individual being approached to make verbal declarations that will result in him being obliged in some way to carry out a request or take advantage of a proposal. The door-in-the-face technique, similarly to foot-in-the-door, has generated significant interest among scholars. It essentially consists in the assumption that one can be induced to carry out a rather difficult request when we start with an even more challenging one. The addressee will most likely reject it, but if the easier request is then presented, he will be likely to accede. Empirical studies have demonstrated the efficacy of this technique, as well as the two conditions on which it depends. First: both requests must be made by the same person. Second: the target request must be made immediately following rejection of the initial request. This technique also has led to discussions on the psychological mechanism responsible for its success. The most commonly cited one is the reciprocity rule. An individual who rejects a request to fulfil a difficult request sees how the person making the request reduces his expectations and formulates an easier request. This, in turn, leads the addressee of the requests to feel obliged to make a concession, and he agrees to the second request. Another theoretical model proposes that rejection of a difficult request often leads to a feeling of guilt, and by complying with an easier request we can ameliorate that unpleasant feeling.

The next sequential technique analyzed in this chapter is foot-in-the-face, which is a merging of foot-in-the-door with door-in-the-face. This technique is based on the assumption that, prior to formulating the target request, another request of a different nature but similar level of difficulty should first be advanced. If the addressee fulfils this request, the mechanisms responsible for the success of the foot-in-the-door technique are activated. If he rejects it, the mechanisms that generate the effectiveness of the door-in-the-face technique are set in motion. Thus regardless of the decision concerning the first request, the chances grow that the second one will be carried out. The dump-and-chase technique, in turn, consists of persistent repetition of the same request while simultaneously convincing the addressee to discuss the reasons for the refusal. In the course of the discussion those arguments become less convincing and counter-arguments are presented. Studies on this technique are still in their initial phase, but we can assume that under certain conditions it is a successful method. The last of the techniques presented in this chapter is the "low ball". It is based on issuing a proposal to an individual that seems very attractive. After the addressee becomes cognitively and emotionally involved in carrying out the particular activity, it turns out that the offer is not quite as beneficial as it was initially made out to be. In spite of that fact, the addressee continues down the course he had set out on. While it was initially assumed that this was the result of the activation of mechanisms of engagement in activity and consistency, the newest research indicates that the feeling of an obligation towards an individual with whom we have entered into an interpersonal relationship is the key factor.

3

TECHNIQUES INVOLVING EGOTISTIC AND SELF-PRESENTATION MECHANISMS

People can hold good or bad opinions about themselves. These opinions relate to particular characteristics, competences and skills, or they can be of a more general nature. Psychologists are generally in agreement that such convictions are of importance, but controversy arises around the reasons why this is so. High levels of self-esteem obviously result in an individual experiencing positive emotions: it is pleasing to think of oneself as competent, humorous or physically attractive. This is why people try to find the good in themselves, applying an incredibly broad range of strategies and techniques that enable them to defend and even enhance their positive self-image. For example, they attribute success to themselves rather than others, while chalking failure up to others instead of themselves (e.g. Gilbert, 1995), they are eager to disclose any link they may have to famous people, which gives them pride and satisfaction (Cialdini, Borden, Thorne, Walker, Freeman & Sloan 1976), and they also exhibit tendencies towards bias in comparing themselves to others, maintaining their belief that they are better (Wills, 1981). It would, however, be an oversimplification to make the assumption that all of these efforts are based solely on the desire to experience pleasing emotions. Researchers emphasize that an affirmative view of oneself is a condition of effective task performance, as well as of making both short- and long-term plans (Taylor & Brown, 1988). Thus, striving to view oneself in even a slightly exaggerated positive light is adaptive. Yet another aspect is highlighted by Sheldon Solomon, Jeff Greenberg and Tom Pyszczynski (1991), authors of terror management theory. According to this notion, humans are the only entities on earth aware of their own mortality, this awareness being the source of fear and of threats. However, an individual can maintain the pretence of being immortal in both the literal and symbolic sense. Literal immortality is offered by the vast majority of religions, promising everlasting continuation of the soul and a second life after the one on earth. Symbolic immortality, on the other hand, is ensured by participation in broadly-taken culture, whose lifespan is far longer than that of an individual. High self-esteem allows individuals to feel they are valuable elements of culture (or a part of it, such as a nation or a group of a football club's fans). Thus, maintaining positive beliefs about oneself is a means of reducing the terror that results from being aware that our life must, eventually, end. Roy Baumeister and Dianne Tice (1990) do not concur with these assumptions. They do not directly dispute the theory itself that awareness of mortality gives rise to fear, but they rather feel that the bulk of people's daily anxieties are grounded in the threat of exclusion from the community in which we function. A strong majority of communities accepts competent, honest and valuable individuals. The conviction that one fulfils these requirements leads to a weakening of the afore-mentioned fear. So, while Solomon, Greenberg and Pyszczynski on the one hand, and Baumeister and Tice on the other, posit completely different sources for the majority of human beings' fears, they are in agreement that the antidote to them is positive self-assessment.

Most people are concerned, not only with what they think of themselves, but also with how they are viewed by others. We try to manipulate the impression we make on others so that they think of us in a manner consistent with our own interests. Sometimes we desire for people to like us, other times we want them to fear us, or even to treat us as helpless and in need of immediate assistance (e.g. Leary & Allen, 2011). When others react in the way we desire, this also contributes to *helps* improving and maintaining our self-esteem.

Concerned by others think of them

In recent decades, an increasing amount of empirical data has begun to indicate that processes associated with one's feeling of self-worth are not necessarily con-scious ones. Anthony Greenwald and Mahzarin Banaji (1995) propose applying the term 'implicit self-esteem'. People are not aware of their special relationship to things associated closely with the "I", even while those things are totally unrelated to their attitudes, skills and level of competence.

not conscious

While the effects associated with people's tendency to care for their positive self-image and to make the desired impression on others are strong and undisputed, the question is rarely addressed in research of how mechanisms associated with this can be used in successfully exerting influence over others. It appears that such stud-ies are focused primarily on four social influence techniques using the name of one's interlocutor; emphasizing one's incidental similarity to that person; drawing attention to discrepancies between publicly declared and actual behaviour; and exploiting the presence of a witness to the interaction. In this chapter I will discuss each of these techniques in turn.

Using the name of one's interlocutor ①

When Napoleon's army occupied the Netherlands in 1811, the emperor issued a decree ordering all residents of the country to officially register their surnames. Family names were not widespread at the time in the Netherlands but were the exclusive domain of people at the top of the social ladder. For many of those at the bottom of it, Napoleon's decree must have seemed a needless extravagance.

The Dutch thus began thinking up quite exotic surnames for themselves, such as: Naaktgeboren (Born Naked), Den Boef (Swindler) or Poepjes (Little Halfwit). While surnames may have seemed unnecessary in some countries and during some periods of history, since the dawn of human civilization no one has questioned the need to use first names. The status of an individual without a name can be compared to one stripped of honour, or even of humanity (Koole & Pelham, 2003). As a result, for many years a person's name has borne exceptional significance.

Jozef Nuttin (1984) described his impressions from a holiday he took with his wife. At one moment he observed that some of the licence plates on cars passing him were evoking warm feelings. After thinking about it, he concluded that this was probably from the plates that contained the letters of his name or digits corresponding to his date of birth. This constatation served as a starting point for a sterling series of empirical studies in which Nuttin demonstrated that people do, in fact, exhibit an unusual preference for the letters that compose their name.

Further studies conducted around the world demonstrated that the first letters of a name in particular seem to have impressive power. It turns out that individual letters are liked more by people whose names begin with just those letters (Kitayama & Karasawa, 1997; Koole, Dijksterhuis & van Knippenberg, 2001). In our experiments (Dolinski, 2005), the first letters of names were described by participants as having a more pleasing shape (perhaps a surprising conclusion) than letters that did not form a part of their own names. This effect was also observed in respect of letters printed from the commonplace computer programme Word for Windows (the fonts Courier and Times New Roman were used), as well as decorative letters, such as can be found at the beginnings of chapters in older volumes.

Brett Pelham, Matthew Mirenberg and John Jones (2002) demonstrated that the initial letters of first names have an influence on professional careers and on the places that people inhabit. For example, among American **den**tists there is a large number of people named **Den**nis (and vice versa, many people named **Den**nis are **den**tists), while a far greater number than chance would indicate of women named **Virginia** live in **Virginia** Beach. People with the first name or surname of **S**aint, more often than coincidence could explain, decide to take up residence in **S**aint Louis, **S**aint Paul or **S**aint Joseph. The special role of one's first name is also attested to by the cocktail party effect.

During a cocktail party, people generally stand around in small groups, and in this intimate company discuss various things. The selectivity of top-down attention means that they can block out voices coming from other small groups, focusing on what someone in their immediate vicinity is saying. The din, often loud, bothers them a bit, but they are able to tune it out to such a degree that, in a sense, they don't hear it. However, if their own name pops up in this ignored murmur, not only do they register it immediately but they also begin listening to what the person who has just used their name is saying. People are thus both ignoring and not (completely) ignoring this din at the same time: one's own name is a stimulus so strong that it has the fascinating power to divert others' attention. In the context of this chapter, the cocktail party effect constitutes an outstanding example of the importance of one's own name. From a purely practical perspective, it advises us to avoid speaking the name of the person we would like to gossip about. We mustn't be deceived by the fact that Christine is standing some distance from us and seems to be completely absorbed in her own, private conversation.

Sometimes it occurs that we recall someone's name following a chance encounter. However, other situations occur more frequently. We know that we have been told several times the name of that tall, blonde woman, or of the balding man in the glasses, but we are simply incapable of recalling what their names are. Fortunately, certain situations occur that demonstrate we are not exceptions in this regard: after all, we encounter people who themselves are utterly unable to remember our names.

If someone meets us just once, then later can recall and use our name while making some request of us, does that mean there is an increased chance that we will fulfil this request? Daniel Howard and Charles Gengler (1995) asked themselves this very question. They began with the assumption that the starting point for an analysis of this issue should be the psychological consequences of someone remembering our name. Those, in turn, are very strongly dependent on how we view the causes underlying this fact. In Howard and Gengler's opinion, the consequences will be minor if the cause is viewed as something associated with external circumstances, such as a short period of time ("It's no surprise that she remembers my name. After all, I was introduced to her just a minute ago"), or something exceptional occurring at the time ("I was sure he'd remember my name, because just after we met I got caught up in my dress and fell on the floor, then I spilled a whole glass of red wine on myself"). In other cases, the fact that someone remembers our name can give rise to a wholly different set of consequences. Setting aside particular situations like the one just described, this fact means that we have become a person of importance to someone else. This sort of consideration fulfils the need to have our ego stroked (e.g. Bowerman, 1978; Bradley, 1978). It also causes us to feel positively about the person who is providing us with such pleasant and desirable experiences. As a rule, we like people who are quick to remember our names. In turn, if we like them, we should be particularly inclined to fulfilling requests they target us with.

In an experiment designed to shed light on this question, a natural situation involving a meeting between a professor and students was used. The professor asked each of them in turn to introduce themselves to the group, and then conducted a standard introductory lesson. The next day, the professor sought out the students on campus and asked them to participate in a study he was conducting. What he wanted was for the students to fill in and return a questionnaire as quickly as possible. In half of the cases, the professor addressed the student by name, while in the remaining ones he indicated that he knew he was speaking to his student but couldn't remember that individual's name. Regardless of how the professor addressed the student, he explained that one of the areas explored by the research was the effect of the time of day on cognitive functioning, and that students were asked to write down the exact time at which they began and finished filling in the questionnaire.

None of the students refused to take the questionnaire and complete it. (It would have been odd had someone done so, taking into consideration the asymmetric relationship of professor/student.) We should keep in mind that the investigator emphasized it was of importance that the student return the completed questionnaire as quickly as possible. Thus, indicators of a positive reaction to the request were the time at which the student began and completed work on the questionnaire, and the time between the completion of this activity and the return of the papers to the professor (he had said that he would wait in his office until 11:00 pm). Analysis of the results demonstrated that students whom the professor had addressed by name began filling in the questionnaire more quickly (on average after around 2.5 hours) and brought it to his office a shorter time after completing it (on average around half an hour) than students whose names the professor appeared to be unable to recall (on average, after 5 hours and 1.5 hours, respectively).

In another experiment (Howard, Gengler & Jain, 1995), the researchers examined whether remembering someone's name and addressing a person by it increases the likelihood that the person will make a purchase, the proceeds of which would go to benefit a charity. Indeed, almost every handbook for salespeople in America advises them to remember the name and surname of their regular customers and to address them personally, but this advice is rather based on the intuitive feeling that such behaviour will increase their sales, not on any proper studies that would unequivocally confirm this.

As in the previous example, the experimental design assumed a natural situation. During the first lesson, students introduced themselves to the teacher. Following that, the teacher declared that he would like to meet each of them individually and discuss their expectations concerning the course, as well as past experience in the area the classes would focus on. The students signed up on a list, selecting the most convenient time. When a student appeared in the professor's office, the professor greeted the person either by name and surname, or impersonally, or gave a clear signal that he was not able to recall the student's name. (By differentiating these three groups, it was possible to reject the hypothesis that it is not so much remembering someone's name that increases the chance that person will fulfil later requests, but rather that a visible inability to remember someone's name will make that person exceptionally unlikely to accede to them.) After a short conversation with the student, the professor mentioned that his wife was selling cookies, and that the proceeds from sales would go to a church conducting various charitable campaigns. A record was kept of whether students bought cookies or not, and also the number of packages purchased. Initial analysis indicated that neither the decision to buy nor the number of packages bought differed between the group of students greeted impersonally and the group of students whose names the professor could not recall. This allowed for exclusion of the hypothesis that individuals observing that their name has clearly been forgotten would be particularly unlikely to fulfil requests targeted at them. Both of these groups taken together did, however, differ from the group of students addressed by their name and surname. Those students purchased cookies with more frequency and in greater quantities.

The results of the aforementioned experiment are consistent with the one described before it. This does not, however, conclusively prove that the foundation of greater inclination to fulfil the request of a person who addresses us by name is a feeling of affinity. An alternative explanation can involve the roll of one's mood. A large number of studies have indicated that people in a good mood are more eager to help others than those who are in a neutral mood (e.g. Baek & Reid, 2013; Isen & Levin, 1972; see also Chapter 6). We may assume that the constatation that someone remembers our name and surname after the first meeting puts us in a good mood (because we have turned out to be important, interesting and of significance), which then inclines us to help others.

The legitimacy of this interpretation was tested in a successive study based on a design similar to the one in the experiment previously described. This time, however, students who had arrived for an individual meeting scheduled in advance with a professor were asked to fill in a special survey concerning their classes, place it inside an envelope, seal the envelope and place it in a box located in the office of another professor responsible for evaluations of courses and instructors. The questionnaires filled in by the students included questions about the attitude of the professor towards students, as well as a scale to determine the mood of the respondent while filling in the survey. Again, analysis of the results demonstrated that people who were addressed by name purchased cookies more frequently and in greater amounts than participants from the remaining groups. It also turned out that individuals addressed by their name rated the professor's attitude towards students more highly, and they were in a better mood than the other respondents. It was also shown that addressing study participants by name had a greater impact on their attitude towards the person interacting with them than the mood they were in. While both the attitude towards the professor and the degree to which their mood was positive impacted their readiness to buy cookies at the professor's request, the strength of the former association was greater than that of the latter. These results allowed the authors to adopt the assumption than an interpretation grounded in the mechanism of liking has a greater justification than the alternative interpretation linked to the mechanism of positive mood.

It should be noted that the hypothesis assuming that the effectiveness of the technique of addressing individuals personally (by name) is based on good mood can be verified in an even more direct and conclusive manner. In order to achieve this, an experiment's design should include conditions in which a request is formulated by an individual other than the one who used the name of the participant. If this were to generate an increase in readiness to fulfil the request, it would indicate that a good mood is the key factor. However, if no differences were observed between those participants who had previously heard their name (remember: from another person) and those whose name was not used by anyone or could not be recalled, this would be direct evidence that such an interpretation was off the mark. Such a study has been carried out in Poland (Dolinski, 2005). The experiment was conducted by a student of Polish language and literature doing a teaching internship in the fifth grade of a vocational secondary school. During the first class she asked the pupils to introduce themselves and to say something about their favourite books. At the end of the last lesson that day (in another subject), the teacher excused the pupils one at a time, at half-minute intervals, in an order established beforehand with the experimenter. Although the investigator did not have as phenomenal a memory of names as Howard (Howard & Gengler, 1995), she knew the name of every pupil leaving the room because they had been written down for her. She read out the name of every pupil before the student left the class, and in doing so she created the impression that she remembered them.

The aforementioned researcher stood together with her colleague, another intern, in the corridor just outside the door to the classroom. Upon seeing a pupil exiting, she either addressed the youngster personally: "Oh, hello James, you're from the fifth grade, is that right?", or impersonally: "Oh, hello, you're from the fifth grade, is that right?" In addition, either the experimenter or her colleague made a request of the pupil. In the latter situation, the researcher stepped a few metres away, distancing herself from the interaction between her colleague and the pupil. The request addressed to the student involved "completing a survey at home", which consisted of 60 questions concerning fears related to school-leaving exams, assessment of one's prospects for the exams and future plans. Pupils were told that if they agreed to participate in the survey study they had a week to return the completed survey, but also that returning it sooner would make the work easier for the individual undertaking the study, so it would be fantastic if they could bring it back the following day or the day after. The experiment was conducted with the participation of pupils from three groups preparing for their school-leaving exams.

Nearly all of the pupils handed the surveys in, and the four experimental groups recorded equal levels of unreturned questionnaires. However, the result was that in conditions when the experimenter addressed the pupils by name and made the request herself to bring the completed surveys back as quickly as possible, the pupils returned them quicker than in the other conditions. When the experimenter addressed the pupils by name but the request to fill out the survey was made by her colleague, the pupils returned them later, to be precise, with the same delay as in the two conditions in which the experimenter did not remember their names. So, we may assume that this study justified a rejection of the interpretation of results recorded by Howard et al. (1995), in categories referring to the consequences of improving the mood of the person being addressed. By the same token, the most likely mechanism that would explain the compliance of people whom we address by name remains an increase in the interpersonal attractiveness of the person formulating the request.

In their last experiment, Howard, Gengler and Jain (1995) accumulated additional data indirectly confirming the accuracy of just such an interpretation. This particular study was based on the assumption that an egotistic reaction to the sound of one's own name would be the response primarily of people whose faith in their own capacities had been shaken. A situation was thus set up in which, prior to addressing the participants either by name or impersonally, they performed a task at which they either succeeded or failed. The task was an intellectual one, consisting of discovering the rule explaining the connection of two stimuli into a pair, and information on the participants' success or failure was supplied in a random manner. It turned out that the effect of hearing one's own name on the inclination to purchase cookies was particularly evident in respect of those students who had failed at the task just a moment earlier.

The question thus arises of whether it is really the case that increased fondness of the requester, and the desire of targets of the request to demonstrate gratitude for remembering and using their name are what come into play, or if there is also a fear (or at least anxiety) that failure to fulfil the request (or fulfilling it with insufficient zealousness) may result in the requester exacting some revenge. Of course, from a subjective perspective, such revenge is all the more likely when the person making the request identifies us personally and wields great influence over our situation; it is, therefore, more likely when this individual knows and remembers our name than when that person is unable to recall it, or doesn't even bother to try, and also more likely when the person in question is our professor or teacher rather than someone of similar status to us. In their next study, Howard, Gengler and Jain (1997) made an attempt to confirm the hypothesis of the motivation for revenge as the mechanism underlying pliability in the situations under analysis. As in previous experiments, participants were students asked during their first seminar with a professor to introduce themselves and to discuss their areas of expertise and interests. At the end of the class, the students were informed that a longitudinal study was being performed to evaluate courses, and that they would receive additional credits for participation. Those interested were able to sign up for the research. Because everyone declared their participation, the next day the professor met with them again in order to give them the evaluation surveys. The study was of an individual nature. Depending on the experimental conditions, the professor either addressed students by name, or stated that he was unable to recall students' names and requested that they introduce themselves again. Participants then anonymously (in a separate room) filled in the questionnaire, which addressed such issues as the perception of the professor's attitude towards students and the degree to which they feared that assessment of their work during the course and of their competencies could be based on something beyond substantive considerations. The students then returned to the professor's office, at which time they received a document confirming the additional credits received for participation in the study. At the same time, the experimenter proposed that they purchase cookies. In half of the cases he pointed to a table on which students could find the cookies and a piece of paper with information that they cost 25 cents each, as well as a box for money. In the other cases, the professor informed them that the cookies were in another room, and the students could go there and purchase them if they wished. The self-service cookie point of sale was arranged in a similar way. It can thus be said that the potential purchase of cookies was either of a public nature (the student knew that the professor was aware of the decision taken) or a private one (the student did not think that the professor would see). The analysis of results revealed that students whom the professor addressed by name generally bought cookies more frequently (77%) than those whose name was not mentioned by the experimenter (38%). It should come as no surprise to us that students addressed by name did so with particularly great frequency in public conditions (92%). That said, what is symptomatic is that even in purely private conditions those students bought cookies more often (64%) than those whose names the experimenter "forgot" – both in private (25%) and in public (50%) conditions. This pattern of results is entirely consistent with the assumption that the fulfilment of requests by people we address by name results from their desire to repay us for doing so.

An analysis was also undertaken of the answers provided by the student participants to questions contained in the instructional evaluation questionnaire. It transpired that students whom the professor had addressed by name rated his attitude towards them slightly higher than those whose names the professor had "forgotten". Responses to the question concerning fears over transparent assessment by the professor were not, however, a function of whether he remembered their names or not. This result also indicates clearly that the effect discussed here is not grounded in the fear of people addressed by name that refusal to accede to a request will result in their being poorly treated by the person making the request.

Incidental similarity

In one experiment by Jerry Burger, Shelley Soroka, Katrina Gonzaga, Emily Murphy and Emily Somervell (2001), female student participants filled in a questionnaire that they were told was a personality test. Next, they received feedback on the results of the test. In some conditions they learned that another person who had filled in the questionnaire together with them received a very similar personality profile. In the following stage, that very person (who was in fact collaborating with the experimenter) turned to the experiment participant with a certain request. It concerned providing assistance with a task that the collaborator had received during a class in English literature, which involved finding and asking a previously unknown individual to provide an honest assessment of an essay the collaborator had written. The essay was eight pages long, and the idea was for someone to give a sincere review of the argumentation contained therein and to write a one-page review. Would the person targeted with the request agree to it? The outcome was that this request was fulfilled much more often when the participant and the requester had allegedly similar personalities than in conditions under which no mention was made of a comparable personality profile. How can this result be explained? The simplest assumption would be to say that, since we generally like our own personality traits, the consideration that someone else shares them should result in a positive attitude towards that individual. From this positive prejudice it should follow that we are more inclined to fulfil requests made by that person.

Jerry Burger, Nicole Messian, Shebani Patel, Alicia del Prado and Carmen Anderson (2004) began, however, with the assumption that people may be particularly likely to accede to the requests of people exhibiting any – even a purely coincidental – similarity. In the first of their experiments the researchers informed female participants that they were conducting studies on the link between personality and signs of the zodiac. Situations were arranged so that the participant sat in a room with the experimenter, who pretended to be another participant. At the very beginning, the experimenter peeked at the birthdate of the participant, who had given it in a questionnaire containing demographic information. In half of the cases the experimenter provided an analogical date as her birthday, and in the remaining cases a different date was given. After a moment, the person conducting the experiment entered the room occupied by both women and explained that the personality test they would be given depended on their astrological signs. She then asked her collaborator, who was only pretending to be a participant in the study, about her date of birth. As a result, in half of the cases the real study participant was able to take into consideration that she shared a birthday with the other "participant". The person conducting the study then asked the real respondent about her date of birth (who, in the case of concurrence of dates usually made mention of her surprise at this unusual coincidence), after which she gave personality tests to both women. After the allegedly completed study, both women exited the laboratory, and in the corridor the experimenter made the request to review an eight-page essay she had written. It emerged that prior constatation of the coincidence of birthdates generated almost a twice-greater chance that this request would be fulfilled. While under conditions in which there was no concurrence of birthdates, just over 34% of participants agreed to fulfil the request, when this concurrence did occur the rate of compliance was over 62%.

In their next study, the experimenters set two objectives for themselves. First, they decided to examine whether analogical effects would occur in the case of a slightly induced conviction of an incidental similarity. Second, they changed the nature of the request. Whereas in the experiment previously described the request was of a personal nature, and accession to it provided the person making the request with immediate benefits, in this case the request had a socially beneficial essence. Here participants were invited to an experiment concerning creative thinking. They were asked to select one of the items placed on a desk, and then spend five minutes describing all of its possible applications. With knowledge of each participant's name, during these five minutes a scenario was arranged to take place following the participant's exit from the laboratory. An experimenter stood in front of the building collecting donations on behalf of a severely ill girl. She wore an ID badge and held a picture of the sick girl in her hands. Depending on the experimental conditions, the ID badge worn by the experimenter had either exactly the same name as the study participant, or a different one. In the latter case, different names of the sick girl on the picture were also given. Sometimes the signature under the photograph indicated that she had the same name as the study participant, whereas in other cases the names were different. The researchers did not provide data on the percentage of people making a donation in particular experimental conditions, limiting themselves to the average sums donated by participants in individual conditions. The results of this study are presented in Figure 3.1.

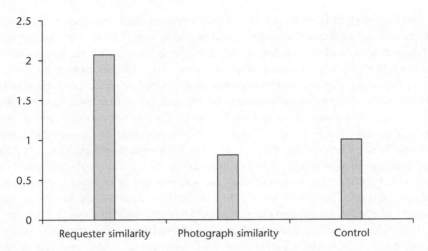

FIGURE 3.1 Mean amount of money donated in Burger et al. (2004) experiment

As can be seen, when the study participants ascertained that the volunteer had the same name as they did, they gave significantly larger sums of money than in the remaining two conditions. The observation that they share a name with the victim in need of assistance did not, however, result in such generosity. The perception by the target of the request of similarities to the person issuing the request is of key importance (see also Pandelaere, Briers, Dewitte & Warlop, 2010).

Nicolas Gueguen, Nathalie Pichot and Gwenaelle Le Dreff (2005) invited students via e-mail to participate in a questionnaire study. It transpired that they were far more successful in recruiting participants for such studies in conditions when the person lodging the request signed with the same surname as the person invited to participate. Randy Garner (2005) investigated the persuasive influence of name similarity on questionnaire return rates. He demonstrated that both undergraduates and college professors completed and returned questionnaires more frequently if the name on the cover letter was similar to their own. This effect was independent of name familiarity. Angelique Martin and Nicolas Gueguen (2013), in turn, stopped passers-by on the pavement and asked them to answer a series of questions. They began with purely demographic questions (date of birth, marital status, etc.), proceeding to slightly intrusive and intimate (the age at which their virginity was lost), until reaching the level of clearly "taboo questions" (e.g. "Do you use sex toys?"). It is known that people very often refuse to answer such intimate questions (Tourangeau & Yan, 2007). Such refusal occurred with far less frequency in conditions under which the experimenter, upon hearing the respondent's day of birth, stated with feigned surprise that he was also born on the same day of the same month. Other studies have demonstrated that people declare their intention to take advantage of a dental care programme or recreation centre programme more often when they "discover by chance" that they were born on the same day and month as the individual making the pitch to them (Jiang, Hoegg, Dahl & Chattopadhyay, 2010).

Although the similarity induced in the studies discussed above concerned rather trivial things, it was sufficient to increase the tractability of people towards requests targeted at them. It is worth observing that the likelihood of such a coincidence occurring was rather minimal. The odds that another person was born on the same day and in the same month as us are 1/365; the probability that someone else has the same name as we do is more difficult to estimate, and depends on the degree of originality of our name in a given population, but we can safely assume that the chances of this happening are not great. The question arises of whether the low probability of a similarity occurring is a condition that enhances submissiveness? In attempting to answer this question, Burger et al. (2004) informed study participants that they were involved in a study dedicated to the links between personality and biological traits. As part of this study, thumbprints were taken from the participants. Individuals taking part in the experiment were then informed that they had a type E fingerprint. As one might expect, another study participant also had the same type of fingerprint. The experimenter also mentioned either that type E fingerprints could be found in just 2% of the population, or that it was the most common type, occurring in 80% of humans. In the control group, thumbprints were also taken from participants, but nothing was said to them about the type of fingerprint they had. Next, the official portion of the experiment was concluded, and an experimenter playing the role of a participant asked an individual actually taking part to review an essay she had written. The same request was also made in the control group. It transpired that only an exceptional similarity to other individuals inclined people to fulfil their requests. While in conditions when type E fingerprints were allegedly present in only 2% of the population the request was fulfilled in the vast majority of cases; in conditions when it was said that type E was the most prevalent one, only about half of the participants complied with the request. The rate of compliance in this group was not significantly higher than that observed in the control group. The results of this experiment are presented in Figure 3.2.

One particularly distinctive form of similarity is imitation of the behaviours exhibited by an individual we begin interacting with. As was demonstrated by Tanya Chartrand and John Bargh (1999), people usually unconsciously imitate gestures (e.g. wiping one's face, foot tapping) made by the person with whom they are speaking. In another experiment, the authors also proved that people are generally more positively predisposed to those who subtly imitate them. It is this last discovery that served as a natural impetus to undertake a series of studies concerning social influence. The hypothesis that the subtle imitation of partners make them more likely to comply with our requests and suggestions has become exceedingly obvious. The results of experimental studies are quite definitive. Rick van Baaren, Rob Holland, Kerry Kawakami and Ad van Knippenberg (2004) demonstrated that when an experimenter imitated the position of an interlocutor's hands and legs, there was a greater likelihood of receiving assistance from the study participant in gathering coins that had allegedly spilled onto the floor by accident. In other experiments results indicated that waiters who repeated the words spoken by

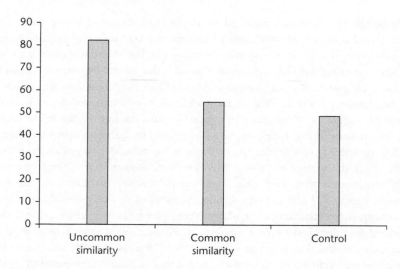

FIGURE 3.2 Percentage agreeing to the request in Burger et al. (2004) experiment

customers while taking their orders received larger tips (van Baaren, Holland, Steenaert & Knippenberg, 2003), and sales staff in shops with electronics equipment (Jacob, Gueguen, Martin & Boulbry, 2011) and cosmetics (Kulesza, Szypowska, Jarman & Dolinski, 2014) sold more of it. Wojciech Kulesza, Dariusz Dolinski, Avia Huisman and Robert Majewski (2014) demonstrated that similar techniques can induce people to make donations for charitable causes, and that copying the words used by our partner in an interaction results in an effect of equal strength, regardless of whether the order of those words is observed or not, as long as the sense of the utterance is maintained.

Copying the behaviours of an interlocutor can, moreover, concern both behavioural and verbal reactions simultaneously. Robin Tanner, Rosellina Ferraro, Tanya Chartrand, James Bettman and Rick van Baaren (2008) invited participants to sample a new beverage named "Vigor". In some cases, while speaking about the product, the experimenter imitated the gestures and repeated the words spoken by the participant, allegedly to be sure that he had properly understood the statement. He did not do this with the other participants. It turned out that participants from the former group rated the taste of the beverage more highly.

Induction of hypocrisy

At the beginning of the 1990s, Elliot Aronson, Carrie Fried and Jeff Stone (1991) described a technique that they termed 'induction of hypocrisy', which is based on inducing individuals to understand clearly that their behaviour is inconsistent with their public declarations. Such an observation of one's own hypocrisy and inconsistency in behaviour is an unpleasant experience, and motivates people to behave in a manner befitting of their previous public statements.

The induction of hypocrisy technique consists of two stages. In the first, individuals are encouraged to openly declare support for a viewpoint or idea they really do (at least on the level of verbal declarations) accept. In the second stage, their attention is focused on their own behaviours that are inconsistent with that declaration. In a series of experiments Aronson et al. asked students to make short speeches on camera about the sensibility of using condoms. Next, they held conversations with the students during which they asked the participants to recall all the situations in which they failed to use condoms. Study participants then had the opportunity to purchase condoms. Results indicated that the students subjected to the induction of hypocrisy technique bought more of them than those who were assigned to another group during the experiment – those who only made statements on camera about the necessity of using condoms, or those who only had to recall situations in which they did not use them.

In another study involving the induction of hypocrisy technique, students at a swimming pool were asked to sign a declaration that the obligation of every conscious human being is to avoid wasting water. They were then asked to respond to questions in a survey whose alleged objective was the implementation of a water conservation programme. The questions were formulated so that students responding to them were inevitably led to the conclusion that they did not conserve water. They were thus made aware of their hypocrisy (I will sign an appeal about saving water, but I won't do it myself) and a lack of consistency in their behaviour. As it turned out, students subjected to this influence later began limiting the time they spent taking showers in comparison to those who were not asked to respond to the survey nor to sign the petition (Dickerson, Thibodeau, Aronson & Miller, 1992). Using a similar approach it was also possible to prompt people to recycle packing materials (Fried, 1998), and to use sunscreen to reduce the risk of skin cancer (Stone & Fernandez, 2011).

What, exactly, explains the success of the technique being described? Aronson claims that the mechanism underlying its effectiveness is the individual's experience of a state of dissonance. In contrast to Leon Festinger, creator of the theory of cognitive dissonance (1957), who defined this phenomenon as an inconsistency between two convictions or between a conviction and a behaviour, Aronson (1969, 1997) also perceives its essence in a threat to one's feeling of self-worth and the integrity of the "I". Cognitive dissonance in his definition is linked with the need to see oneself as an intelligent and moral person, and it emerges only when this perception is under threat. The successful reduction of dissonance is a condition in which individuals can again view themselves as moral and intelligent beings.

The induction of hypocrisy technique leads to people becoming consciously aware of the discrepancies between what they feel is important and proper (and what they publicly declare support for) and their real behaviour. This state places their values under threat and wobbles the conviction of the integrity of the "I". It motivates individuals to behave in accordance with prior public declarations. Their manifestation makes it possible to rebuild the conviction of self-worth and the view of self as an individual who behaves in a consistent, coherent manner. It is worth stressing that the induction of hypocrisy technique also works when, following an individual's realization of the differences between beliefs and behaviours, the opportunity is then created to boost the threatened self-appraisal in a manner other than adapting actions to declared opinions. Jeff Stone, Andrew Wiegand, Joel Cooper and Elliot Aronson (1997) first asked participants to videotape a speech for a high school AIDS prevention programme about the importance of using condoms to prevent AIDS, and then encouraged them to admit they themselves had on occasion neglected to use condoms. It was made possible to recover one's sense of self-worth either directly (participants were offered the chance to buy condoms, thus behaving in a manner consistent with their professed beliefs), or indirectly (participants could make a donation to benefit the homeless, and thus feel they were morally just). Even though participants were given the chance to recover their self-esteem indirectly, they preferred to take the direct route, adjusting their behaviour to their declared views. This demonstrates the strength of the induction of hypocrisy technique in altering people's behaviours.

Valerie Fointiat (2004) decided to examine whether the induction of hypocrisy technique is based in dissonance. She began with the assumption that dissonance should be felt particularly acutely by people whose feeling of self-worth is uncertain or is being threatened. If the technique presently analyzed is particularly effective towards just these kinds of people, it will constitute a strong argument for a foundation in dissonance.

In a study conducted in a supermarket car park, housewives were approached. They were randomly assigned to one of four groups. In three of them, participants were first asked to sign an appeal with the words "Everybody has to respect speed limits. When you drive slowly, life goes on". Then, participants were asked to respond to a series of questions about whether in the last two months they had been speeding, and to discuss the place, time and circumstances surrounding these incidents.

Next, the women were offered to have a recording tachometer installed in their cars – a special device that registers the speed at which a car is driven. They were also informed that this would be free of charge.

In two of the aforementioned three groups an additional manipulation of the integrity of participants'"I" was introduced. In one of the groups, the experimenter stated at the very beginning that although 95% of people exceed the speed limit, it didn't seem that the participant would belong to this category (reinforcing the feeling of integrity); in the second group, the experimenter did just the opposite, expressing the belief that the participant did, at least sometimes, exceed the speed limit (a threat to the feeling of integrity).

In the fourth (control) group a portion of participants were asked to sign the appeal, and the other to answer a series of questions. The results of this experiment have shown that individuals in whom hypocrisy was induced (and thus those who first signed the appeal, then responded to questions about their own behaviours behind the wheel) agreed more often to the installation of a tachometer in their car than did those from the control group who either signed the appeal or answered survey questions. The effect of the induction of hypocrisy was strong in those experiencing a threat to their own feeling of self-worth, but was absent in those who had this feeling reinforced.

Thus the experiment by Fointiat (2004) not only provided another piece of evidence as to the effectiveness of the induction of hypocrisy technique, but also proof of its grounding in dissonance. While keeping in mind empirical data attesting to the effectiveness of this technique, it should also be considered that its effectiveness is limited to particular areas of reality. Indeed, it is only useful when we desire to induce people to behave in a manner they support and value in the verbal layer. Other studies by Fointiat and her collaborators (Fointiat, Somat & Grosbras, 2011) also show that changes to behaviours do not occur if, immediately after becoming aware of one's hypocrisy, the participant is given the chance to trivialize the discrepancies between words and deeds. In one of their experiments, participants were made aware of their hypocrisy regarding observance of speed limits, and were then asked to participate in volunteer work for a road safety organization. If this request was made just after the induction of hypocrisy, the result was a greater tendency on the part of the participants to engage in altruistic behaviour. If, however, the offer to be involved in work for a road safety organization was preceded by a questionnaire filled in by participants in which they had to rate how important it was to adhere to the rules of the road regarding speed, they applied a different method for reducing cognitive dissonance: trivialization. They usually responded that observing speed limits isn't a particularly important matter, and then demonstrated no eagerness to become involved in altruistic work for the benefit of a road safety organization. In another article, Fointiat (2008) presents data that suggests the circumstances in which individuals become aware of their hypocrisy may be of importance. The effects of changes to behaviours are stronger when a norm governing how people should behave is negotiated during a discussion with others rather than a situation in which they are asked individually about it.

This last issue brings us closer to another area of social influence – the potential presence of others (outside observers) in situations during which we are asking someone for something.

A witness to an interaction

One of the more well-known and classic books by Erving Goffman (1959) bears the title "The presentation of self in everyday life". In essence, individuals are often not entirely themselves, but actors showing others their various faces, staged for the needs of particular audiences. People do not want others to know they are irritated; they desire for others to see them as intelligent and to admire their sense of humour; on the beach they suck their stomachs in to show how attractive and thin they are. These types of behaviours are referred to in psychology as "self-presentation". Activities involving self-presentation can exhibit a very wide range of features. It has been shown in many studies that this often lies at the foundation of offering help to others. Generally, readiness to provide assistance is reduced when people are unobserved (e.g. Finkiel & Baumeister, 2010; Gottlieb & Carver, 1980). When there are witnesses, however, people can demonstrate their altruism.

With this in mind, Bruce Rind and Daniel Benjamin (1994) came to the conclusion that certain types of requests will be more readily fulfilled by people when there is another person witnessing them. It would be best if the witness was an emotionally close person, whose opinion is of particular importance to the target of the request.

With a view to testing this assumption, Rind and Benjamin conducted an experiment in the period immediately preceding Christmas, at a small restaurant in a shopping centre. The study participants consisted of young men. The experimenter approached men sitting at a table either alone, or in the company of a woman. Next, he offered the man a chance to purchase a lottery ticket. The main prize was a weekend for two in Bermuda, and the proceeds from the lottery were to benefit a charity. The gauge of request fulfilment was the average number of tickets purchased in the two conditions compared with each other. It turned out that the men purchased nearly twice as many tickets when they were in the company of a woman (on average two tickets) than when alone (on average just over one ticket). It was also the case that half of the men sitting alone were not even interested in listening to the entire pitch given by the person selling the tickets, while in conditions in which a female was in their company, only six percent of the time did the men interrupt the ticket salesman before he had finished speaking. These results could suggest that the need to make a good impression on the witness to an interaction between a requester and the target of the request inclines the latter to a greater level of amenity and to complying with the request. This need could thus form the basis for an effective technique exploiting the presence of an observer.

Some questions, however, arise from this experiment. First and foremost, the issue of whether the desire to cast oneself in a good light before a person of importance to us is really at work here. Conditions in which someone offers to sell a lottery entry to a man sitting with a woman induce him to listen to the entire pitch, not because he wants to look good to his partner, but because the situation itself becomes unclear and ambiguous. When a man is sitting alone and concludes after hearing just a few words that he is not interested in the proposal being made by a stranger, he can express this directly and interrupt the monologue. If, however, he is accompanied by someone else, he might assume that the proposal he himself is not interested in could be an attractive one for his female friend. This fact precludes him from interrupting the salesman's monologue. Another problem with Rind and Benjamin's experiment concerns the nature of the request itself. The lottery ticket salesman mentioned that the main prize was a trip for two people to Bermuda. This could have rendered the chance to take a punt more attractive for a man sitting at a table with a partner (he could go with her to Bermuda) than for a person sitting alone (who would be more likely to think that he wouldn't have anybody to go with, so there would be no point in buying a ticket). The sorting of participants into groups is also difficult to label as random. Men spending their time alone can differ in many ways from those sitting with women.

The first of these issues was examined by Renata Koscielniak (1998) in a study based on a concept applied by Rind and Benjamin, but with an enhanced experimental design. She assumed that if the need for positive self-presentation is what motivates people to hear someone out to the end when confronted with situations like the one created by the American researchers, then the readiness of the person to whom the request is addressed should be a function of who the witness of the interaction between the asker and the asked is. A situation in which a young man is with a young woman he knows should provide a greater impetus to self-presentation than one in which a man happens to be with another man, or with an unknown woman.

The research was conducted on the streets of Wrocław, a city in south-west Poland. The target participants were young men either walking alone, or in the company of another man, or in the company of a woman. A female experimenter approached participants, introduced herself as a representative of a children's foundation, and asked them to do something on behalf of the foundation (depending on the conditions, this could be purchasing a ticket for a lottery in which the main prize was a television; purchasing a ticket for a lottery in which the main prize was a New Year's Eve package in the mountains for two; or making a donation for a particular charity). The experimental design also included conditions in which the targeted man was with an unknown woman for only a short moment. In these cases, a female collaborator of the experimenter approached a man walking alone and asked him for directions. Next, the experimenter appeared and made her request, while the collaborator remained as a passive observer of the interaction. As it transpired, participants were more inclined to purchase lottery tickets than to make a donation, but in none of the conditions did the presence of an additional person and witness to the interaction increase participants' readiness to fulfil requests compared to conditions in which they were walking down the street alone. Koscielniak's second experiment precisely replicated that of Rind and Benjamin, but her results also failed to demonstrate a reduced interest in acceding to requests made by an unknown individual on the part of men who were alone compared to those of men accompanied by women.

These results potentially suggest that there are differences in models of self-presentation between the United States and Poland. It cannot be ruled out that in the USA, a person who wants to make a good impression on someone else makes a demonstration of generosity and eagerly buys a lottery ticket whose proceeds will benefit a charity. In Poland, this type of self-presentation is most likely far less common, and people try to make an impression on others in an entirely different way. It could even be supposed that people in Poland want to show their assertiveness during a situation in which someone probably wants to cheat them out of money. However we look at it, the effectiveness of the technique of exploiting a witness's presence requires further exploration, including of the intercultural dimension.

Summary

This chapter has provided analysis of social influence techniques whose common denominator are the mechanisms underlying their effectiveness. These mechanisms appeal to a fundamental human need: most people want to see themselves in a good light, and they want others to think well of them.

The first technique is very simple. It only requires that we quickly and correctly remember the name of the person we are interacting with, and then use this name during future contact. This simple operation (requiring a very sharp memory) results in a greater propensity on the part of another person to comply with our requests. People treated in this manner feel they are favoured and appreciated when they consider that during the first, brief meeting someone has bothered to remember their name. This generates increased goodwill to the individual who is presently formulating a request towards us.

The second of the techniques consists in displaying a similarity, if just an incidental one, to the individual asked to fulfil a request. This could be a shared birthdate, or some unusual trait (in the experiment discussed this trait involved fingerprint characteristics). Interestingly, research has shown that even similarities in respect of entirely trivial (but rarely occurring) characteristics are sufficient for a marked increase in amenability. Compliance can also be induced in others by imitating their gestures, or by repeating their verbal communiqués.

The third technique described in this chapter is more complex. The induction of hypocrisy is comprised of two phases. In the first of them, individuals are encouraged to declare their support for a view or idea that they in fact (at least at the level of verbal declarations) accept. In the second phase, the focus shifts to their behaviours that contradict the declaration. When people become aware that their own behaviours are inconsistent with their public statements, this evokes a feeling of dissonance. The desire to rid oneself of this feeling induces people to undertake behaviours consistent with previous public declarations. It must be emphasized that, while the technique is effective, this effectiveness is limited to situations in which the aim is to induce an individual to engaging in behaviours in line with openly declared convictions.

The fourth of the techniques placed under analysis is based on the assumption that many human behaviours are associated with the need for self-presentation. We behave a bit differently in the presence of others than in entirely private situations. American studies demonstrated that if the request concerns engaging in charitable activity, men are more eager to fulfil it when they are in the company of a woman than when they are alone. In Poland, this result could not be replicated. Perhaps this is the result of culturally determined differences.

4

THE ROLE OF WORDING
THE REQUEST

The overwhelming majority of human interactions involve a verbal component (Clark, 1985). It goes without saying that the same trait is true of the majority of social influence techniques. For example, in the case of sequential techniques described in the Chapter 2 of this book, an initial request is first issued verbally, and then the target request is also presented verbally. Even when the role of non-verbal interaction is being studied, such as in the case of techniques based on making eye contact or holding the addressee of a request by the arm (see Chapter 5), these gestures are accompanied by a request expressed verbally. Words thus lie at the heart of social influence. In this chapter, we will take a special look at words by examining techniques in which the word takes centre stage. We will analyze the role of subtle differences in the content of messages addressed to other individuals. It will become clear that seemingly superficial differences can in fact be of key significance, and that what seems obvious to us is not always so.

"Please" – is it always the magic word?

Most of the time, being polite will not only increase the chances that our request is agreed to, but will also give rise to a symmetrical politeness when it is carried out. We can imagine a situation in which someone asks for directions to a building, like a university library. This exceedingly simple request can be formulated in at least a dozen different ways. For example, we can ask "Where's the university library?", "Excuse me, where is the university library?", or "I'm so sorry to bother you, but would you be so kind as to tell me where the university library is?" Herbert Clark and Dale Schunk (1980) conducted a series of studies in which they asked their students to read a list of similar requests and then write down the answers they would provide to them. The pattern in the results showed very clearly that the more polite the question, the more polite the response. This gives rise to the question of whether being polite always increases the strength of social influence. The body of empirical work examining this particular question, while admittedly small, gives us firm grounds to doubt that it does.

Michael Firmin, Janine Helmick, Brian Iezzi and Aaron Vaughn (2004) examine the extent to which including the word "please" when making a request increases the likelihood that it will be carried out. They called several hundred students and offered to sell them chocolate cookies, while informing them that the proceeds from the sale would go to help people suffering from hunger. A cookie cost 50 cents. Half of the time, the pitch was concluded with the words "Will you purchase a cookie?", and in the other half the word "please" was added to the question. The frequency with which people bought the cookie differed between the two conditions, but as it turned out, in conditions where the word "please" was added to the end of the request they were bought less often (65.3%) than in conditions where that word was absent (79%). While this result was quite surprising for the authors of the experiment, they made an effort to explain it. In my opinion, at least two of the potential explanations they offered for the results of their experiment deserve our attention.

First, it is highly probable that the word "please" in the context of a minor request submitted in the course of an experiment might seem strange, inappropriate or even suspicious to the experiment's participants. "Please" is a word used in order to persuade people we do not know during interactions with them, so it may be the case that hearing that word at the end of a sales pitch for cookies leads to a heightened sense of caution.

Second, the appearance of the word "please" at the end of a message may redefine the object which is receiving the aid. When the situation consisted of the study participant being informed that by purchasing a cookie he would help those suffering from hunger, his positive decision was associated with providing aid to people who have nothing to eat. The word "please" may lead to a change in the perception of that situation. Agreeing to buy the cookie would be more likely associated not with the hungry, but rather the person who most clearly has a direct interest (that is, the person who is making the request). Naturally, it is more sensible to think that buying a cookie will help those who are suffering from hunger rather than someone who is likely sitting comfortably in a chair, talking over the phone as part of his everyday job.

In another experiment, Aaron Vaughn, Michael Firmin and Chi-en Hwang (2009) examined the degree to which the word "please" could help a dishonest person avoid having his fraud uncovered. They took advantage of the fact that some students were supposed to take a test on general knowledge of psychology. The students were invited to come in pairs into a room; one of the students was an actual student (the study participant), while the other was a confederate who was only pretending to take the test. A teaching assistant handed out the test to both of them, informed them that they had 10 minutes to complete it, and left the room. The confederate copied multiple answers from the student's test on several occasions. A minute before the examiner's return, the confederate turned to the participant and asked him to keep his cheating a secret by saying "Don't tell the teaching assistant I cheated, I need your help", while in half of the cases this message was preceded by the word "please". In the control conditions he said nothing to the study participant. It was then recorded whether the study participant reported his colleague's dishonesty to the teaching assistant (the confederate quickly exited the room, leaving the participant alone with the examiner). It turned out that in the control conditions 24% of participants informed the examiner of the other student's cheating. In conditions in which the "student" politely requested that the participant keep his secret, the results were similar (28.6%), while in the conditions in which he simply said "Don't tell . . ." they shot up to 52.2 %. What explains this pattern of results? Perhaps the very appeal not to expose the cheating focused participants' thoughts on the dishonesty and violation of ethical norms by their partner in the interaction, and for this reason they reported the fraud more frequently in the "Don't tell" conditions than in the control conditions. "Please", in turn, awoke a feeling of sympathy and had the opposite effect, minimizing the inclination to expose the dishonest partner in spite of the focus on his reprehensible behaviour. One way or another, the polite request was, indeed, more effective than a simple message, but it was not as effective as silence.

In two field studies which I conducted with Barbara Dolinska (Dolinska & Dolinski, 2006), we examined the role of the sex of partners in an incidental interaction, involving conditions of formulating a request either politely or rather impolitely. In the first study, the experimenter pretended to be looking for a lost gold earring, which was supposed to be a present for his/her mother; in the second, help was sought in guarding a bicycle as the experimenter needed to drop by his/her aunt's flat on the eighth floor of a block of flats in which the elevator was out of order. In half of the cases the request for help was formulated very politely ("Would you be so kind as to help me . . ."), while in the other half it came across as an order ("I've lost a precious gold earring here. You must help me look for it!" or "Watch my bicycle so no one will steal it."). It turned out that if the interaction took place between individuals of the same sex, the polite request was clearly more effective than the order (this probably comes as a surprise to nobody). Surprisingly, however, it turned out that if a woman addresses an unknown man, or a man addresses an unknown woman, a quite impertinent order is more effective than a polite request! In attempting to explain this pattern of results, we assumed that an order constitutes an emphasis on the part of the person giving the message of his/her privileged position in relation to the addressee of the message. In Western culture (European/American), men generally enjoy higher social status than women, something that also concerns situations involving communication (Carli, 1990). Men therefore perceive that it is their right to order a woman to do something. On the other hand, the same culture acknowledges that women, due to the disparity in physical strength between women and men, have the right to demand assistance and care from the opposite sex, therefore they have the right to issue orders to men. Both men and women are thus entitled to emphasize their privileged status during interactions with people of the opposite sex, which they may do by way of direct orders. The addressee of such a message clearly does not call this privilege into question and provides the necessary assistance to the person issuing the order.

To tell the truth, I am not entirely sure if this is the right interpretation, but I am not able to come up with a more convincing one. Either way, the experiments presented in this part of the chapter demonstrate that the word "please" – contrary to what our instincts tell us – does not always boost our chances of success in having someone carry out a request.

Even a penny will help

Robert Cialdini and David Schroeder (1976) draw attention to the fact that people do not experience great difficulty in refusing difficult requests. Indeed, if someone turns to us with a request that would cost us a lot of money, place heavy demands on our time, or would in some other way prove burdensome, we are capable of providing many reasons for which we cannot accede to that request. What is more, these reasons generally enjoy social acceptance. Other people (including the one formulating the request) should, in turn, acknowledge the sensibility of our arguments. Easier requests, however, are an entirely different matter. First, it is difficult to provide rational, convincing arguments why we cannot agree to them; second, refusal to carry out simple requests may have negative implications for self-perception. A person who refuses to do some small thing that would bring joy to someone close to him will have to deal with the feeling that he is unhelpful, insensitive and unsympathetic.

The situation is thus quite disadvantageous from the perspective of the person issuing a request. If he asks for a lot, there are few who will agree. If he asks for a little, the request will definitely be agreed to by more people, but each donor will give only a minimum. Cialdini and Schroeder indicate the way out of this paradox. They suggest employing a message in which we do not state exactly what level of help is expected, while at the same adding that any help at all – even the smallest amount – is highly valued and will be accepted with gratitude. It is sufficient in the case of a standard request for financial assistance to add on the phrase "Even a penny will help". In this manner, a person hearing the request will be prevented from thinking "I would do it, but I can't afford it", or "I'm not rich either". To put it more simply, the addressee of such a request will not be able to identify rational arguments justifying a refusal to provide assistance. On the other hand, we are not simply asking for a small amount of help (we are not saying that we want precisely one penny). The chance remains that the assistance offered will be more than symbolic.

In an experiment testing the effectiveness of the "even a penny will help" technique, people presenting themselves as members of the American Cancer Society went door-to-door in the suburbs, and after introducing themselves they stated that they were collecting donations for the fight against that awful disease. The experimental group added the phrase "even a penny will help" to the standard pitch for donations. It turned out that in the control group just under 29% of those approached were willing to make a donation, while in the experimental group this number reached 50%. Interestingly, those from the experimental group who made a donation to those engaged in the fight against cancer gave them, on average, the same amount of money as those approached in the control conditions. Thus the experimental group collected a much higher sum than the control group. We can clearly observe that those who were told "even a penny will help" did not limit themselves to giving a just a penny.

We may, however, question whether the information "even a penny will help" really accomplishes what the authors claim it does, which is to stop the addressee from explaining to both himself and others the reasons for not providing assistance in such terms as "I can't afford it", and thus becoming a factor that enhances the generosity of those approached; an entirely different mechanism from the one just described may, at least potentially, come into play. The information that any sum of money will help could imply that the organization seeking donations is in a perilous financial situation. In such a situation the factor inducing people to offer assistance is rather a feeling of pity and the resulting obligation to support those who would not manage on their own.

To examine which of these mechanisms played a real role in the study being discussed, Cialdini and Schroeder conducted an additional empirical study in which they applied four experimental conditions. Along with the standard request and the appended "even a penny will help", this time they added "We've already received some contributions, ranging from a penny and up, and I wonder if you would be willing to help by giving a donation", or it was said that "even a dollar will help". It turned out that the information about previous benefactors giving "from a penny and up" provoked a positive reaction on the part of those approached with roughly the same frequency as the phrase "even a penny will help". Because this message does not evoke the image of a charitable organization in a dramatic financial situation (something which Cialdini and Schroeder examined in yet another study), we may in fact assume that by providing information about the acceptability of a minimal donation, we are able to neutralize self-justifying interpretations for refusing to help, by the same token inducing people to reach for their wallets. This interpretation is also supported by the fact that a larger sum was collected from the group which heard "even a dollar will help" as a part of the pitch for a donation than in the case of the control group.

James Weyant and Stephen Smith (1987) decided to examine whether the 'even a penny will help' technique could be successful when applied in the context of a charity drive conducted via direct mail. A fundamental difficulty in using the literal formula, however, was the cost of organizing a campaign of that nature. The symbolic penny was not enough to cover the costs of printing and postage. The researchers therefore decided to replace the phrase "every cent" with a suggested minimum donation of $5. For the experiment, people living in the suburbs were sent letters from the American Cancer Society. The letter was accompanied by an index card designed to simplify the donation process. In some cases there was no suggestion of a minimum donation that should be made, while in others there were various dollar amounts suggested, such as $50 (a typical number for a charity drive) or $5 (a very unusual figure, incredibly low). It turned out that when the minimum suggested donation was $5 the total sum of money collected was significantly greater than when no minimum donation was proposed, and also when the proposed donation was given as $50. At the same time, the average value of donations from those who offered their support to the American Cancer Society was similar in all three experimental conditions. Thus it can be said that in the case of direct mail the principle "ask for less to get more" is also applicable. It should, however, be mentioned that when William DeJong and Arvo Oopik (1992) tested the "even a penny will help" technique when approaching potential benefactors for a donation via direct mail, their results did not demonstrate a greater proportion of people offering help. Perhaps this resulted only from the fact that study participants were sent a large number of very diverse materials, as a result of which most of the addressees of the appeal might not have even read it.

The "legitimization of a paltry contribution" technique (this is a more official alternative name for the influence technique under analysis here) is not limited exclusively to situations involving the pursuit of monetary donations. Junko Takada and Timothy Levine (2007) recruited volunteers to help in administrating orientation programmes for new international students by approaching young people walking around campus who appeared to be students. They explained that various activities could be helpful, such as picking foreign students up from the airport or showing them around campus. In half of the cases the appeal to volunteers was concluded with the words "even a few minutes would help". It turned out that this increased the percentage of people declaring readiness to provide assistance from 14% to 23%. (However, owing to the small size of the cohort, this difference did not achieve statistical significance). In our experiments we approached residents of Wrocław, a large Polish city, and asked for their help in distributing flyers among their acquaintances promoting the organization of the World Expo in Wrocław. In half of the cases the appeal for help was concluded with the phrase "Every single distributed leaflet will count". The result was that, by adding this phrase, the percentage of people who accepted a packet of leaflets for distribution rose from just under 31% to over 43% (Dolinski, Grzyb, Olejnik, Prusakowski & Urban, 2005).

A range of studies using the technique under analysis in other areas than collecting monetary donations have been conducted by Nicolas Gueguen. Interestingly, information that even a minimal level of contribution is legitimized was not stated verbally in these experiments. Study participants could, however, get the message . . . by reading the t-shirts of experimenters. In one such study (Gueguen, 2013a) students were encouraged to donate blood. Those who were engaged in recruiting donors were dressed in jeans and red t-shirts. In half of the cases the t-shirts bore the slogan "Even one donation in your lifetime will help". It turned out that the presence of this slogan on t-shirts increased the percentage of people donating blood from under 10% to over 16%. Celine Jacob, Virginie Charles-Sire and Nicolas Gueguen (2013) also dressed experimenters in t-shirts, but this time they stood in front of the entrance to a supermarket. The study was conducted just before Christmas and involved the collection of food donations for impoverished families. When the t-shirts displayed the slogan "Even a single package of pasta will help", the proportion of people who deposited food purchased from the store into specially prepared shopping carts increased from around 20% to over 29%. In yet another study, based on a similar design, the experimenters demonstrated that donations could be successfully increased just by wearing t-shirts with the slogan "Even a single marble will make him/her happy" (Gueguen, Martin & Meineri, 2013).

But you are free!

Many legends of psychology have rightfully emphasized that people place a high value on personal freedom, and that they react with aversion when someone wants to restrict that freedom (e.g. Brehm, 1966; deCharms, 1968). Taking this very assumption as their point of departure, Nicolas Gueguen and Alexandre Pascual (2000) formulated the hypothesis that direct semantic evocation of the subject's freedom in making a decision facilitates compliance with the request. In their experiment they randomly divided shoppers walking alone around a mall into two groups. In the control conditions, a young man approached such an individual and said "Excuse me Sir/Madam, could I ask for some change to take the bus, please?" In the experimental conditions he added the phrase "But you are free to accept or to refuse". It turned out that while 10% of people in control conditions were inclined to agree to the request, in experimental conditions this number shot up to 47.5%! In addition, it turned out that participants who decided to make a donation gave on average twice as much in the experimental condition. What is fascinating in this study is that none of the participants in the experiment had any reason to feel compelled to carry out the request. Objectively speaking, freedom of action was the same in the control and the experimental conditions. Verbal emphasis of the freedom to choose, however, had an exceptionally simple effect!

In another study conducted by the same authors (Gueguen & Pascual, 2005), the individual conducting the experiment approached passers-by and requested their participation in a survey that would take around 5–8 minutes. It was explained that the study was to focus on the perception of local merchants and craftsmen in their town. The offer to participate in the study turned out to be quite an attractive one for local residents, as 75.6% of those approached agreed to take part. Could this already high number be boosted even further by emphasizing the freedom to choose? This time, the relevant words were spoken in the experimental condition at the very beginning. The experimenter addressed passers-by with the words "Excuse me Sir/Madam, I would like to ask you for something but you are free to accept or refuse", and then explained that he was asking for their participation in a survey. In these conditions, 90.1% of those approached agreed to participate.

Further studies have demonstrated the effectiveness of the "evoking freedom" technique as applied to a broad range of requests (Gueguen, Joule, Halmi-Falkowicz et al., 2013). It turned out that by telling people "you are free to accept or refuse", we increase the chances that they will share a cigarette with us, and also that they will agree to watch a video for 5 minutes and then fill in a questionnaire. Study participants to whom experimenters repeated the aforementioned phrase were also much more likely to buy pancakes when the proceeds from their sale were intended to fill the coffers of a charitable organization. Another experiment examined whether the evoking freedom technique can be successful assuming a longer time horizon (Gueguen, Joule, Halmi-Falkowicz et al., 2013). Study participants were asked to participate in an environmental campaign, and their involvement would consist of recording their trash-sorting activities in a special diary for one month. The researchers examined whether they would agree to the request and whether they really did perform the task which they had consented to do. The results of this experiment are presented in Table 4.1. As we can see, the technique proved successful in both respects.

Further studies have demonstrated that the "evoking freedom" technique is also effective when we attempt to convince someone to do something over the phone, via traditional post and by e-mail. It has also been shown that the phrase "you are free to accept or refuse" is not the only effective wording for emphasizing personal freedom, as "do not feel obliged" and "do as you wish" also turned out to be equally effective. What will happen if we initiate the conversation by saying "You are free (. . .)" and finish it with "Do not feel obliged"? As it turns out, the technique is even more effective!

The feeling of personal freedom is particularly important for people living in individualistic cultures, in which strong emphasis is placed on the value of the possibility to determine one's own fate. At the same time, we may assume that the technique under examination here should prove less effective in societies with a collectivist orientation, as the need to decide about one's own life is less acutely felt. Significantly, multicultural studies conducted in France, the Ivory Coast, Romania, Russia and China (Pascual et al., 2012) demonstrated that the technique is outstandingly effective in the first of those countries, and also works well in Romania (a country where, particularly in recent years, an individualistic orientation has begun to dominate over a collectivist one), while in Russia and the Ivory Coast the rate at which requests were complied with in experimental conditions (e.g. with the phrase "But you are free . . .") was only slightly higher than in the

TABLE 4.1 Frequencies of participants who complied with the request for money in Gueguen, Joule, Halmi-Falkowicz et al. (2013) experiment

	"But you are free . ." condition	*"Do as you like . . ." condition*	*Control condition*	*Total*
Male participants	83.7% ($n = 43$)	81.3% ($n = 43$)	60.4% ($n = 43$)	75.2% ($n = 129$)
Female participants	67.4% ($n = 43$)	72.1% ($n = 43$)	20.9% ($n = 43$)	52.7% ($n = 129$)
Total	75.6% ($n = 86$)	76.7% ($n = 86$)	40.7% ($n = 86$)	64.3% ($n = 258$)

control conditions (without that phrase). In China, the most collectivist, there was practically no difference at all.

Michael Patch, Vicky Hoang and Anthony Stahelsky (1997) draw attention to another aspect of the freedom of an individual approached with a request. This time, a particular limitation in the freedom to choose comes into play, consisting in the elimination of one of the potential decisions. The researchers focused on the feelings that can be experienced by an individual approached by a stranger asking for something. They suggest that such an individual may observe that he has been placed in a rather uncomfortable situation: someone who is neither my friend, nor even my acquaintance, has approached me utterly unexpectedly in order to ask for something. Additionally, the request goes beyond trivial matters such as giving directions or the time. Unwritten and vague cultural norms are violated, according to which a stranger is not entitled to make such requests. Yet it is also undesirable to remind him of this fact. Thus the addressee of the request refuses to assist the stranger, but keeps his reasons to himself.

What, however, will happen if the person making the request says directly to his interlocutor that if he feels the request is an inappropriate one for an interaction with a stranger, or if he feels pressured, he can just say so? Paradoxically, this does not make the task easier for the addressee of the request, but rather makes it more difficult! The option "I won't help you, and I'll keep my reasons private" is, at least to a certain degree, made inaccessible. Indeed, the addressee of the request is actually encouraged to state directly why he doesn't want to provide his assistance. Thus he is left with only two possible choices in his decision tree: to refuse and to explain that he feels the request is inappropriate, or to accede and comply with the request. Owing to the fact that explaining to a stranger – who happens to be a polite one – that he has violated some code of conduct regulating interpersonal contacts is a confrontational and rather stressful act, people may simply prefer to comply with the request being made of them.

In one of the experiments dedicated to examining the effectiveness of this technique, students were asked to help by conducting interviews among their acquaintances concerning the ways in which they spend their free time. It turned out that those who were encouraged to state their reasons for refusing actually agreed to fulfil the request more often (49%) than participants from the control group (34%).

The question emerges of whether the effectiveness of the technique being analyzed here simply results from the fact that an individual who, when making a request, asks the addressee to declare if he feels uncomfortable, is perceived as more polite than one who does not do so. In order to exclude this possibility, Patch et al. (1997) conducted an additional experiment whose participants responded to a series of questions concerning their perception of individuals formulating a request in various manners. This study succeeded in excluding the aforementioned interpretation. As it is, the most likely interpretation would seem to be the one suggested by the very authors of the studies under discussion here. When facing the dilemma of "how to behave", people believe it is less undesirable to fulfil a request addressed to them than to enmesh themselves in the confrontational and stressful process of explaining to a stranger that they feel uncomfortable.

Labelling and asking questions

There are a great number of situations in which people happen to overhear opinions about themselves. Sometimes these opinions take the form of so-called labels. Someone labels another as a brute, or a slob, others are called unreliable or untrustworthy. These types of labels, however, need not necessarily be negative ones. Labels can be comprised of such words as "reliable", "hardworking" or "gentleman". Robert Kraut (1973) suggests that by applying various labels to people (labelling), in some circumstances they can believe that they really are what the labels say they are, and in consequence they begin to behave in accordance with the label they have received. Of course, this can lead to positive or negative effects depending on the content of those labels. Richard Miller, Philip Brickman and Diana Bolen (1975) supplied pupils, from selected classes in a school, information about them suggesting that they were neat and liked to maintain order in the classroom. After a certain time it turned out that in those classes there was a visible improvement in cleanliness, and pupils took very close care to ensure that objects in the classroom were in their proper place. However, no improvements in hygiene were recorded in classes where traditional persuasive methods were applied. Edvin Schur (1971), in turn, analyzed "labelling" of particular people as aggressive deviants. He stated that a certain time after being given this label, he could often observe changes in their behaviour, consisting of growing aggressiveness. The labelling most likely led to so-called dispositional self-attribution in accordance with the content of the label. The "labelled" thus came to the conclusion that "this is just the way they are" (the attribution is internal, stable and uncontrollable), and then begin to behave in a manner consistent with the image of themselves they had come to accept.

Of particular interest from the perspective of the issues analyzed in this book are studies on the consequences of labels referring to altruism. A textbook example is supplied in a study by Angelo Strenta and William DeJong (1981). In the first phase of their experiment, participants (students taking an introductory course in psychology) responded to a 49-question survey ostensibly designed to measure particular aspects of their personality. The questions were displayed on a computer screen, and respondents answered them using a keyboard. Next, the participants were provided randomly with information as to what their answers indicated. Some of them were told the results suggested that they were kind and thoughtful. Others received information that they were more intelligent than the majority. Further participants were informed that the results would be calculated within a week, and one of the characteristics of particular interest to the researchers was kindness to others. The last of the groups was not given any feedback. When the participants left the laboratory they experienced an unexpected event (which, in reality, had been meticulously arranged by the researchers). One of the experimenters "dropped" a pile of 500 index cards. It was observed whether a given participant would spontaneously act to assist in gathering the cards, and the number of cards each participant picked up was counted. The amount of time between the cards landing on the floor and the participant's engagement in providing assistance was also measured, as well as the entire amount of time spent helping out. It turned out that those who had been given the label of altruists displayed different behaviour in all of the aforementioned respects when compared to the remaining groups. This group saw 70% of its members provide assistance, while 50% of those from the group that did not receive feedback and the group that was informed that the results would be analyzed later on did so, and a mere 36% of those from the group that was given a label associated with intelligence elected to help out. Participants from the group given the label of altruist also picked up far more index cards than the people in other conditions. Measurements related to time were equally definitive. Participants labelled as altruists reacted the quickest and devoted the greatest amount of time to providing assistance.

Of course, in order for labelling to be effective, it is necessary for the person being labelled to believe in the accuracy of the label. This can be most easily achieved when a label appears immediately after the individual has engaged in behaviour consistent with the label; for example, just after offering someone help, one is told that he is helpful. It should come as no surprise that experiments devoted to social influence techniques often combined labelling with a technique we have already learned about in Chapter 2: foot-in-the-door.

One such study was conducted by Morton Goldman, Mark Seever and Margaret Seever (1982). These authors assumed that a positive label associated with altruism would magnify the effects of the foot-in-the-door technique applied to efforts at increasing people's inclination to provide help to others. A negative label could lead to reduction in the effectiveness of the aforementioned technique. The experiment was conducted in a university library. One of the experimenters stopped people headed towards the entrance of the library and asked them for directions to one of the buildings on campus. After receiving directions they either thanked the person (foot-in-the-door conditions), or offered a rather unique comment on the help they had received. In the conditions involving foot-in-the-door joined with a positive label, the experimenter said: "You are very helpful. Thank you very much, you've really been a big help." In conditions of foot-in-the-door combined with a negative label, the response was different and went: "You're not very helpful. You didn't really bother to explain how to get there, and I still have no idea where to go." Each of the study participants then entered the library, where they encountered the next experimenter who asked them if they would be willing to sacrifice 2 hours in the following month to assist a charitable organization that serves disabled children. The work was to consist of working a shift answering phones. The same request was addressed to participants from the control group, who had not been approached by anyone at the library entrance. It turned out that while in the control conditions 17% of participants responded positively to the request to donate 2 hours answering phones, this result improved to 40% when the "pure" foot-in-the-door technique was applied. When the aforementioned technique was combined with a positive label, the percentage of those ready to donate their time to help disabled children jumped to 67%. However, when a negative label was applied, this number plummeted to 20%, more or less the level recorded in the control group (the difference between the two groups did not reach statistical significance).

A series of interesting experiments concerning the effect of labelling in the area of marketing was conducted by Gert Cornelissen, Siegfried Dewitte and Luk Warlop (2007). They demonstrated that if study participants first learn that they are very concerned with the environment and ecologically conscious, they then go on to select environmentally friendly products with a clearly greater frequency, and also prefer biodegradable product packaging.

An unusually original technique, which may be treated as a particularly specific variation of labelling, has been proposed by Anthony Pratkanis and Yigal Uriel (2011). The researchers call the technique the "expert snare". While the classic labelling technique generally refers to the personality traits or character of the person we wish to influence, this particular technique involves labelling the target as an expert in a given field. The request that subsequently appears is related to that very subject. The first experiment dedicated to the expert snare technique was conducted on the beach of Santa Cruz in Santa Monica, California. Surfers were asked to endorse the proposal that the belly of all new surfboards be painted yellow with purple polka dots. Before this request was made, some of the surfers were complimented on their skills. It turned out that such a compliment led to twice as many surfers signing what was in essence an idiotic petition. Perhaps the compliment put them in a good mood, and this led to them agreeing to the request? Maybe the receipt of a compliment from a stranger activated the mechanism of reciprocity – now the surfers should be polite. From the start the researchers foresaw the potential for such interpretations and introduced conditions into the experimental design in which the surfer was given a compliment, but the remark was not associated with his prowess as a surfer. Rather, he was praised for his nice wetsuit (or other swimwear). It turned out that this compliment did not serve to boost the inclination of study participants to sign the petition placed before them.

Why did the surfers who were given the label of experts sign an absurd petition? It may be significant that the petition bore the title "Polka Dot Safety Petition". If you're an expert in surfing, you should definitely have heard that polka dots enhance the safety of beginning surfers. You haven't heard about that? Maybe you should ask. But should an expert ask questions about that sort of thing? No, he should know about it, and he should support it.

A second experiment was equally as creative as the one described above. This time, the participants were Frisbee players and recreational dancers. A portion of them were initially complimented for their proficiency, while others were not told anything related to their skills. Participants were asked to sign a petition concerning students who were beginning their university education. The petition concerned a requirement for students to take an orientation course in Tanzimat Frisbee or root dancing. It turned out that "being an expert" made people more inclined to sign the petition, but only when the course that new students would be required to take was related to their own area of expertise. As it was, those labelled Frisbee experts more frequently signed petitions concerning the course in Tanzimat Frisbee than Frisbee players from the control group, but when the petition concerned a course in root dancing there was no difference between the groups. By the same token, when recreational dancers given the label of experts were asked to sign a petition concerning root dancing for students, they did so with greater frequency than dancers from the control group. However, if the petition referred to a Tanzimat Frisbee course, there was no difference between the two groups of dancers. Thus, the issue of flattery is not the one in play here. Rather, the idea is that if you are an expert in some area, then you should be knowledgeable on various topics in that area and support sensible initiatives. As for things in another area in which you are not an expert, you are not expected to know everything and do not have to support such initiatives. One important detail about this experiment should be mentioned at the end: Tanzimat Frisbee and root dancing do not exist – they were fabricated by the experimenters.

A very interesting variation on the labelling technique is one called image induction, proposed by San Bolkan and Peter Andersen (2009). While in the classic version of the technique the person exerting influence is also the one providing the label to the person who is being influenced, in the case of image induction it is the very person targeted by social influence who comes up with labels for him-self! How can this be? Bolkan and Andersen respond that it is sufficient to use "a single question to get targets to apply a label to themselves without any previous interaction and which asks them to comply with a direct request" (p. 318). In a simple but equally clever experiment, the authors asked each participant at the beginning of the experiment whether they felt they were a helpful person (every-one responded in the affirmative), and then asked if they would agree to help the experimenter by volunteering to take part in a 30-minute communication survey at a later date. It turned out that 77% of participants agreed to this request. In the control conditions where the request was issued at once (without the initial ques-tion of whether participants viewed themselves as helpful), only 29% of participants consented. In a second experiment, participants were given the initial question "Do you consider yourself to be somebody who is adventurous and likes to try new things?", or this question was not given. Next, all of the participants in the exper-iment were asked to provide an e-mail address in order to receive information about a new brand of soft drink. It transpired that when the request was made at once, 33% of participants gave their address, while when the aforementioned ques-tion preceded the request 75% of them did so. The third experiment, in contrast with the previous ones, was not conducted face to face, rather participants completed a questionnaire. In the experimental conditions they initially responded to the question of whether or not they viewed themselves as helpful. In the control conditions this question was not present. Next, participants were asked if they would help the experimenter with his work on survey studies. In the experimental group 50% of participants agreed to help out, while only 32% did so in the control group. In another version, a portion of people were first asked if they were adventurous, and then asked to give their e-mail address in order to forward them information about a new brand of soda. In this case, 55% of those who had previously defined themselves as adventurous gave their e-mail address, compared to 30% of those who had not.

As it is, posing questions is itself a very effective social influence technique. Steven Sherman (1980) demonstrated that people's behaviours can be influenced without resorting to orders or requests. It is enough to ask them to predict how they would react if they encountered a given situation. Sherman assumed that people generally make inaccurate predictions regarding their own responses when the behaviours described are either socially desirable or undesirable. In respect of the former, people naturally overestimate the likelihood that they will engage in a given behaviour, while in respect of the latter they underestimate this likelihood. Formulating predictions as to one's own behaviour very often activates the script for engaging in a given behaviour (or for refraining from a given behaviour) with oneself playing the lead role.

In one of Sherman's experiments (1980) participants were asked to write an essay the content of which would clearly contradict their own attitudes. Over two-thirds (67%) of those approached agreed to do so. Other participants were asked to declare if they would agree to write such an essay when asked by someone else to do so. Only 29% of respondents said that they would. Sherman thus declares that if people estimate the probability of engaging in undesirable activities, their estimates are below the mark. Interestingly, when the same group of people who had estimated the chances that they would agree to write such an essay were asked a few days later to actually write it, only one-third (33%) of them expressed their consent. A second experiment delivered similar results. This time, the activity in question was singing a song over the phone. In the case of the control group 68% agreed to do so, but when other people were asked whether they would agree to such a request from someone else, only 44% said "yes". When these same people were then asked to engage in the behaviour, 42% of participants agreed to do so. Writing an essay that does not correspond with one's own attitudes and singing a song over the phone during a conversation with a person we do not know are, indeed, behaviours that do not enjoy the highest level of social acceptance, and may even be a source of embarrassment. What will occur, however, if people are asked about the likelihood they will engage in behaviours that enjoy social acceptance? In his next experiment Sherman (1980) asked participants to join in a charity campaign consisting in a three-hour collection drive gathering donations for the American Cancer Society. Only 4% of respondents agreed to help out. Meanwhile, nearly half of those from the group asked to declare if they would hypothetically agree to participate in such a campaign said that they would. When these same people were then asked to actually engage in the campaign, nearly one-third of them consented to pitch in!

Sherman claims that in these cases we encounter a very interesting mechanism: while people do make erroneous estimates of the likelihood they will engage in various behaviours (as people in comparable control groups whose real reactions were tested behaved in diametrically different ways), they then proceed to behave in a manner consistent with their own prediction.

Anthony Greenwald and a group of collaborators (Greenwald, Carnot, Beach & Young, 1987) explored whether people's voting patterns could be influenced in a similar manner. They called individuals who had already registered for elections and asked them what they were going to do until the announcement of the results of initial exit polls. As it turned out, the majority of people mentioned that, among other things, they intended to visit their local polling station. Of particular interest, however, was that among those who were engaged in such a conversation, 86.7% of them did in fact cast their vote. This result was higher than the one recorded among a comparable cohort of individuals who were not called (61.5%).

The "ask about" technique also proved successful in conditions where it was used to encourage students to sort packaging material as part of a recycling campaign. Residents of some dormitories were asked to complete a sociological survey in which they were asked, among other things, if they would sort their trash. When containers were then placed in the dormitories for aluminium beverage cans to be recycled, they filled up more quickly in the locations where the survey had been conducted (Sprott, Spangenberg & Perkins, 1999).

Eric Spangenberg (1997) began his research by reviewing a list of members of a particular club whose primary objective was to maintain the health and physical condition of its members. Spangenberg selected those who had not visited the club for at least a month for his study. Participants were then assigned randomly to one of two groups. In the experimental group, Spangenberg phoned and asked the participant if he planned to visit the club in the near future. In the case of the control group, he did nothing. The fact that twice as many people from the experimental group visited the club over the following week compared to the control group should come as no surprise, considering the results of previous studies on the effectiveness of the technique being discussed here. What is fascinating, however, is that when six months later Spangenberg examined the frequency of members' visits to the club, it also turned out that people from the experimental group went there twice as often as those who had landed in the control group – in spite of the fact that members of the experimental group had only been called once, without any further contact!

In yet another study it was demonstrated that this technique can be applied successfully on a mass scale. One day, in front of the entrance to a university building, an electronic notice board displayed the message "Ask yourself . . . are you going to recycle?" The corridors and entrances to the building were littered with bins for paper, aluminium cans, etc. The message on the board led to the bins filling up much more quickly than on other days when no such message was displayed (Spangenberg, Sprott, Grohmann & Smith, 2003).

It is also worth drawing attention to two important advantages of this technique. First, it is exceptionally easy to apply. All that needs be done is to ask people what they would do in a hypothetical situation. Second, it can be used both to increase the probability of engagement in socially desirable behaviours and of elimination of socially undesirable ones.

How are you feeling?

The technique I would now like to present to you is also based on asking a question. There are many reasons, however, for which it is deserving of its own section. Daniel Howard was primarily interested in the effectiveness of techniques that could be applied when collecting donations for charitable purposes. He observed people working on behalf of charitable societies and participated extensively in various internal courses and training sessions designed to boost qualifications.

> Before you ask anyone for a donation, you first ask them how they are feeling. After they tell you they're feeling good, and you tell them you're glad they're feeling good, they'll be more likely to contribute to helping someone who isn't. (Howard, 1990, p. 1185)

This is the advice Howard heard during one of those courses; he then observed that it is, in fact, applied quite frequently (particularly during telephone conversations) by people seeking donations for charitable causes. As a scientist, Howard was naturally interested not only in the mere efficacy of the recommended technique, but also the psychological mechanism that could explain why people in such situations succumb to the requests of others.

Howard assumed that the foundation of this technique was the mechanism of commitment and consistency. In his view, a person who publicly announces his good mood then feels obliged to care for the emotional well-being of those who do not feel good. Compliance with a request to make a donation to a charitable cause is then a means of fulfilling the obligation as it is understood in this particular situation.

In Howard's first experiment, an individual presenting himself as an employee of a charitable organization placed phone calls to randomly selected residents of Dallas, Texas. In the control group, the interlocutors were informed that in their neighbourhood they would soon have the opportunity to purchase cookies at a price of 25 cents, and the proceeds from the sale would go to benefit the organization of a holiday meal for those suffering from hunger (the experiment was conducted in the period before Thanksgiving). Participants were asked if they would allow the person selling the cookies to visit them at their home. In respect of the experimental group, after introducing himself the researcher first asked the interlocutor how he was feeling, and then – depending on the answer – said he was either glad or sorry to hear that, after which he proceeded to explain that a charitable cookie sale was being organized and asked if they would be interested in purchasing some cookies. It turned out that people from the experimental group agreed with greater frequency (25%) to have a cookie salesperson and representative of the charity committee visit them than those from the control group (10%).

Nevertheless, the question arises whether the more frequent compliance of people from the experimental group did not result from the simple fact that the person conducting the telephone conversation came across as more polite. It could be assumed that asking how one feels and responding with satisfaction when the answer is positive (or with sympathy when the answer is not so positive) is polite behaviour. Indeed, it would not be a strange thing for people to consent more often to a request from a person who is behaving pleasantly compared to the same request issued in a less pleasant manner. In order to exclude this interpretation, Howard conducted a second experiment in which an additional experimental group was introduced. In this case, the person conducting the study started the conversation by expressing the hope that his interlocutor was feeling well. It turned out that compliance among participants in that group was equal to that recorded in the control group, and was half that of the experimental group. This pattern of results led Howard to accept that the factor of politeness exhibited by the individual asking for help could not explain the differences in compliance rates across individual groups.

In his third experiment Howard undertook a precise analysis of the responses of those asked how they felt, demonstrating that the better their declared mood, the more often they expressed willingness to admit the cookie salesperson into their home and the more cookies they bought. People from the experimental group who declared they were in a bad mood were equally unlikely to participate in the charity drive as those who were not asked about their mood.

In his interpretation of this pattern of results, Howard emphasizes that it is not a simple function of a good mood being favourable to altruistic behaviours, as people from the control group did not declare a worse mood yet they were clearly less inclined to comply with requests to join in the charity drive (while it is true that control group participants' moods were not recorded, the random assignment of people to individual conditions should lead to that particular effect). Thus of key importance is not necessarily the experience of a good mood, but rather of the public declaration of such feelings. Daniel Howard therefore concludes that asking people about their mood and expressing joy when they declare that they feel good is an effective social influence technique. He also proposes a name for this technique, calling it "foot-in-the-mouth".

Results similar to Howard's were recorded by Valerie Fointiat (2000), who did not conduct her study by telephone, as did Howard, but rather in face-to-face interactions. Participants were asked to make a donation in support of those suffering from hunger. In the control conditions this request was made directly – people were approached with the question of whether they would like to provide financial support for hungry residents of their city. In the foot-in-the-mouth conditions this request was preceded by a question about their mood, to which the majority declared that it was good, at times responding even more enthusiastically. Fointiat also introduced a third group into the experimental design, as she was interested in the effect generated by the combined application of the foot-in-the-mouth tech-nique and a technique familiar to us from the second chapter, door-in-the-face. In this case, the participant was first asked how he felt, then his response was heard and commented on, after which a very difficult request was made. This request involved making a donation of food for the hungry once a week over a period of at least three months. When participants refused to fulfil this quite problematic request, they were immediately asked to do something much easier – to make a one-time donation to residents from their city who were suffering from hunger. It turned out that compliance with the target request was the lowest in the control group, higher in the group where the foot-in-the-mouth technique was applied, and the highest in conditions involving the joint application of that technique with influence based on the concept of door-in-the-face. Valerie Fointiat managed not only to replicate the results achieved by Howard, but also demonstrated that the technique he described works equally in conditions where the contact between the person making the request and the addressee did not involve a telephone call.

The results of the experiments conducted by Howard and the study done by Fointiat – who refers to his proposed theoretical interpretation when discussing her results – demonstrate that asking people how they feel and then declaring satisfac-tion upon hearing of their good mood serves to increase those people's inclination to comply with a request to participate in a charitable campaign. Insofar as this particular result does not give rise to any doubts, the issue of the mechanism under-lying this truth is a different matter. It does not seem that Daniel Howard succeeded in convincingly proving that the mechanism of commitment and consistency lies at the heart of compliance when applying the foot-in-the-mouth technique.

First and foremost, it is not entirely clear why people who declare they are in a good mood should feel obliged to ensure those who have no reason to feel good themselves experience the same feeling. In reality we are not dealing with an obli-gation that would directly and logically result from a public declaration (as we would in the case of a declaration such as "I believe we should help people who are experiencing difficulties in life"), but at most with a discrepancy between one's declaration of a good mood and the implied information that there are some who have no reason to be in such a good mood. Also, by accepting Howard's interpreta-tion, we should assume that the participants in his second experiment who heard that they felt good and did not dispute this should also (at least to a certain degree) feel obliged to help improve the mood of others. Meanwhile, in the case of this group the rate of compliance was practically identical to that in the control group.

In many psychological studies it has been demonstrated that the experience of a worsened mood does not facilitate engagement in altruistic behaviours (e.g. Milberg & Clark, 1988; Forgas, 1998). The results of Howard's third experiment are consistent with this principle. Individuals declaring they did not feel good when asked about their mood were equally disinclined to engage in helping the needy as people from the control group. We may assume that in American culture, with its social norm of reporting one is in at least a good mood; admitting to a more negative disposition occurs when one is in fact in a very poor mood indeed. It should thus come as no surprise that people who report precisely just such a mood rarely engage in altruistic behaviours. We may, however, ask the question of whether we would record a similar effect in a culture where the norm is to declare a bad mood. If it turned out that people declaring this kind of mood engaged in altruistic behaviours with greater frequency than those from a control group, such a pattern of results could not be interpreted in the manner Howard proposes (after all, "If I am in a bad mood, I don't feel any obligation to do something in order for others to feel good"). One of what is likely a very small number of countries where a norm of complaining exists is Poland (Czapinski, 1993; Wojciszke & Baryla, 2005). A good illustration of how complaining is a cultural norm in Poland is the results of a simple survey study in which respondents were asked about everyday conversations. It turned out that 61% of Polish respondents declared that they liked to talk about high prices, 56% about the spread of poor manners, and 47% about the ineffectiveness and amorality of Polish politicians (Wojciszke & Baryla, 2005). Cultural differences between Poland and the majority of other countries in the world (including the USA) are also reflected in declarations of one's emotional experiences. The most spectacular illustration of these differences would seem to come from the studies which I will now proceed to discuss.

In 1937, one of a small number of contemporary psychological journals published a brief report of results from studies conducted by Winifred Johnson. The participants in this study were a 30-person cohort of American students who responded to just one recurring question. They were asked to estimate their mood in comparison to how they usually feel, using an 11–point scale with extremes of −5 and +5. The middle of the scale was 0, representing a "like usual" mood. Of course, one person's mood is subject to greater or lesser variations. While we generally feel "like usual" (in Johnson's study we would select 0), we can experience days when we feel worse than usual, as well as days when we feel better than usual. We should have, on average, as many better days than worse ones. The average result generated by each of the participants should, therefore, oscillate around zero. Johnson's calculations, however, showed that the respondents must have generally felt better than usual, because the average result recorded by each of them over a 65-day period was +1.2. In the 1990s I replicated Johnson's experiment in Poland (Dolinski, 1996), extending its time frame to 100 days. It turned out that all of the Polish respondents achieved a lower result than the neutral point of zero, and in the majority of cases (19 of 24) I recorded a statistically significant effect. For Polish students, it was typical for them to feel worse than usual!

Taking advantage of the fact that Poland is ensconced in a culture of complaining, Magda Nawrat (1997) conducted an experiment designed as a cultural test of the correctness of the interpretation suggested by Howard. Let us observe that the foot-in-the-mouth technique requires those asked "how do you feel" to respond that they at least feel good. This technique works in the United States (as shown by Howard), France (as shown by Fointiat), and probably in the vast majority of other countries because most people reply in just this way when asked about their emotional state (and only those people consent to the request to engage in a charitable campaign more often than participants in the control group). However, because it can be expected that the standard response in Poland will be a reaction like "not so good", "bad", or at best "not too bad", this technique should prove ineffective (to put it more precisely: it should not be successful if the mechanism of commitment and consistency as proposed by Howard lies at the heart of the technique's effectiveness). As a result, and somewhat paradoxically, the ineffectiveness of this technique in studies conducted in Poland (or in other countries where a culture of complaining holds sway) would provide an argument in support of Howard's interpretation of the psychological mechanism driving the effectiveness of the social influence technique he studied.

In the aforementioned experiment by Magda Nawrat, participants were drawn from residents of dormitories in Wrocław. Participants identified in a dormitory and assigned to the control group were given information about the organization of a campaign to support a young children's home. This campaign, they were told, consisted of collecting money, books and toys. They were informed that the drive would be starting soon, and then asked to give their address or telephone number in order to arrange the details. In the experimental group the request for assistance was preceded by a question about their mood. Participants were asked "how they were doing" in the face of the upcoming examination session.

It turned out that participants from the experimental group (asked about their mood) were more likely to provide contact information (62.5%) than participants from the control group (27.5%). It was also the case that from among the 40 people from the experimental group, only 15 declared a positive emotional state. The level of compliance among those people did not differ from that observed among the 25 people who declared a different mood (i.e. negative or neutral). As in the case of Howard's study, it transpired that asking people about their mood increased the chances that they would agree to the later proposition to take part in a charity drive. However, in contrast to his experiments, the declaration of a negative or neutral mood also served to boost engagement.

Another test of the hypothesis that the foundation of the foot-in-the-mouth technique's success is the mechanism of commitment and consistency could be a situation in which the request to be fulfilled is not related to a charitable campaign, but rather to a clearly commercial venture. If it were the case that also in these circumstances people asked about their mood complied more frequently with suggestions addressed to them, it would prove difficult to continue supporting an interpretation based on the aforementioned mechanism. Howard acknowledges this explicitly, suggesting that the regularities he recorded should only be limited to situations in which the addressee of the request knows that the person making the request will not personally benefit from it being carried out. Magda Nawrat, Iza Rudak and I decided to examine whether this significant limitation actually occurs (Dolinski, Nawrat & Rudak, 2001).

Our study's participants were 100 women walking along the sidewalk in the centre of the city; 50 of them were randomly assigned to the control group, and the same number was assigned to the experimental group. A young woman served as the experimenter. She greeted participants from the experimental group, and then asked them how they were feeling. If the participant responded that she was feeling good, the experimenter responded by saying: "I'm glad to hear that you're feeling good". If the participant responded by declaring something different than a good mood, the response went: "I'm sorry to hear that you're not feeling particularly good." Regardless of the mood declared by the participant, the experimenter immediately followed up with the statement "I am selling aromatic Indian pastilles. Would you like to buy a box from me?" In the control group, people were greeted and immediately presented with the proposed transaction.

In the experimental group 11 out of 50 people decided to purchase the incense. In the control group, only 3 people did so (the difference in the proportions of people in both conditions who complied with the seller's request was statistically significant). From among those asked about their mood, 21 declared a positive emotional state, while the remaining participants reported feeling either bad or not very good. It turned out that the declared mood had no influence on the tendency to purchase the pastilles: in the experimental group they were bought by 5 of those who had declared a good mood, and by 6 of the remaining participants.

We can again observe that asking people about their mood boosts the chances of inducing compliance also in situations when they declare feeling bad. Importantly, this experiment also demonstrated that the foot-in-the-mouth technique, contrary to the predictions made by Howard (1990), proved equally successful in conditions involving a request of a clearly commercial nature rather than a charitable one.

We now know what is *not* the source of the reported pattern of results: as Howard himself demonstrated, it is not one's mood. In turn, studies conducted in Poland suggest that it is also not the mechanism of commitment and consistency assumed by Howard. Why, then, is the foot-in-the-mouth technique effective? To what psychological mechanisms does it owe its success?

An interesting interpretation of the phenomenon under analysis here has been proposed by Kelly Aune and Michael Basil (1994). In their view, asking people about their mood and then expressing satisfaction that it is good leads to the formation of a bond with the person asking the question. Asking about someone's emotional state is something qualitatively different from asking for the time, or for directions to the university library. Someone who asks us how we are doing is expressing interest in us as people, while someone who asks us for the time or for directions is only interested in his or her own problems. An inquiry about mood thus constitutes an expression of interpersonal warmth and emphasizes that the asker and the asked are on some level not indifferent to each other. It could be said that asking this question leads to a particular relationship of intimacy and closeness. This relationship leads to the person being approached for assistance incurring an obligation to help. Indeed, there is a social norm requiring us to help those with whom something binds us, particularly if providing such assistance does not result in a significantly negative impact on our own interests; this was precisely the case in both Howard's experiment as well as in the others discussed in this section.

Of course, a question about mood is only one of many ways in which we can establish a relationship of intimacy and closeness with another person. Aune and Basil thus conclude that compliance with a request can also be induced in other ways than expressing concern for well-being and the verbal techniques involved in creating the aforementioned relationship. They additionally present their own study, in which the experimenter either directly asked students encountered at a university campus to donate to a charity; asking first how they were feeling and then requesting the donation; or asking first if they studied at that university and then, upon receiving confirmation, declaring that she did too and following this up with a request for a donation. The first group was the control group. The second was a copy of the conditions set up by Howard in which, depending on the theoretical assumption adopted, either the mechanism of consistency or a relationship of closeness was activated. The third created conditions in which a feeling of closeness was established resulting from membership of the same community. It turned out that participants from the last group complied with the greatest frequency, while those in the first group did so the least (see Table 4.2).

A second, complementary experiment conducted by these authors was done using "paper and pencil". Study participants were given descriptions of the three experimental scenarios described above, and were asked to assess the relationship between the participants in the interactions (i.e. the experimenter and the person she approached). It turned out that this relationship was perceived as being the closest in the conditions where the conversation involved studying at the same university, while it was the most distant when the experimenter directly addressed the participant with a request for a donation. In the authors' opinion, this indicates that the perception of closeness in interpersonal relationships constitutes the mechanism responsible for compliance in both Howard's experiments and their own.

It should be added that establishing a relationship of closeness could also be the mechanism responsible for the effects noted in the Polish studies conducted by Nawrat (1997) and by Dolinski et al., (2001). The mere question about one's mood builds a relationship of closeness, and this in turn induces people to agree to carry out requests involving engagement in a charity drive, as well as to react positively to proposals with a commercial slant.

My collaborators and I, however, have offered yet another interpretation of the effects recorded in studies on the foot-in-the-mouth technique (Dolinski et al., 2001). Because this issue goes beyond a simple explanation of the mechanism

TABLE 4.2 Compliance by group in Aune and Basil (1994) experiment

	Complied	Refused	(n)
Standard	5	46	51
FITM feeling-state	13	38	51
FITM relational obligations	24	27	51

Source: Journal of Applied Social Psychology, 1994, vol. 24, p. 551
Copyright: 2006, John Wiley and Sons.

facilitating compliance on the part of people subjected to this technique, it is worthy of its own section, which follows.

Dialogue involvement

In the preceding section we analyzed the "foot-in-the-mouth" technique. Let us recall that in Howard's experiments the experimenter called up participants and introduced himself as an employee of a charitable organization. In the control conditions, he then immediately asked his interlocutor to purchase some cookies and informed him that the funds collected from their sale would go towards organizing a holiday meal for people suffering from hunger. In the experimental conditions, before the sale of the cookies was mentioned, he asked his interlocutor about his mood, listened to the answer, commented on it appropriately and only then formulated the request to buy the cookies. People asked about their emotional state bought the cookies far more frequently than those who were not asked. Howard assumed that the sole difference between the control and the experimental groups was that participants in the latter group had been asked about their mood. In my opinion, there was yet another difference: in the control group the contact was based on a monologue, whereas in the experimental group it was grounded in a dialogue. In the control group, the study participant was informed of the character and the objective of a charity drive, and then asked to take part. In the experimental group, the participant was given a question, responded, heard a comment on the response, and only then was the request issued. The same procedure was used in our experiments as well, in which we tested the technique described by Howard. Both when we attempted to convince students to join in a charity drive (Nawrat, 1997) and when we sold Indian incense to passers-by (Dolinski et al., 2001), we used a monologue with the control groups, while we engaged participants from the experimental groups in a dialogue. The studies of Aune and Basil (1994) and Fointiat (2000) were also constructed in an analogical manner. The control groups were directly asked for something (using a monologue), while the experimental groups experienced a dialogue between someone who asked for something shortly after the dialogue had been established and someone who was asked for that thing.

Why might different modes of communication have an effect in respect of social influence? Dialogue and monologue are the primary modes of interpersonal communication. While monologue as a form of one-sided communication would seem "cold", a dialogue, whose essence consists in the mutual exchange of information between participants in the interaction, would seem "warm".

It could be said that a monologue is associated with avoiding a deeper interaction with the other person. If someone addresses us in the form of a monologue, we usually just listen to him and then conclude the interaction. We can also merely pretend to be listening, or we can even ignore what that person is saying. Dialogue is a completely different case. This form of communication demands cognitive activity. In discussing with someone we are forced to listen to him in order to respond to his ideas and arguments. These are not the only differences between dialogue and monologue. It would seem that while the convention of verbal communication rooted in monologue is typical of interactions between those who do not know each other, dialogue is primarily characteristic of interactions between people who are familiar with one another. It could also be judged that in the case of a drastic decline in the relationship between two people who know each other, their mode of communication shifts from dialogue to monologue. Workplace colleagues in conflict with each other do not engage in conversation (they do not use dialogue), but they can, if the situation demands, exchange terse messages based on monologue (such as "The boss wants you to prepare a report", or "Last week I wrote the report, now it's your turn"). Also, a frustrated parent engaged in punishing his child who has seriously abused his trust can say "Listen to what I have to say to you now" and launches into a monologue, while generally communicating with the child in the form of a dialogue. The transition from dialogue to monologue is thus associated with a sudden and radical decline in a mutual relationship.

If we agree with the assumption that in conditions of interaction between people who know each other well the dominant mode of communication is dialogue, while in conditions of interaction between strangers it is monologue, this will have real significance for explaining the results of all of the experiments presented in the preceding section. Indeed, if we accept that a given mode of communication can serve as a stimulus that activates a given reaction pattern, then a monologue would activate the pattern of behaviour assigned to strangers, while a dialogue would activate the pattern of behaviour assigned to people we are familiar with. Because people are more inclined to comply with the requests of people they know rather than of strangers (e.g. Argyle & Henderson, 1984; Roloff, 1987), dialogue may serve to motivate them to comply with a request more effectively than monologue. We could thus assume that it is precisely for this reason interactions based on dialogue between the experimenter and the participant (typical for those familiar with one another) led to more frequent compliance in the studies presented above than did contacts rooted in monologue (characteristic of people who do not know each other).

From this perspective it could be said that in Howard's (1990) experiments the key aspect was not that participants were asked about their mood, but that they were asked about anything at all, and then something related to their responses was said. Along the same lines, in the experiment performed by Aune and Basil (1994) what was crucial was not that participants were asked if they were students from the local university, but simply that a question was asked of them, and then their answer was commented on. In both cases the study participants were ensnared in dialogue.

In our experiment, dedicated to verifying the assumption that it is the engagement in dialogue that plays a key role, we approached students on the campus of a Polish university. They were randomly assigned to one of eight experimental conditions, with 50 people in each group. Independently of each other we differentiated the mode of communication (monologue – dialogue), posed or did not pose a question about mood, and fostered or did not foster closeness based on social identity. For example, in conditions of monologue, a question about mood and absence of closeness, the experimenter (a 20-year-old woman) addressed participants in the following manner:

"I hope you are doing well today. I am collecting money for children with special needs. Would you like to contribute, please?"

However, in conditions of dialogue, without a declaration of mood and without fostering closeness, the experimenter asked participants:

"I guess you're a student here. May I ask what you major in?" After receiving the answer, she said, "Well, do you consider it worth studying?" listened to the answer, and asked for a donation.

The analyses later conducted showed that participants in conditions of dialogue more frequently (31%) agreed to the experimenter's request for a donation than in conditions of monologue (11%). The average sum given was also significantly higher in conditions of dialogue than those of monologue.

The conditions of monologue that did not broach the subject of mood and did not foster closeness can be treated as the base conditions for estimating the effectiveness of various means of exerting influence on people's submissiveness, applied in the remaining seven experimental conditions. In other words, these conditions can be treated as a control group. A series of pairwise comparisons between the 'control' group and each of the seven remaining groups demonstrated that compliance was greater across all four groups in which dialogue was applied compared to the control group. The average sums raised in each of those groups compared to the control group was also higher. However, all of the differences between each of the three groups in which monologue was applied and the control group were far from statistically significant. The results of this study are presented in Table 4.3.

TABLE 4.3 Proportion of persons complying with the experimenter's requests, average amount of donation (in parentheses), and average duration of the interaction (in seconds) in each condition in Dolinski et al. (2001) experiment

	Closeness			
	No		*Yes*	
	Mood		*Mood*	
	No	*Yes*	*No*	*Yes*
Monologue				
Compliance	08 (.044)	08 (.090)	16 (.108)	12 (.084)
Time	10.22	17.54	16.36	20.78
Dialogue				
Compliance	32 (.262)	24 (.250)	36 (.398)	32 (.294)
Time	23.52	18.44	16.42	31.78

Source: *Personality and Social Psychology Bulletin*, 2001, vol. 27, p. 1400

These results are very consistent with our hypothesis, which assumes that the activation of dialogue as the mode of communication increases people's readiness to comply with requests made of them. Emphasis on a relationship of closeness or of an interlocutor's good mood in the context of monologue turned out to be an insufficient way of inducing submissiveness. However, if our assumption is correct that the key is to ensnare the other person in a dialogue, then a similar pattern of results should be achieved in conditions where the subject of the conversation is neither one's emotional state nor something referring to a shared community identity. What is more, engaging someone in dialogue should prove equally effective in a situation that is purely commercial.

Thus we decided in another of our studies to sell Indian incense sticks on the street. In the monologue conditions we simply pitched our product to passers-by, encouraging them to make a purchase. In conditions of dialogue we asked passers-by who they thought was more sensitive to smell, men or women? After hearing their response, we asked for a justification. After our interlocutor provided some arguments, we offered to sell them some incense. It turned out that, while in conditions of monologue we succeeded in selling the incense to roughly 1 in 17 people, this number was 1 in 5 when conditions of dialogue were used. We also noted the responses of participants regarding which sex they felt was more sensitive to smells. One might assume that the mechanism of commitment and consistency would lead to those responding that their own sex was more sensitive to smells would be more inclined to purchase incense than those who declared that it was the opposite sex whose olfactory senses were more acute ("Since I'm particularly predisposed to take pleasure from smells, then I should take advantage of this opportunity"). However, it turned out that this aspect was of no significance. This experiment was yet another demonstration of how using dialogue to ensnare a person whom we are attempting to exert social influence over is a means of increasing his readiness to comply with our request.

A similar effect was recorded by Sebastien Meineri and Nicolas Gueguen (2011). In their experiment, they asked participants to take a telephone survey about their local newspaper. In the control conditions they made the request at once, while in the experimental conditions they began by saying "I hope I'm not disturbing you, am I?", waiting in half of the cases for an answer from the respondent while in the remaining cases proceeding immediately to the request for participation in the survey. It turned out that, in comparison to the control group, only those who were allowed to respond to the statement "I hope I'm not disturbing you" agreed more frequently to participate in the survey. Those who were told this but had no opportunity to respond consented to take the survey as rarely as participants from the control group. The key element, therefore, was the presence of dialogue.

Because we assumed that the use of a dialogue-based mode of communication would automatically activate the scenario "conversation with an acquaintance", it could be thought that particular sequences of that scenario associate with a positive reaction to the request will be automatically and without reflection carried out also when the conversation concerned banal issues of minor importance for the individual. However, if the conversation were to turn towards important things, then a more detailed analysis of the issues under discussion should be expected – the individual should function on a more reflexive level. These expectations are a reflection of the rich literature on mechanisms of persuasion. Many studies have demonstrated that a high level of interest in information coming to us leads us to process it in a highly regimented manner, clearly engaging our cognitive resources in effortful mental processes. In turn, insignificant interest in the content of information coming to us results in a more superficial and automatic processing of information, and is associated with a very low level of cognitive engagement, referred to as noneffortful mental processes (see e.g. Chaiken, Liberman & Eagly, 1989; Chaiken & Stangor, 1987; Maio & Olson, 1995; Petty & Cacioppo, 1990). In the last case, people pay less attention to the content of the information, and more to so-called peripheral issues such as whether the author of the message is nice, is an authority, is physically attractive, etc.

In respect of the issue of interest to us here, it may be accepted that, in the event, the conversation involves an issue of significance to the individual, not only the activation of dialogue will be important but its content will be as well. A person being approached in these conditions will pay attention to what his interlocutor is saying, as well as his attitude towards the issues under discussion. However, if the conversation concerns relatively unimportant matters, the simple fact of employing dialogue as the mode of communication will be the key issue. Dialogue as a mode of communication in this situation plays the same role as authority or the pleasant appearance of the person communicating the message does in studies on persuasion. Dialogue creates a positive attitude on the part of the addressee towards the person speaking with him, but also renders him less active, and as a result he will not engage in deep reflection on the information reaching him.

Thus, from the perspective of boosting compliance – which is of interest to us here – of importance in a dialogue on a subject of minor significance is not whether the initiator of the conversation espouses the same attitude as the person being approached or a different one. In the event of a discussion on important subjects, this issue may take on real significance. Only a dialogue based on a consensus of opinions should aid in boosting compliance. To examine whether this is really the case, we conducted another experiment in which we took advantage of the dramatic situation residents of Wrocław experienced following a giant flood that washed over the city. The experiment (Dolinski et al., 2001) was conducted in the streets of the city just after the flood waters had receded.

In the control group, the experimenter informed passers-by that studies were being conducted concerning various issue associated with daily life in the city, and issued a request that they respond to a few questions concerning the local press. He added that this would take about 15 minutes to do.

In the experimental conditions this question was preceded by a dialogue with the study participant, about a topic of either minor interest or of great interest. The topic of minor interest was the yellow colour of the new phone booths that had

just been put up on the streets of Wrocław. The experimenter asked some participants if they liked the new phone booths or not. The topic of great interest was
the issue of eliminating the consequences of the flood in the city. The experimenter asked these participants if they felt the clean-up after the flood was
proceeding quickly and in an orderly manner, or not. In the case of both dialogues
the experimenter's reaction to the opinions voiced by participants was differentiated.
Regardless of the opinion formulated by a participant, in half of the cases the
experimenter declared that he was of the very same opinion, while in the remaining cases he said that he did not agree and had an entirely different opinion on that
subject. Immediately after this, the experimenter asked the participant to sacrifice
15 minutes in order to respond to questions about the local press.

It turned out that, whether a participant agreed to the 15-minute interview
depended on the level of engagement brought about by the initial conversation, as
well as its course. The results of this study are presented in Table 4.4.

The rate of compliance in groups where communication with study participants was done by way of dialogue (34.6%) was greater than the analogical statistic
for the control group, in respect of which monologue was applied (20%). A series
of pairwise comparisons between the control group and the four experimental
groups, however, demonstrated that the rate of compliance in the group discussing
the topic of great interest with an experimenter expressing an analogical opinion
was higher than in the control group, but the rate of compliance in the group
discussing the topic of great interest with an experimenter expressing a contrary
opinion was similar to that of the control group. When the subject was of little
interest, agreement or disagreement with the experimenter generated similar rates
of submission, which themselves were higher than in the control group.

The results of the experiment thus turned out to be in line with our expectations. In conditions where the dialogue touched on issues of minor importance,
the simple fact of activating that mode of communication was sufficient to induce

TABLE 4.4 Percentage of persons complying with the experimenter's request to devote 15
minutes of their time to answer questions about the local press in Dolinski,
Nawrat and Rudak (2001) experiment

	Compliance (%)
Monologue	20.0
Dialogue	
Low involvement	
Disagreement	36.6
Agreement	35.0
High involvement	
Disagreement	23.3
Agreement	43.3

Source: *Personality and Social Psychology Bulletin*, 2001, vol. 27, p. 1403.

compliance among participants, while in conditions involving an important discussion only those participants whose opinion the experimenter claimed to share demonstrated increased compliance.

In a series of experiments we succeeded in demonstrating that the initiation of a dialogue with a stranger makes that person more likely to comply with a request subsequently directed towards him. Considering that the subjects broached in the conversations concerned various questions, and the requests involved various actions, we may assume that the rule we have uncovered is of a largely universal character. The results of the last experiment presented in this section also demonstrate certain limitations of this rule: when the conversation relates to important issues, dialogue only serves to increase submissiveness when the interlocutors are in possession of analogical opinions.

The power of imagination

Our brains store an incredible amount of all sorts of information. While certain cognitive content is very readily accessible, gaining access to other content can be significantly more difficult. The essence of this phenomenon is illustrated in a study by Amos Tversky and Daniel Kahneman (1982), who asked over 100 people whether there were more words in English beginning with the letter *k* than those in which the letter *k* appeared as the third letter of the word. While in fact there are more than twice as many words in which *k* is the third letter, compared to words which begin with *k*, the large majority of study participants declared the opposite.

Why do people commit such obvious mistakes? The problem is that the manner in which our memory is organized is favourable to searching for words based on their first letter, but it does not facilitate a search for letters in the middle. To simplify even further, it was easier for people to recall words beginning with the letter *k* than to recall those in which *k* was the third letter. The more that something is directly "accessible" to our memory or our consciousness, the more it seems likely to us.

Psychologists interested in the above rule discovered by Tversky and Kahneman decided to examine to what degree it constituted a general principle, and also if it could be applied to social phenomena. From the perspective of interest to us here, the most interesting question was posed by John Carroll. In an article published in 1978 he wondered whether imagining certain events would lead to an increase in the subjective probability that they could actually occur.

In his experiments – which today constitute classics in the literature – Carroll supplied participants with a scenario for some incident in which they themselves were the focal point (e.g. they took part in a trip to another continent, passed an exam at university, communicated successfully in a foreign language they were not fluent in) and asked them to imagine such a situation. It turned out that following this suggestion, people estimated the possibility of a given event taking place in their real life much higher than those who were simply asked to estimate the potential that they would experience an analogical situation. In Carroll's opinion, the act of imagining a given event – according to a properly constructed scenario – renders the event more cognitively accessible, and by the same token it seems subjectively more likely to the individual.

Larry Gregory, Robert Cialdini and Kathleen Carpenter (1982) began with the assumption that this rule can be used in social influence, and proposed a technique whose essence consists in saying the words "Imagine that . . .". The researchers conducted a thought experiment, in cooperation with a television station from the city of Tempe, Arizona, just outside Phoenix. Suburban home-owners were unwitting participants in the study. They were randomly assigned to one of two groups – control and experimental. Each of the participants was visited by a female experimenter. In the case of the control group, she applied typical marketing techniques – she said that the company offered a broad selection of entertainment and informational channels. She also added that buying a subscription was a great way to save money: rather than spending it on fuel and child care – normal aspects of spending time outside the home – they could spend time in a very pleasant manner in the home, with the family, with friends or alone. In the case of the experimental group she also presented basic information about the cable TV offer, declaring that it contained a broad range of informational and entertainment channels, but she then appealed to the imagination of the participant by presenting a scenario. She used arguments such as "Take a moment and think of how, instead of spending money on the babysitter and gas, and then having to put up with the hassles of 'going out', you will be able to spend your time at home, with your family, alone or with your friends" (p. 95).

Participants were then asked to respond to a few questions concerning such topics as whether they felt people would like to have cable TV in their homes, would they be inclined to buy a subscription, would they have a positive attitude towards it, and would they be interested in receiving additional information. Study participants who had been asked to engage their imagination responded more positively to these questions.

The next portion of this experiment produced even more interesting results. After a few weeks had passed, each of the study participants was visited by another person. This time, it was an employee of the cable television company unaware of the group to which a given person had been assigned. He offered a one-week free trial loan of equipment for receiving the cable TV signal, as well as the opportunity to purchase a full set of equipment and programmes if the customer decided to get a subscription following the end of the one-week period.

It turned out that in the group on which the "Imagine that . . ." technique was used, more people decided to borrow the equipment for a trial week than those in the control group. The differences between the two groups become even more visible when we compare the purchase decisions they made after the trial week. In the "Imagine that . . ." conditions, nearly two-and-a-half times more people decided to purchase a cable TV subscription than those in whose case more conventional marketing methods were applied.

A similar pattern of results was reported by Anna Schlosser (2003), who replaced the cable television subscription with a digital camera, and real behaviour with the declared intention to purchase the camera. The "Imagine that . . ." technique in her experiment also proved more effective than conventional means of convincing an undecided customer to make a purchase.

Why is such a simple technique not applied on a widespread basis? One of the important limitations in its effectiveness could be the difficulty involved in imagining oneself in particular situations. In one experiment, student participants were presented with a story about an illness that spread around a university campus. Some of them were asked to imagine that they were exhibiting symptoms of the disease; half of these participants were given symptoms that are easy to imagine, while the other half were given symptoms difficult to imagine. The experimental design also included a control group that was not asked to imagine anything. Study participants were asked to estimate the likelihood that they could contract the disease. It turned out that participants given more easily imaginable symptoms felt they were more likely to fall ill than the control group, while those with symptoms more difficult to imagine felt they were not in danger of catching the disease (Sherman, Cialdini, Schwartzman & Reynolds, 2002).

Petia Petrova and Robert Cialdini (2008) recorded a similar effect in studies concerning social influence. They proposed to their American subjects that they consider the possibility of spending their next vacation in Central Europe. In the standard conditions they were shown pictures of the landscape in Bulgaria and encouraged to take advantage of the opportunity to take a vacation there. In the experimental conditions, the participants were asked to imagine themselves spending time there. Half of those asked to do so were shown a crisp, clear picture while the other half were shown a fuzzy, unclear image. The latter group experienced difficulty in imagining themselves in the scenario that was presented to them. It turned out that the "Imagine that . . ." technique was only effective when participants in the experiment saw pictures they could make out easily. This means that the technique ceases to be effective when imagining oneself in a given situation is difficult. To put it differently, the technique fails when activating the imagination of a scenario involving oneself as the star runs into problems.

Difficulties in imagining something can occur for a wide range of reasons – both objective (something can be considered highly unlikely, thus rendering it difficult to imagine) and purely technical (as in the experiment of Petrova and Cialdini). All of them, however, can render the technique of activating the imagination an ineffective one.

Our attention is drawn by Shelley Taylor and her collaborators (Taylor, Pham, Rivkin & Armor, 1998) to another important issue related to the effectiveness of imagining various situations in the context of evoking behavioural changes. While the authors do this in the context of people ridding themselves of various problems in their lives and achieving their desired outcomes, as we will soon see, their work also turned out to have important implications for the psychology of social influence and served to initiate a series of studies on that subject. Taylor and her collaborators drew attention to the fact that imagining a positive state of affairs is an extremely frequent recommendation made in popular self-help literature designed to help people improve their lives. The aforementioned authors undertook a critical review of studies addressing this issue and stated that giving ourselves up to our dreams does not always bring us closer to our goals.

They therefore proposed drawing a distinction between two types of imagination concerning desirable states of affairs. The first is imagination focused on the process of achieving a given state of affairs, while the second is imagination focused on an end result. In respect of the former, people imagine themselves engaging in activities that lead to their dreamed-of result. This type of fantasizing contains a sequence of actions exhibiting a causal link with some desired objective. It serves to facilitate the development of plans and courses of action, and as a result leads one to believe that the likelihood of achieving the dreamed-of goal is relatively high, but on condition of engaging in very clearly-defined actions. Such dreams focused on the process of achieving a goal are usually very constructive and do, in fact, increase the chances it will be accomplished. However, things look entirely different when considering dreams focused exclusively on an end result, where the imagination consists of only the desired final effect. This does not provide a foundation for mentally working out various means of achieving that goal and developing plans. As a consequence, after being jolted awake from their dreams, people see only the contrast between the dull reality and the objective they wish to reach. Since the means of reaching the goal were not an element of the fantasizing, the goal itself seems equally (in extreme cases even more) unreal as it did before the daydreaming began. This sort of imagination is not as effective at improving the likelihood of an individual achieving a desired goal. To illustrate the idea, an alcoholic should imagine that he is capable of resisting the urge to lift a glass rather than being happy because he does not even feel drawn to alcohol. One who dreams of becoming a famous athlete, in turn, should imagine the difficult, day-to-day training, and gradually improving his personal bests rather than dreaming of standing on the top of the podium listening to the strains of his national anthem over the applause of the crowd.

This differentiation of two types of dreams quickly attracted the interest of researchers on social influence. Jennifer Escalas and Mary Luce (2003) explored whether inducing people in a different way to dream could impact their readiness to purchase certain products. Students served as participants in their study, and the product was a non-existent vitamin formula – Millennium – whose formula was supposedly designed with students in mind. The students were asked to allow themselves to engage in fantasizing associated with the product; some of them were asked to think about how their health would improve while using the product, and the others were asked to focus on how they would incorporate taking the product into the rhythm of their everyday activities. As it turned out, students from the latter group declared their desire to purchase Millennium more often than their fellow students from the former group. The researchers recorded similar results in later experiments during which they examined people's readiness to purchase shampoo (Escalas & Luce, 2004). In conditions of concentration on the process, the participants were supposed to imagine how they would feel washing their hair using the shampoo. In conditions of concentration on the result, they were supposed to imagine how they would feel when using the shampoo improved their appearance. The authors also draw attention to the role of their discovery in marketing. While advertisements often appeal to the imaginations of their targets, it would seem that they order us to imagine final effects rather than the processes leading to them.

The aforementioned results demonstrate that the "Imagine that . . ." technique can prove effective in affecting people's decision-making when making consumer purchases, but only in certain circumstances. The real problem for practitioners, however, is not how to induce desire and make people imagine buying various, often utterly needless, items; it is also important that they do not spontaneously imagine how they will run out of money for the things they really need.

Summary

Words play a very significant role in social influence processes. Many studies have shown that seemingly unimportant differences in the wording of a message may have a serious impact on people's readiness to carry out requests and orders addressed to them. The results of some experiments flew in the face of conventional wisdom. While it is most certainly the case that adding the word "please" to a standard request will generally increase the chances of it being fulfilled, this is not an unconditional rule. Studies have shown, for example, that if a request for a donation to a charitable cause is made by a person who is only organizing the help (and is not a beneficiary of it), then adding the word "please" to the message may in fact weaken its effectiveness.

One of the most well-known techniques exploiting the power of the word is "even a penny will help". We often refuse various requests to support charity campaigns, justifying the decision by saying that we can't help everyone, or that we are not rich enough to support each worthy initiative. However, it turns out that if the phrase "even a penny will help" (or something similar) appears following a standard request, this manner of thinking is blocked and people are more likely to carry out requests being made of them.

Another technique discussed in this chapter is based on the fact that people often refuse to carry out small requests without justifying the reasons for such a decision. It turns out that if they are directly asked to explain why they have refused to help out, their desire to avoid becoming ensnared in embarrassing justifications boosts the chances that they will carry out the request. A similar increase in compliance is noted when emphasis is placed on the fact that the choice of whether to agree or not belongs solely to the addressee of the request. Most likely, people feel more appreciated when they establish that it is solely dependent on them whether they choose to help, rather than when they think their decision results to a greater or lesser degree from external pressure.

Many studies have been devoted to the phenomenon of labelling. Defining people using dispositional traits often leads to them behaving in a manner consistent with the content of those labels. This is especially likely when the source of the label is trustworthy, and the label itself refers to areas of an individual's self-awareness in respect of which he is not entirely sure who he really is. This technique also has some interesting variations such as asking questions leading the individual to label himself, and the expert snare in which the competences of the individual in a given area are emphasized.

The next technique discussed in this chapter was foot-in-the-mouth. According to this technique, in order to increase the chances that a person we approach with a request to make a donation on behalf of a charity will react positively, we should first ask how he is feeling. After receiving a response that he feels good, we should express our satisfaction, and only then make our request for his support for charitable activity. Some believe that this technique's effectiveness is based on the mechanism of commitment and consistency. Someone who has publicly declared that he feels good should feel an obligation to act in a manner that will help others to feel good as well. An alternative interpretation of this effect refers to a relationship of intimacy and closeness that is formed when the question about well-being is asked. Yet another interpretation assumes that of key importance is not so much the question about mood, but questions themselves. The answer to a question sets a conversation in motion. According to this interpretation, ensnaring our interlocutor in a dialogue about a neutral subject should boost later submissiveness.

Another interesting social influence technique is inducing an individual to imagine particular circumstances. In one related experiment it was demonstrated that people who were induced to imagine that they could keep tabs on social and political importance, while also being provided a rich selection of entertainment, were more likely to purchase a cable television subscription than people approached in a more traditional manner. Later research on the consequences of imagining various conditions demonstrated that the effectiveness of this technique is limited to conditions in which the individual does not experience any difficulties in imagining particular conditions or behaviours.

5

INTERACTION DYNAMICS AND THE SURPRISE FACTOR

The techniques discussed in this chapter are based on a particular course of events during an interaction between the requester and the person targeted with the request. We are not concerned here with a sequence of two subsequent requests, as in the case of the techniques discussed in Chapter 2, nor with a subtle appeal to the feeling of the target of a request's self-worth, as in Chapter 3, but rather with the situation itself in which a dynamizing element is involved in the formulation of expectations. There is always something exceptional taking place, something that removes the course of events from the sphere of the typical and routine. This unusual happenstance is, of course, no accident. The individual formulating the request is aware that without it, the chances that the request will be fulfilled would be significantly lower.

Underlying the effectiveness of such social influence techniques is the assumption that we quite often vacillate as to our decisions: Should we buy a particular car or not? Should we vote for one presidential candidate or another? Should we sign a petition supporting the introduction of the death penalty or not? In the majority of such cases, our indecision results from weighing up the arguments "for and against", with the scales failing to tip significantly in either direction. Even if we are inclined to follow one path over the other, the arguments in support of the remaining option are not so easily dismissed that we could take a decision with absolute certainty as to its correctness.

The techniques described in this chapter are grounded in the common assumption that by introducing a particular dynamizing element into the structure of a situation we can ensure that, at least in the key moment during which the decision is taken, the individual targeted with the request will be convinced of the greater merit of the option that the requester would prefer to be chosen. Let us examine some of these social influence techniques.

That's not all

Although it would seem that the lower the price of a given product, the more people there are ready to buy it, salespeople know that quite often the opposite is the case. Indeed, customers often regard the price of a product as an indicator of its quality. They assume that "the more expensive, the better". This way of thinking is particularly typical of situations when estimating the quality of some item on the basis of measurable criteria is difficult, or when we lack sufficient knowledge in a given sphere.

Discounts present us with a special kind of situation. For example, if we know that a washing machine nominally costs $800, but because the end of the year is approaching the store's management is holding a sale and has reduced the price of the washing machine to $300. We know that it is a device of good quality (the high initial price tells us so), while at the same time we are now able to afford it, because it is no longer expensive. From the psychological perspective, a discount draws its strength from the fact that the situation is initially characterized by arguments supporting the purchase of the aforementioned washing machine (it's expensive, so it's good), and by arguments against doing so ($800 is a lot of money for a washing machine). The exceptional opportunity created by the shop's management results in the arguments "for" retaining their immediacy, while removing the arguments "against". If there were no discount and the washing machine's price was always $300, people who were not well-versed in home appliances would have no idea that this particular washing machine was so good.

Situations involving price cuts are generally static. The customer sees the old (higher) price and compares it with the new (lower) one. The "that's not all" social influence technique is even more effective than a simple discount; what differentiates it is its dynamic character. This technique was first described and subjected to empirical verification by Jerry Burger (1986). As in the case of many other techniques, the impetus came from observing a trick played by some salespeople. Burger noticed that when asked about the price of a product, they gave customers an answer, but seeing that customers were wavering, they intervened and prevented them from saying "no" by immediately providing additional information that can be metaphorically represented as a sort of "that's not all" statement. So, salespeople can say such things as "only today" or "for selected customers" a free gift comes with a purchased product. They can say that a "special offer" makes the price slightly lower, or that "until the end of the day" customers will get not one, but two packages of product for the same price. The application of the "that's not all" technique can be easily spotted in TV commercials, where the main product is introduced first and additional bonus items are presented later using the "if you call now" format. In general, this technique is based either on leaving the base price untouched while offering an additional freebie, or by dropping the price of a given product.

In the first experiment dedicated to examining the effectiveness of the "that's not all" technique, those selected as participants were people who approached a stall where cookies were being sold and asked about their price. The prospective clients were randomly assigned to one of two groups. In the control conditions, they were informed that the cookies were being sold in a set composed of two packages, and the price of the set was 75 cents. In the experimental conditions, the salesperson said that the cookies cost 75 cents, then after a short pause added that this was the price for a set containing two packages. As it turned out, while 40% of customers purchased cookies in the control conditions, this number jumped to 73% of customers in the experimental conditions.

It was thus demonstrated that the "that's not all" technique is effective when a potential customer, wavering as to whether to buy, is unexpectedly informed that an additional product will also be given. Will this technique be equally successful if the price of the article is unexpectedly lowered? Burger decided to attempt to answer this question in his next experiment. This time, having asked about the price of cookies, participants from the experimental group were told they would have to pay $1. Next, the salespeople exchanged a few remarks with each other, and then the customer was told that since they were getting ready to close up shop, the cookies would be sold at a reduced price of 75 cents. Participants from the control group were informed at the beginning that the price was 75 cents. The "that's not all" technique was effective in this case as well. Cookies were purchased by 44% of the control group, but by 73% of the experimental group.

Why is this technique an effective social influence strategy? We may assume that the principle of reciprocity comes into play – a mechanism described previously during discussion of the "door-in-the-face" technique. In the case of the "that's not all" technique, this principle provokes an intellectual reflection in the form of "if the salesperson makes a concession, I should buy the product".

Burger's next experiment was dedicated to confirming the correctness of the aforementioned interpretation. He assumed that if the technique under discussion is based on the principle of reciprocity, it should be particularly (and perhaps exclusively?) effective when the interaction between buyer and seller resembles a negotiation, as was the case in the two experiments discussed previously. A similar situation was created for one of the conditions in the following experiment. The seller reduced the price from $1 to 75 cents, explaining that this resulted from the desire to finish work quickly. In another group, the price was also lowered from $1 to 75 cents, but the situation clearly involved no negotiating. Here it was the case that a misunderstanding had occurred: the seller was just beginning work, and had been told by a colleague that the cookies previously cost a dollar, but were now on sale for 25 cents less. The control group was, of course, told straight away that the price was 75 cents. It turned out that more customers decided to purchase the cookies in the two experimental conditions (85% and 70%, respectively) than in the control conditions (50%).

In another experiment the effectiveness of door-to-door sellers was tested. In the control group, they offered to sell candles for $2. For the group in which a price cut of a negotiated character was applied, one of the sellers gave a price of $3, but the second partner loudly remarked that the real cost was a dollar lower because "(they) had agreed to sell them for $2 in order to sell more". In the group for which the discount was not of a negotiated character, the partner of the seller who had given a price of $3 remarked that $3 was the price of some other candles, while the ones they were offering now cost $2. In the control group the candles were offered at a price of $2 from the very beginning. While under the control conditions the candles were bought by only 14.3% of participants, the non-negotiated conditions saw this number rise to 37.1%, and in the negotiated conditions it jumped to as high as 57.1%. Before we proceed to other considerations, let us stop for a moment and examine the procedure followed in this experiment. It is worth noting that, despite the intentions of the experiment designer, the conditions in which a $1 discount was provided differed not only in the level of negotiability. In the first group the participants were informed that they had the opportunity to purchase the very same candles that had been sold earlier for $3. In the second group, they were offered candles for $2 that had always been available at that price (it was other candles that cost $3). Only in the first condition was the price an exceptional one.

Regardless, we can easily see that, while the rates at which participants purchased cookies and candles were higher in groups involving a seller/client negotiation-style interaction, this was not a precondition for the technique's success. These results thus indicate that the principle of reciprocity is but one of a number of mechanisms underlying the effectiveness of the "that's not all" trick. Burger, seeking an additional mechanism that would serve to explain this technique's success, referred to a "changing the anchor" effect. In one classic study (Kenrick & Gutierres, 1980), men rated the attractiveness of a woman presented to them in a photograph quite highly. This score was lower, however, if just before they had watched an episode of *Charlie's Angels*, in which unusually attractive and sexy actresses had appeared. If we view this regularity through the lens of "that's not all" technique and recall the experiments previously discussed, we can say that hearing a price of 75 cents just after having heard "$1" seems to be a more advantageous offer than 75 cents without the $1 "anchor".

In one simple experiment, participants were provided information about the price of cookies thus: some people were told that the price was 75 cents, others that the price was a dollar, while at the same time being asked how much they would be willing to pay for the cookies and what they felt was a "fair price". Results indicated that people from the group informed that the regular price was $1 declared their readiness to pay more, and that they regarded a higher price as a fair one, in greater numbers than the group informed that the price was 75 cents. During a subsequent experiment in which the sale of cookies for a price of $1 was accompanied by information from the seller that they had previously been marketed for 25 cents more, there was no greater interest exhibited on the part of buyers than in the group that was simply told the price was $1 (again, significantly greater numbers of participants purchased cookies when the "that's not all" technique was applied, reducing the price by 25 cents under the pretense of quickly winding up the day's work).

These results do not provide confirmation for the supposition that the mechanism responsible for the effectiveness of the analyzed technique results from supplying the targeted person with an anchor for judging the profitability of a decision to buy. To put it more precisely, such an anchor does not, in and of itself, increase one's readiness to take advantage of an offer, which led Burger to conclude that the primary mechanism at work is the previously mentioned principle of reciprocity. It is possible, however, that of key importance is the surprise with which the new anchor appears in the "that's not all" technique and is linked with the removal of an argument that previously justified refusing the offer, occurring in the moment at which the wavering customer was mentally reviewing the reasons "for and against" the purchase.

Ian Brennan and Kenneth Bahn (1991) drew attention to other problems in the search for the psychological mechanism underlying the effectiveness of the "that's not all" technique. They observed that, in the interaction this technique assumes between the requester and the target of the request, there is no element of rejection by the target of the initial query (as was the case in the "door-in-the-face" discussed previously). It is thus not the case that the person issuing the request makes some sort of clear concession benefiting the target of the request, which would in turn provide motivation for that person to offer some sort of concession. What is more, a reduction in price by the seller may be perceived by the client as being motivated by the seller's own self-interest (i.e. desire to close the stall) rather than as a favour for the customer. As a consequence, in conditions that Burger treats as reciprocity, essentially a mechanism of contrast takes the fore. The price of $1.25 acts as an anchor point against which $1 appears reasonable. In situations that Burger views as a contrast effect condition, the price of $1.25 is, in turn, a weaker and less-definitive anchor point, coming as it does only after the real price of $1 is given. Brennan and Bahn (1991) thus conclude that the issue concerning the mechanism responsible for the effectiveness of this technique is not resolved. Yun-Oh Whang (2012) also feels that the mixed results recorded by Burger failed to provide a clear theoretical explanation for the process. Whang observes that, from the perspective of the contrast effect, the attractiveness of the discount offered by the seller is not associated with the amount of the difference as much as whether the final offer consists of a price higher than the anchor point or lower. If, for example, a customer feels that a particular television should cost $200, a discount from $240 to $210 fails to be attractive, while one from $220 to $190 renders the offer tempting. From the perspective of the principle of reciprocity, we can say that in both cases we are dealing with a concession – the price has been lowered by $30. In one experiment conducted by Whang, students were invited to participate in a computer simulation of a purchase decision-making task. They were initially asked how much they would be willing to pay for a 27-inch LCD TV, and this figure was treated as the anchor point (Whang uses the term "reservation price"). Next, the participant's computer screen displayed an offer to sell that very television at a price slightly higher than the declared reservation price. In the control conditions, information was simultaneously provided about a price change: the television could now be bought at a reduced price. In the "that's not all" conditions, the information about the price change appeared after 15 seconds. Independently of the conditions, the value of the bonus was constructed such that in half of the cases the final offer remained higher than the anchor point (or, as Whang calls it, the level of the reservation price), while in the remaining cases it was lower. At the end, participants were requested to indicate on a 7-point scale the likelihood of their taking the opportunity to purchase the television. The effectiveness of the "that's not all" technique will be confirmed if this declaration is stronger in conditions when the information about a drop in price appeared following a delay, as opposed to analogical conditions in which this information was provided alongside the regular price. As it occurred, in the case of the unattractive conditions (i.e. when the final price remained higher than the anchor point), the technique described here was effective (increase in declared inclination to buy from 3.92 to 5.00), while in the attractive conditions (i.e. when the final price was lower than the anchor point), this technique was not effective (inclination to accept the offer remained at the same level: 4.77 and 4.82, respectively). In Whang's opinion, these results offer little support for the contrast mechanism – indeed, contrast should bring the technique's mechanisms to life in attractive conditions, not in unattractive ones. The author concludes that it is the principle of reciprocity that constitutes the psychological mechanism activating the technique described here. Be that as it may, how can we explain the fact that it only functions in conditions viewed as unfavourable? It is worth noting that in the attractive conditions, the participants had already declared a rather strong inclination to buy. The attractiveness of the offer itself was at work in this case. The technique had no opportunity to improve the situation, it could not increase the likelihood participants would buy the television. These results, besides casting a certain light on the mechanism underlying the effectiveness of the "that's not all" technique, would also seem to be of practical value: this sales trick should be applied first and foremost when the final asking price remains quite high. If the proposed discount proves to be truly attractive, it is sufficient to offer a traditional reduction in price without any dynamizing element. The question arises, however, to what degree the effect achieved by Whang can be generalized and applied to all situations involving sales. We should keep in mind the fact that this researcher explored decisions by consumers related to the purchase of a television, which is a product used in the private sphere (at home), technologically advanced and quite costly.

Carrie Pollock, Shane Smith, Eric Knowles and Heather Bruce (1998) observed that people behave in different ways when making the decision to purchase various types of products. If we focus on the aspect of price, in the case of inexpensive items the customer does not carefully review all the information provided by the seller. It is sufficient that the interaction gives the impression of a price negotiation, and that the seller backs down from the original price, for the customer to be likely to purchase the article in question at the lower price. This would serve to explain why, in Burger's experiments, situations in which a lower price was quoted following a higher one was sufficient to induce greater customer interest than conditions in which the sale price was given at the start.

The aforementioned researchers feel that the concept of automaticity developed by Ellen Langer (1978) can be helpful in understanding the behaviour of Burger's research participants.

In many social situations we react automatically, limiting the volume of data processed and the complexity of the processing itself to a minimum, reducing our cognitive activity. The simplest way to convince ourselves of this truth is to ask people the time after they have just glanced at their watch. They will invariably look at their watch again, and this time they will do so for a bit longer. As another example of mindlessness, we may cite the course of an experiment I conducted some time ago with my collaborators (Dolinski, Gromski & Szmajke, 1988). We were interested in judgements about the responsibility of the perpetrator of a bad act, more specifically, in the effect of being the person wronged by said perpetrator. The design of the experiment thus required that a portion of participants experienced the feeling of being harmed. To achieve this aim, we decided to cheat the participants out of some money (which we naturally returned to them after the experiment had finished). One of us came into a lecture hall occupied by first-year students, introduced himself as an employee of the university and announced that the students had paid too little during registration. The researcher then took out a plastic bag that already contained a small sum of money, as well as a clean sheet of paper, and began taking payments. We did not present any documents to the students, nor did we issue any sort of receipts. As the design of our experiment was rather complex, we had to repeat the situation four times. In each case, we observed to our surprise that nobody expressed any concern; students who didn't have any cash on hand borrowed some from their classmates, and all of them were careful to ensure that their names were written down on the piece of paper. We collected money from several dozen students, and in half of the cases the sums were significant.

While it may be debated whether automaticity is the product of our mind's limitations, as suggested by Michael Posner and Charles Snyder (1975) and Shelley Taylor (1981), or rather from motivational deficits, as would argue Ulric Neisser (1976) and David Navon (1984), in a range of situations we apply ready schemes of behaviours learned and formulated in the past. Langer (1978) suggests that if a message targeted at us is structurally similar to ones we have reacted positively to in the past, it is highly likely that we will refrain from analyzing its content and the context in which it is transmitted; rather, we will mindlessly and automatically activate an established response pattern. An example of this manner of functioning is supplied by Ellen Langer, Arthur Blank and Benzion Chanowitz (1978). In this study, individuals waiting for a copy machine were asked to give up their place in line. Depending on the experimental conditions, the person doing the asking either made only a simple request ("Excuse me . . . may I use the Xerox machine?"), or added a fragment with only the grammatical and structural form of a justification for the request ("because I have to make a copy?"), or appended the request with a real justification ("because I am in a rush?"). When the experimenter added that there were only 5 pages to be copied, participants gave up their place in the queue equally often in cases when the justification was a real one (being in a rush) as in those when it was spurious (needing to make copies), even though in the second situation the content of the remark provided absolutely no additional real explanation. It was obvious that the person addressing the participants wanted to make photocopies. Clearly, nobody would use a photocopier to fry pancakes. At the same time, participants very rarely allowed experimenters to jump the queue when only a request without any sort of justification was provided. Because participants in the past had probably reacted to requests aimed at them and accompanied with a justification on multiple occasions, in the situation described above they simply activated mindlessly the script for agreement to displaying politeness. The oddity and novelty of a situation involving a request with no justification at all, however, put them on their guard and shifted their reaction to a qualitatively higher level of reflection. Participants also reacted in a reflective manner when the experimenter said that there were 20 (and not 5, as in the conditions described above) pages for copying. In this situation the experimenter was far more likely to receive consent to use the photocopier when the provided justification was a real one than when only an apparent one. Automaticity here would be too costly (significant loss of time). Thus, the participants analyzed not only the structure of messages targeting them, but also their content. Langer et al. (1978) suggest that in these situations there is sufficient motivation to shift one's attention from the simple structural characteristics of the message to its semantic elements, which results in processing of the actual information streaming in.

Pollock et al. (1998) suggest that the "that's not all" technique exploits the fact that customers being offered inexpensive goods are in a state of automaticity. If this is essentially the case, it may be assumed that the technique will cease to be effective when the item in question is expensive. This should generate a shift in the individual's functioning to a reflective level, as well as neutralizing the effect of information about circumstances making it cheaper to buy at the present moment. In addition, by applying the technique of Langer and her associates involving the use of real or apparent justifications for requests or propositions, it is possible to determine whether and when people are in a state of automaticity or are not.

In one experimental study, the reactions of people given the chance to purchase sweets were observed. In some conditions these were small bombonieres, sold for $1. In the version involving the application of the "that's not all" technique, the initial price was $1.25; following a short conversation between sellers, it was announced that the bomboniere cost $1. In other conditions, the bombonieres were significantly larger, and their price was $5. When the "that's not all" technique was used, a price of $5.25 was first quoted, and after the sellers engaged in a brief conversation between themselves, a price of $5 was subsequently given. In addition, in some cases the sellers provided an additional remark designed to justify the purchase of the bomboniere. Similarly to the experiment by Langer et al., sometimes this justification was real while in others it was spurious. In the first case, it was said that the manufacturer was a recognized brand, present on the market for many years, and that the chocolates contained titbits hand-dipped in liquid chocolate mixed with cashews. In the case of the spurious justification, it was said that the chocolates were made of chocolate and were sold in that very box. Some participants were not provided with any additional justification for purchasing the bombonieres. Analysis of the results showed that the "that's not all" technique was only effective when the price of the bomboniere was not high. In these cases, 76% of customers purchased them as opposed to the 45% who did so in the control group. If, however, the bombonieres were expensive, the differences between the control group and the group on which the technique under analysis was applied was no longer statistically significant. Additionally, it turned out that if the sweets cost $1, the spurious justification was equally effective in boosting customers' readiness to buy them as the real justification. The opposite was the case, however, when the bombonieres were expensive. Without any justification at all provided for making the purchase, roughly the same number of participants decided to buy them compared to those receiving a spurious justification; the percentage of those buying the bombonieres was significantly higher when a real justification was given. These results thus suggest that people stop behaving mindlessly in the case of relatively costly purchases. The "that's not all" technique also ceases to be effective in these situations.

It would seem, however, that a lone experiment is not a sufficient basis for claiming that the analyzed technique is never effective in such cases. Perhaps, if the discount or additional product offered is of substantial value, the individual receiving the offer can make a more or less rational decision to take advantage of it. Although I have not conducted any empirical research in this area, I have been led to this conclusion by observing the behaviour of a knife salesman working in the main railway station in Wrocław, the city where I work and live. He offers passers-by a set of knives in a wood block for $50, and when he observes they are taking a moment to think, he adds that as part of a grand promotion every purchasing customer can receive a surprise gift worth $100. Tempted by this highly exceptional opportunity, customers often purchase the knives and then receive their surprise gift of ... two additional sets of knives (each worth $50).

It would seem that the essence of the "that's not all" technique's effectiveness consists primarily of the initial offer itself being rather attractive (for example, it is worth noting that in the aforementioned experiments, cookies were bought by around 40% of people in the control group, while the small bomboniere was purchased by 45% of participants). At the moment when someone is wavering and exploring the arguments for and against both potential decisions (buy/don't buy), a new argument suddenly appears, which often tips the scales. Unlike those researchers who refer to the theory of automaticity, I do not think that this argument proved decisive only in conditions involving the potential purchase of inexpensive goods. I would rather say that in the case of cheaper products, it is enough that the aforementioned argument is simply raised. In the case of expensive items, however, it must be of significantly greater weight.

Disruption-then-reframe

The disruption-then-reframe (DTR) technique is based on the assumption that people of whom some request is made then experience an approach/avoidance conflict. The approach is associated with the desire to provide assistance to another person who needs and asks for it. It can also be linked with the desire to acquire particular goods. Avoidance, however, is related to the necessary effort or loss of time and/or money. Individuals thus resist the thing others are encouraging them to do. Many social influence techniques are oriented on enhancing the incentive to do something, such as by highlighting the benefits that can result. The best example of this may be the "that's not all" trick discussed above. The technique to be discussed now consists of both reducing resistance and boosting incentive. What lies at its core? The act of "knocking someone out of their comfort zone", of making the course of an interaction a bit surprising and unusual, then presenting a new argument to encourage our interlocutor to accede to a particular request.

Barbara Davis and Eric Knowles (1999) suggest that at least two psychological theories provide a foundation for the prediction that a cognitive reframing technique will be effective. The first of them is based in the work of Erickson – the founder of modern hypnosis. Erickson (1964) observed that people came to him in order to be subjected to a state of hypnosis, but at the same time they experienced a feeling of resistance. To overcome this recalcitrance, it becomes necessary to do something that will put them off balance, at least for a moment. For example, we may suddenly and forcefully squeeze a patient's hand during our greeting. This event will occupy the patient's conscious thoughts, at the same time preventing the exercise of control over self in the face of hypnosis. This particular state of confoundment results in an increased submissiveness to the efforts of the clinician/hypnotist, maximizing the chances for successful hypnosis therapy. Of course, the content of the hypnosis itself is a new cognitive quality, and can be expressed in categories of cognitive reinterpretation.

The second concept mentioned by Davis and Knowles is action identification theory, which is the work of Robin Vallacher and Daniel Wegner (1985, 1987). These psychologists drew attention to the fact that not only do individuals function rationally and assign meaning to their behaviours, but that they can also identify them cognitively on multiple levels. A handyman pounding a nail with his hammer can identify this activity in such ways as active recreation or building a shelf for books, but also as pounding in a nail or hitting a nail on the head with a hammer. More general and abstract labels (e.g. active recreation) are viewed by Vallacher and Wegner as the equivalent of action identification on a higher level. Specific and detailed identifications (such as hitting a nail on the head with a hammer) are equivalent to identifying de facto the same action on a lower level. From this perspective, of interest to us here is one particular element in Vallacher and Wegner's theory: people generally prefer higher levels of identification (because they give their actions meaning and place them in the service of some objective), but various situations that disrupt their routine functioning generally cause this level of action identification to temporarily shift lower. One particularly suggestive illustration of this truth can be found in experiments by Wegner and his collaborators concerning consumption. In one of them, study participants were given a cup of coffee, and then asked to give a description of what they were doing. Some of them were drinking coffee in normal coffee cups, while the remaining participants were served coffee in cups weighing 1 pound. People in the former group generally stated that they were drinking coffee, giving themselves a shot of energy, or satisfying their caffeine addiction. Those in the latter group generally identified their actions on a lower level, declaring that they were raising a coffee cup to their lips with some difficulty, that they were sipping, or that they were swallowing coffee (Wegner, Vallacher, Macomber, Wood & Arps, 1984). Participants in another experiment were given snacks to eat, with some being allowed to grasp them normally (using their fingers), and others in an atypical manner (using chopsticks). People in the former group generally identified their actions with such designations as "I'm eating", "I'm satisfying my appetite", or "I'm filling up". The latter group's participants, in turn, applied such terms as "I'm placing food into my mouth" or "I'm chewing".

Vallacher and Wegner emphasize that a disruption in routine behaviour results in people shifting their focus to details, which enables them to regain their bearings in the situation at hand. Only after this is accomplished can the individual engage in shifting action identification to a higher level. Davis and Knowles, concurring with this view, simultaneously draw attention to the fact that this level need not be the same high one as before. In particular, if we engage in cognitive reframing then the probability is increased that this level will be a different one.

Thus, as Davis and Knowles (1999) conclude – from both the perspective of Erickson's work on the conditions for effective hypnosis as well as from that of the theory of action identification advanced by Vallacher and Wegner – that subjecting people to a sequence of disruption to the normal course of interaction, then cognitive reframing, should constitute an effective social influence technique. These psychologists present four research studies that are designed to establish that this is in fact the case.

The experiments involved the sale of either Christmas cards (study 1) or note cards (studies 2 and 3). They were sold by door-to-door salespeople, who declared that the income from the sale would go to support charitable organizations. Faced with the choice to buy or not to buy, those queried experienced the aforementioned approach/avoidance conflict. Why might one decide to purchase the cards? Doubtlessly, the desire to support a charitable organization and, in doing so, to help people in need. The cards themselves may also be of some benefit. If we have yet to send out our Christmas cards, these will be "just the job". Note cards can also be useful in some way. What reasons could we then have for not buying? The necessity to engage in extended contact with an unknown door-to-door salesperson, to open the door, to spend money and, perhaps, to deal later with the unpleasant feeling that we have succumbed to the pressure of a smooth-talker.

The experimenters applied the following technique: after introducing themselves, they announced the price of the cards in a very unusual way. They said "The price of these notes/Christmas cards is 300 pennies." After a moment they added "That's three dollars. It's a bargain." The wholly unusual manner of giving the price in pennies disrupted the routine course of the interaction. The cognitive reframing here consists of providing an additional, previously unmentioned justification for why the purchase of the cards is a sensible one. This justification is the "bargain".

For the first experiment three groups were formed. Participants from the first group were told of the charitable cause associated with the sale of the cards, and then were told only of their price. They were told that the cards cost $3. The second group was subjected only to cognitive reframing. After giving the price in dollars, the experimenters waited around 2 seconds and then added: "It's a bargain." In the third group, the technique recommended by Davis and Knowles was utilized: first, jolt people out of their routine, then supply them with cognitive reframing. Participants were informed that the cards cost 300 cents, then after 2 seconds they heard "That's three dollars. It's a bargain." In each of the first two groups the cards were bought by 35% of participants. In the third, nearly twice as many (65%) did so.

In the second study, the experimenters added yet another group to the experimental design: only a procedure jolting participants out of their routine was applied. In these conditions, potential customers were told that the cards cost 300 cents, and after 2 seconds it was explained that this was $3. As it transpired, this measure was not sufficient. The percentage of people deciding to buy the cards was only slightly greater than in the group informed about their price in a more normal manner (35% and 25%, respectively: a statistically insignificant difference). However, the technique recommended by Davis and Knowles again proved successful. This time, 70% of participants decided to purchase the cards. Why is jolting people out of their routine not enough? The scholars refer to the concept of action identification. If a cognitive reinterpretation is not performed, following the disorganization resulting from the destabilization of routine the individual in question will return to the previously applied framing of the issue. Such doubts come back into play as "What do I need these cards for?" If, however, a cognitive reframing is proposed in the form of "It's a bargain", this statement, in turn, becomes a new rallying point for the individual's actions. This effect does not take place without disruption to a routinely proceeding activity: in such cases the person will remain focused on the first decision motive ("What do I need these cards for?"). If this line of thought is correct, then the technique proposed by the authors should prove effective exclusively in the following sequence: first, a routine course of events, then supplying a cognitive reinterpretation. Not only would the presence of both elements be of importance, but their sequence would prove decisive as well.

To determine if this really is the case, Davis and Knowles conducted further empirical study. This time, aside from the control group informed of the price in the standard manner, and the group on which the scholars' proposed technique was tested, the experimental design included conditions in which the sequence of elements constituting the technique was reversed. When offering the cards, the experimenter/seller said "It's a bargain", and after 2 seconds added "It costs 300 cents, that's three dollars". It turned out that this procedure was not enough to result in a higher number of people deciding to purchase the cards than in the case of the control group. Again, however, the effectiveness of the technique consisting of disrupting the routine course of events followed by supplying cognitive reframing is demonstrated. The proportion of individuals who complied in the three aforementioned Davis and Knowles experiments are presented in Table 5.1.

TABLE 5.1 Percentage of targets who complied in each condition in Davis and Knowles (1999) experiments

Condition	Study 1	Study 2	Study 3
Disrupt-then-reframe ("They're 300 pennies...that's $3. It's a bargain")	65	70	65
Price only ("They're $3")	35	25	30
Reframe only ("They're $3. It's a bargain"	35	30	–
Disruption only ("They're 300 pennies... That's $3")	–	35	–
Reframe-then-disrupt ("It's a bargain... They're 300 pennies. That's $3")	–	–	25

Source: *Journal of Personality and Social Psychology*, 1999, vol. 76, p. 194.
Copyright 1999 by the American Psychological Association, Inc.

The effectiveness of the technique under discussion was also confirmed by Davis and Knowles in a fourth study. In this experiment, it was decided to exclude the hypothesis that the effectiveness of the technique being tested is an artefact resulting from the occurrence of a self-fulfilling prophecy. Eight experimenters/door-to-door salespeople were employed, each of whom received either the instruction to sell cards using the DTR system, or was additionally asked to give the standard price ($3) and to add "It's a bargain" (cognitive reframing). It turned out that in the first of these conditions, 90% of those solicited purchased the cards, while in the second condition this number was 50%. The methodological value of this experiment is diluted, however, by the fact that its design failed to include conditions involving disruption to a routine and the sequence of reframing-then-disruption.

Bob Fennis, Enny Das and Ad Pruyn (2004) examined whether the DTR technique could be effective in convincing people to participate in a lottery. A female experimenter stood in the main square of a large city and approached passers-by, singing the praises of the Dayzers lottery, which had a structure different from traditional lotteries; instead of one lucky winner taking the whole prize pool, Dayzers gave a million people smaller prizes. In the control conditions she informed people that one entry cost €3.50. In the experimental conditions she gave the price in cents (350 euro cents), and after a moment clarified that this was the equivalent of €3.50. In both cases, the lottery ticket sales pitch was concluded with the argument that it was a bargain. While in the control conditions every fourth person approached took the chance to purchase a ticket; when the DTR technique was applied the percentage of those acceding to the request jumped to 43%. The authors of the experiment also demonstrated that people subjected to the technique being analyzed here were less inclined to present arguments against buying the ticket. They treat this fact as a piece of indirect evidence that cognitive disorientation (resulting here from the reporting of the price in cents) disrupts the efficient processing of thoughts linked with the offer just received, and the additional argument (the bargain) functions as a cue for thinking to take a heuristic turn.

We have also confirmed the potential for using the DTR technique in sales transactions during research in which one of my masters students (Katarzyna Selwant) sold jars of prepared soup at a bazaar. Participants were drawn from customers at the bazaar doing their normal grocery shopping (they had been buying milk, cream, butter, etc.). The saleswoman also offered to sell them soup, producing a jar with its contents. In the standard conditions she said that it cost 2 zlotys and that it was very tasty. In the DTR conditions she gave the price as 200 groszs, and after 2 seconds she explained that this was two zlotys, then provided the argument about the soup's good taste. Results showed that the sales pitch including the '200 groszs' induced roughly twice as many people to buy the soup (Dolinski, 2005). A similar effect was noted by Frank Kardes, Bob Fennis, Edward Hirt, Zakary Tormala and Brian Bullington (2007), selling candies in a supermarket for 100 euro cents while adding the argument "It's a bargain". Of course, giving the price in an unusual manner is not the only use of the DTR technique in a sales situation. "Oddness" can also concern the very name of the product. Eric Knowles, Shannon Butler and Jay Linn (2001) sold cupcakes for 50 cents. In the control conditions, they simply said "These cupcakes are 50 cents, they are really delicious". In the DTR conditions, they only changed the word "cupcakes" to "halfcakes", which was enough to boost sales.

While Davis and Knowles (1999), Knowles et al. (2001), Kardes et al. (2007) and Katarzyna Selwant (see: Dolinski, 2005) demonstrated that the DTR technique can be an effective tool of social influence during commercial transactions, and Fennis et al. (2004) provided evidence of its usefulness in convincing people to buy lottery tickets, Izabela Kubala (2002) showed the potential for it to be applied in an entirely different field. It is well-known that the scourge of research companies carrying out surveys and opinion polling is the high rate of respondents who refuse to participate. This situation generates at least two types of difficulties. First, it renders the sample poorly differentiated, as people refusing to participate may exhibit a range of differences from those who consent to take part. Second, it increases the costs of studies and the amount of time needed to conduct them. Refusal is obviously far more likely in conditions when respondents do not receive any gratification for their participation and spend a long time on it. Even in the case of a short telephone survey, the percentage of those refusing to answer a few questions can be very high.

With these considerations as a starting point, Kubala decided to examine whether the DTR technique could prove helpful in raising the percentage of people agreeing to participate in a telephone marketing study. In the control conditions, the canvasser called randomly selected residents of Wrocław and introduced herself as an employee of the (non-existent) Lower Silesia Social Research Centre. She then asked if her interlocutor would agree to answer a few questions concerning consumer goods, simultaneously confirming that the conversation would last around 7 minutes. In the DTR conditions, instead of 7 minutes it was said that the survey would last "around 420 seconds", and after about 2 seconds it was added that "that's 7 minutes", and then the argument "it'll just take a moment" was thrown in. The experimental design also included other conditions in order to see whether potential differences between the aforementioned groups did in fact result from the application of the disorientation–cognitive reshuffling sequence. Therefore, in another group the order of information given to respondents was reversed. First, the argument that the conversation would be "short" was given, then the statement "around 420 seconds", completed with the information "that's 7 minutes". In another group, only the effect of the additional argument itself was examined. Here it was said that the survey would last around 7 minutes and that "it'll just take a moment". Finally, in the last group the effects of disrupting the routine without appealing to an additional argument were tested. The survey time was given in seconds, then after a moment it was explained that this was 7 minutes.

It was tested whether the person called would agree to participate in the survey, or refuse (in the latter case, no attempt to change people's minds was made and the interaction was concluded). Analyses of results revealed that applying the DTR technique more than doubled the chances that respondents would agree to participate in the survey. The numbers of people consenting to participate in a marketing survey in the remaining experimental conditions did not display significant statistical differences from the control conditions, while they were different from the levels of compliance recorded in the situation involving the DTR conditions.

Izabela Kubala proved that the DTR technique is also effective when individuals are targeted with a request by telephone, and fulfilling the request does not provide them with any benefit. She thus demonstrated that the technique discussed here can also be applied in other spheres than those assumed by Davis and Knowles. The experiment by Kubala was replicated by Christopher Carpenter and Franklin Boster (2009a), who conducted their research, not by telephone, but rather face to face, asking students on campus if they would like to participate in a survey study that would last 20 minutes and would be very interesting. In the DTR version, the phrase "one thousand two hundred seconds" was used, followed by an explanation that this was 20 minutes. In this case as well, more participants agreed to fill in the survey in DTR conditions than in control conditions.

Fennis et al. (2004) decided to examine the effects generated by linking the DTR technique with another classic social influence technique already discussed in this volume: the foot-in-the-door technique. In an experiment exploring this particular issue, a young man appealed to students on a university campus to sign a petition supporting an increase in tuition fees. In half of the conditions, the students were first asked to answer a few questions about studies and scientific research. This was treated as an application of the foot-in-the-door technique. The remaining students were not asked these questions. Regardless of the aforementioned, some of them were told directly that the matter concerned a tuition fee increase of €75, while others heard that the cost of education would go up by 7,500 euro cents ... €75, that is. In both cases, the message was rounded out by the argument that this was quite a small investment. Analysis of the results showed that application of the DTR technique significantly increased people's readiness to sign the petition (from 28% to 63%). Preceding the primary request with a series of questions also generated the expected result (an increase from 29% to 63%). The joint application of both of these social influence techniques, however, proved to be unbelievably effective. The petition to increase tuition fees was signed by 90% of those queried! The DTR technique not only demonstrated its effectiveness, but when combined intelligently with the foot-in-the-door technique it became an extraordinarily successful technique for exerting influence on others.

A meta-analysis of 14 empirical studies performed by Carpenter and Boster (2009b) confirmed the strength of the DTR technique. It also demonstrated that this technique was more effective in a non-profit context than in a sales context. The psychological mechanism itself underlying the success of this technique is not entirely clear. Insofar as the authors of the pioneering paper on the DTR technique referred to the assumptions girding Erickson's hypnosis technique and the concept of action identification by Vallacher and Wegner, other scholars offer still more points of view on the mechanism explaining why people subjected to these influences comply with requests directed towards them. Kardes and his collaborators (Kardes et. al., 2007) make reference to the concept of the need for cognitive closure, proffered many years ago by Arie Kruglansky (1989). He remarked that people are characterized by "the desire for a firm answer to a question and an aversion toward ambiguity" (Kruglanski & Webster, 1996, p. 264); this desire, however, displays different levels of strength in different individuals (individual difference), yet on the other hand, is greater or lesser depending on particular circumstances (situational factor). Kardes et al. (2007) observed a link between DTR and the so-called need for closure. The DTR technique is grounded in creating ambiguity by giving a price in cents/euro cents instead of dollars/euros, or by using a strange word. The argument appearing at the end of the message, in turn, is an element associated with certainty and explicitness. It can be expected that this technique will be particularly effective on people exhibiting a strong need for cognitive closure. On the one hand, they have a strong aversion to ambiguity, and on the other hand they are deeply interested in achieving a state of certainty as to a defined fragment of reality.

The authors spent time on a university campus inviting students to become members of a student interest group, and to pay a related semi-annual membership fee. In the control conditions, they were told that the fee was €3, while in the DTR conditions a figure of 300 euro cents was given, then clarified as €3. In both cases the proposition was concluded with the same argument: "That's a really small investment". Regardless of whether those approached expressed their desire to join the student interest group or not, they were also asked to fill in a questionnaire, which was a de facto measurement of their need for cognitive closure. The DTR turned out to be effective. Compared to the control conditions (13%), the percentage of students deciding to join the interest group and pay the semi-annual fees was clearly higher (30%). Of even greater importance from the perspective taken here is that in DTR conditions the membership fee was paid by 43% of those individuals who recorded a need for cognitive closure score above the median, while only 17% of those whose score was below the median did so. The role played by the need for cognitive closure in the disrupt-then-reframe technique was later confirmed in another experiment by the authors.

Carpenter and Boster (2009a) proposed, in turn, a very simple explanation for the effectiveness of this technique, referring to the Spinozan model of information processing in which comprehension and acceptance happen immediately and simultaneously (Gilbert, 1991). The disruption contained in the DTR technique can prevent someone from comprehending that the subsequent argument is unsound. This model predicts that people who are distracted when exposed to an argument will be more likely to believe it and comply, even if this argument is obviously flawed. In their experiments the authors demonstrated that, indeed, the quality of the argument applied in the message and designed to induce participants to accede to a request or proposition is of no significance for the effectiveness of the DTR technique.

The pique technique – requesting in an unusual manner

While the DTR technique requires quite a complicated sequence of actions (initiating an interaction in a normal manner; doing something surprising and unusual; then presenting an argument after a few seconds designed to induce compliance in the interlocutor) the technique proposed by Michael Santos, Craig Leve and Anthony Pratkanis (1994), itself also based on the appearance of "something strange", is far simpler. During an experiment conducted by the aforementioned authors, a young woman (around 21 years old) dressed in jeans and a t-shirt pretended to be a vagrant. She asked passers-by for money, either using a typical expression ("a quarter" or "any change") or in an unusual manner – for 17 or 37 cents. It turned out that the unusual request led experiment subjects to reach for their wallets with greater frequency. It was the authors' view that if an automatic, habitual refusal of a request is expected, we are better off forming the request in a manner that will induce those to whom the request is made to behave in a less automated manner. It may then turn out that they take a moment to think, and come to the conclusion that in this one particular case the offering of monetary alms is a worthwhile activity. The actual results would seem to confirm this interpretation, considering that when the request was formulated in a standard fashion (a request for "a quarter" or "some change"), people practically never asked any questions (only 0.7% of subjects did so), while when the request was non-standard, far more people did so (11% of participants). That said, it should also be observed that in the latter case asking questions was not a universal practice. Perhaps this resulted from the fact that people did not wish to maintain contact longer than necessary with the vagrant, having their own comfort in mind, or maybe they did not wish to cause her embarrassment with additional questions. Santos et al. thus came to the conclusion that an examination of what people think in these typical and untypical situations would best be facilitated by a closely-monitored laboratory experiment.

Participants were presented one of four real situations from the first experiment (a young female vagrant on the street asking for 17 cents, a quarter, 37 cents or 'some change') and asked them to write down how they would behave in such a situation, as well as what would likely enter their mind. Contrary to the authors' expectations, research participants who were expected to imagine themselves in a non-typical situation reported the same thoughts as those who were asked to imagine the vagrant making a request of them in a typical manner. The former, however, said with greater frequency that they would ask the woman what she needed the money for.

The question of whether an atypical or unusual request in fact shifts an individual's functioning from a non-reflective level (mindless) to a more reflective one (mindful) was the theme of research carried out by Jerry Burger, Joy Hornisher, Valerie Martin, Garry Newman and Summer Pringle, 2007). The authors began from the assumption that an experiment patterned after that of Langer et al. (1978), discussed earlier in this chapter, would be useful in answering the question posed above. Let us recall that if the experimenter asked an individual standing in a queue at a copy machine for permission to push in, adding that there were only 5 pages to be copied, participants let the experimenter go ahead with the same frequency as when the request was accompanied by a sensible explanation ("because I'm in a rush") as when it came with an explanation that essentially didn't explain anything ("because I have to make copies"). Thus in both conditions the study's participants allowed the experimenter to go to the front of the queue with far greater frequency than when the request was not accompanied by any justification. The researchers explained this by claiming that participants asked to fulfil a minor request remained in a state of mindlessness and participants relied on a script that called for them to agree whenever a reason is given. However, if the experimenter said initially that there were 20 pages to be copied, only would a request accompanied by a sensible justification ("because I'm in a rush") lead to more frequent consent to go to the front of the queue compared to situations when the request came with no justification. Langer et al. (1978) suggest that the increased burden of the request (if someone has 20 pages to copy this will lead to a much longer wait) shifts the functioning of the recipient of the request into the reflective domain. In this case the script for automatic consent upon hearing an explanation (of any kind) is not activated, but the content itself of the request is placed under examination.

Burger and his collaborators thus concluded that if those who were asked by the vagrant for 37 cents ceased to function mindlessly and began to think about just what was going on, they should react in the same way as participants in the experiment by Langer et al. who were told that someone had 20 pages to copy. Put differently, they should agree more frequently when the atypical request for a handout comes with a realistic justification compared to situations in which the explanation does not provide any real information. As in the experiment by Santos et al. (1994), a young person asked passers-by for a handout in either a standard manner ("Excuse me, can you spare any change?") or an atypical one ("Excuse me, can you spare 37 cents?"). In conditions when the addressee of the request asked the "vagrant" what the money was needed for, either a concrete response was offered ("Because I need to buy a stamp"), or an answer that in fact failed to clarify anything ("Because I need to buy some things"). It should be emphasized here that no questions of that type came up in conditions when the "beggar" asked for "any change", but in conditions when a request for 37 cents was made, 29.9% of request addressees posed that question.

As for the results of this experiment, in the main the effect generated by Santos et al. (1994) was replicated: in conditions of an atypical request, participants decided with greater frequency to give money than in conditions of a typical request. The former circumstance also led to greater sums being given. In addition, it turned out that both the frequency and the average value of handouts were higher in conditions when, in the course of the interaction between the participant and the "vagrant", questions were asked regarding the purpose for which the money was being collected, compared to when the participant did not pose such questions. However, the content of the response given by the "beggar" turned out to be irrelevant. The generousness of research subjects was nearly identical when they heard "because I need to buy a stamp" (a specific reason), when compared with a situation in which the word "stamp" was replaced by the content-free expression "some things" (a vague reason). Table 5.2 shows the amount of money given and compliance percentage in particular conditions of this experiment.

In a second study, Burger and his collaborators swapped a request for "any change" with entreaties for 25 or 50 cents. The result was that an atypical request (for 37 cents) was more effective in increasing both the frequency of giving and the average sum given, and it again turned out that experiment participants were more likely to reach for their purses when they first asked why the vagrant needed the money and then received an answer to their query. Again, however, the content of the answer was immaterial. This pattern of results suggests that while an unusual request disrupted some participants' refusal scripts, there is no confirmation for the thesis that the atypical request also led these individuals to consider the request mindfully. If, however, an atypically-formulated request does not lead to the addressee of that request functioning in a more mindful manner, how can the increased pliability in these conditions be explained? Burger and his collaborators offered two explanations. The first of them assumes that individuals in these conditions apply the heuristic "I will help acquaintances, particularly when they ask for a small favour" rather than one such as "I don't give money to beggars". This acquaintance script is not, however, restricted to real acquaintances, but is also

TABLE 5.2 Money given and compliance percentage in Burger et al. (2007) experiment

Condition	Amount given (M)	Compliance (%)	N
Control	$0.07	18.8	117
Pique/no question	$0.10	25.9	143
Pique/specific reason	$0.38	87.1	31
Pique/vague reason	$0.37	70.0	30

Source: *Journal of Applied Social psychology*, 2007, vol. 37, p. 2090.
Copyright 2007 John Wiley and Sons.

activated when people unknown to us act as if they were acquaintances. One such situation is a simple conversation. It has been demonstrated in a range of studies that when a request directed at a stranger is preceded by even a brief conversation on an anodyne topic, the chances that the request will be fulfilled are greater (Dolinski et al., 2001; Dolinski, Grzyb, Olejnik, Prusakowski & Urban, 2005) – for more on this topic see the deliberations contained in Chapter 4. We may observe in this context that Burger and his collaborators demonstrated that a strange request in and of itself does not cause a rise in compliance. This effect is only observed when the request for a handout was followed by the subjects asking what it was needed for – thus, in conditions in which they initiated a dialogue.

An alternative interpretation presented by the authors of the article under discussion is based on the assumption that the question about what the 37 cents would be spent on was given by people who had already decided they would give out the money. However, it remains unclear "why disrupting a refusal script with an unusual request led some people to comply, but not others" (Burger et al., 2007, p. 2095). In summary, it may be said that the experiments by Burger provide a clearer demonstration of what mechanism does *not* underlie the effectiveness of the pique technique (i.e. not an increased mindfulness on the part of the addressee resulting from the atypicality of the request) rather than of what mechanism *is* responsible. Further research is thus necessary to explain this phenomenon. It would also be worth conducting studies in another context than that of begging. Indeed, it may be supposed that the unusual formulation of a request may increase the effectiveness of measures intended to induce fellow humans to help in many other situations in which they are accustomed to being constantly asked for something and have already developed the habit of saying "no". The opposite would, of course, be true if the standard, automatic response to a given request were to accept it. In these circumstances, the unconventional formulation of a request would increase the risk of its going unfulfilled.

Gaze

The norms in place in particular cultures provide more or less strict guidelines concerning whom we may address in respect of what matter and in what fashion. At times these norms are very strictly defined, such as in the army, where a private should directly and verbally address his corporal whenever he has any doubts at all. The same private must not, however, disturb the army's generals with the exception of absolutely exceptional situations. In the "civilian" world there is also a wide range of diverse regulations governing this aspect of social life. The greater the difference in the status of an individual wishing to broach a subject and the status of the individual who is to be addressed, the greater the asymmetry in respect of the most appropriate form of contact. There are, however, situations (particularly when there is no evident difference in status) when the choice of form of address is a matter for the individual wishing to make a request. Of greatest significance from the perspective that interests us in this book is whether the greatest success will be had by a request submitted directly in face-to-face circumstances, by telephone, or in writing (letter or e-mail). During a normal conversation we are faced with a situation in which communication takes place via all available channels, and both participants in the interaction are located in the same place. In the case of a telephone communication, the only means of communication is through the use of the faculty of hearing. Although the interaction's participants engage each other at the same time, a spatial divide exists between them. As for a letter or e-mail, the degree of directness in the communication is severely limited. The people engaged in communication are not only to be found in different areas, but they exchange information at different times. As a rule, they also have a significant amount of time to think their decisions over.

Which communication channel is the most effective? In one experiment dedicated to this issue, holidaymakers were invited to take an anonymous psychological examination that would take around 15 minutes (Dolinski, 2005). Some of them were visited in their hotel rooms, others were contacted by telephone, and the rest were issued with a written invitation wedged in their room door. It transpired that as contact became less direct, the frequency with which people decided to accede to the request of the psychologists also decreased. The percentage of individuals meeting the request was the greatest in the case of invitations submitted during a face-to-face conversation (56%), lower in the case of a telephone invitation (28%), and the lowest when invitations to participate were left in doorframes (6%). These results led to simple conclusions about how best to maximize the chances of getting the agreement of others in matters of importance to us, as well as how to arrange situations so as to allow us to behave optimally when confronted with a request that we do not necessarily want to fulfil. Thus, if we would like to turn to someone with a request that is important to us, but we are not sure if we can count on a positive decision, the best course of action is to meet with this person directly and ask directly for consent. On the other hand, if we expect that someone would like to ask us for a favour that would run contrary to our interests, and we have reason to doubt in our capacity to refuse directly, we should attempt to direct the course of events so that the request comes to us in writing, or – at a minimum – limit the contact to a telephone conversation.

Why is this so? Why is it that the more direct the form in which a request is submitted, the greater the chances of compliance? It would seem that directness of contact leads to difficulties in refusing someone asking us for help. Indeed, when we refuse, we risk receiving verbal or non-verbal signals that we have caused someone grief. It is far easier to say "no" when someone asks us for something in writing. We can refuse in writing, or we can leave such a request unanswered. The particularly high effectiveness of requests submitted in conditions of direct interaction may be closely linked with eye contact. A large body of research in social psychology has indicated that people fulfil requests with greater frequency when such contact is maintained by the individual making the request.

For example, it has been shown that if an experimenter deliberately leaves a coin in a pay phone, exits the booth, waits for someone to enter then opens the door and asks the person inside to return the money, the chances of the coin being returned are greater when the experimenter looks that person in the eyes (Brockner, Pressman, Cabitt & Moran, 1982). Similarly, if someone leans out of a telephone booth and asks a passer-by for a coin because of an urgent need to call someone, the chances of receiving the money grow when the request is made while looking the person in the eyes (Ernest & Cooper, 1974). Chris Kleinke and David Singer (1979) demonstrated that when a person handing out flyers looks in the eyes of passers-by, more flyers are taken. This effect was observed when the person handing out the flyers politely encouraged people to take them ("Excuse me. Would you like one?"), when a categorical tone accompanied the distribution of the flyer ("Take one"), and when the flyer was simply placed before passers-by without saying anything. Further experiments led to the conclusion that volunteers making eye contact with those being asked for a charitable donation received larger sums (Bull & Gibson-Robinson, 1981; Linskold, Forte, Haake & Schmidt, 1977). Eye contact may also help people who have had the misfortune of dropping their change (Valentine, 1980) or a pile of surveys (Goldman & Fordyce, 1983), or when they have injured themselves while jogging (Shotland & Johnson, 1978). The beneficial impact of eye contact has also been observed in studies on the effectiveness of hitchhikers. They were picked up more often by drivers if they looked them squarely in the eyes while waving their hands than if they looked off to the side (Morgan, Lockard, Fahrenbruch & Smith, 1975; Snyder, Grether & Keller, 1974).

"Eye contact" is a rather imprecise phrase. Nicolas Gueguen and Celine Jacob (2002) decided to compare a situation in which the requester maintained constant eye contact with the person being asked for something to one in which eye contact was broken off and returned to at intervals. Their experiment consisted of asking passers-by on a city street to participate in a marketing research survey. When eye contact was constantly maintained, 66% of participants consented to fill in the questionnaire, while in conditions when the experimenter's eyes "danced around", only 34% did so.

Why does eye contact increase the chances that a request will be fulfilled? The simplest interpretation of the link between looking in the eyes of people we are directing a request to and their compliance refers to studies suggesting that more desirable personality traits are assigned to those who look their interlocutors straight in the eyes (e.g. Brooks, Church & Fraser, 1986; Droney & Brooks, 1993) and they also benefit from greater affinity (e.g. Cook & Smith, 1975; Scherer, 1974) than those who avoid eye contact. Because there is an assumption that the perception of people's personalities as "better" and greater affinity towards such people are accompanied by a greater readiness to comply with their requests, it should come as no surprise that those who maintain eye contact with their partners in conversation get what they want more often than those who do not establish such contact.

A more nuanced alternative explanation of the connection between eye contact and compliance was offered by Phoebe Ellsworth and Ellen Langer (1976). Their proposed model even attempted to predict situations in which eye contact would enhance pliability and when this effect should not be expected. Ellsworth and Langer observed that emotional excitation increases when we conclude that someone is looking at us. In interpersonal situations, this is usually a signal that some behaviour should be performed. If nothing in particular happens to indicate what behaviour is desired, an unpleasant tension will continue until the moment when the looked-upon individual is able to get away and by doing so terminate the interpersonal contact giving rise to that tension. However, if the feeling that "someone is eyeing me" is accompanied by a clear signal of what reaction is expected from the person doing the looking, a reduction in the uncomfortable tension may be effected simply by engaging in the desired behaviour. The researchers conducted a very clever experiment to examine this assumption. The first of them engaged individuals coming up to the entrance of a shopping centre, informing them that on the other side there was a woman in need of help but that the experimenter herself was in a hurry to catch a train. In addition, half of the experiment's participants were informed specifically that the woman on the other side of the door was behaving as though looking for her lost contact lenses, while the other half were given ambiguous information – they were told that the woman "looks like she's not feeling well". Just behind the door, the second experimenter waited for participants in a rather unusual position – half crouching and leaning against the wall. This position is, obviously, helpful when searching for something that has gone missing, but may also be associated with an individual who has begun to feel ill (e.g. experiencing stomach pain). Regardless of what a given participant said to the first experimenter, the second either avoided eye contact or looked the participant straight in the eyes. As it turned out, looking participants in the eyes enhanced their altruistic tendencies but only when the situation was unambiguous and it was obvious what needed to be done in order to help the woman (look together for her contact lenses). When the situation was left vague, looking participants in the eyes did not increase the likelihood that they would render assistance.

A similar view on the mechanism underlying the connection between eye contact and compliance is held by Chris Kleinke (1977), who suggests that gaze performs the function of a non-specific activator. The conclusion that someone is looking us in the eyes leads to a slight physiological stimulation of the body, and our attention (at least initially) is directed towards the person looking at us. The ascertainment that we are being observed leads in turn to increased public self-consciousness, and we start paying at least slightly more attention to the situation we are in while attempting to ensure that our behaviour complies with social norms and internalized value system (Duval & Wicklund, 1972; Morin, 2011; Wicklund & Gollwitzer, 1987). Extensive experimental data demonstrates that a mere photograph of human eyes "looking at us" can make us more honest. Melissa Bateson, Daniel Nettle and Gilbert Roberts (2006) examined the effect of an image of a pair of eyes on contributions to an honesty box used to collect money for drinks in a university coffee room. University employees tossed three times as much money into the box than in the control conditions where the eyes were not "checking them out". In another experiment, conducted at a supermarket, the

FIGURE 5.1 Eye (left) and control (right) images in situ in the supermarket

Source: *Ethology: International Journal of Behavioural Biology*, 2012, vol. 118, p. 1098.
Copyright Blackwels Verlag GmbH.

researchers displayed either eye images or control images on charity collection buckets for 11 consecutive weeks (Powell, Roberts & Nettle, 2012). Charitable contributions were greater in conditions when they "looked customers in the eyes" – see Figure 5.1.

In accordance with the assumption that the conclusion that someone is watching us sharpens our focus on social norms and activates our readiness to engage in activities consistent with those norms, it may be supposed that gaze will increase compliance only when associated with socially desirable, or at least socially approved, behaviours. (We should note that it was just these types of behaviours present in the experiments described above). What will happen if the request is of a different nature? Kleinke (1980) conducted a pair of studies examining this question. In the first of them, young women approached people walking around an airport. In half of the cases they asked for a 10-cent coin, justifying this by saying that they had no money on them and urgently needed to make a phone call. In the other cases, they said the 10 cents was necessary to buy a chocolate bar. Regardless of the justification, in half of the cases the experimenters made eye contact with the participant while presenting their request, and in the other half they did not. It transpired that directing one's gaze towards a person to whom a request is being issued only increased the chances of that request being fulfilled when it was socially justified. Thus eye contact increased the chance of obtaining the 10 cents needed for using the phone, but it failed to make a difference when the money was for a chocolate bar. In the second experiment it turned out that making eye contact (this time coupled with touching the arm of the person being addressed) actually reduced the chance that change intended to be spent on chewing gum would be received.

Touch

Both animals and people mark their territory and defend it against those who would encroach upon it. Dogs urinate on trees and bushes in the vicinity of their lairs and try to scare off other dogs that enter that area. People erect fences around their homes, build walls or put up signs that read "Private property" or "Entry forbidden". They also have a tendency to defend their territory, but as a rule people are more elastic than animals in matters of territorialism. We eagerly invite guests into our home, or slightly less eagerly permit an unknown letter carrier with a large package to enter our abode. A meter reader from the electricity company is allowed in with still less enthusiasm, but neither do we shut the door in his face.

For people, territory is not inevitably linked with a specific and constant space. Indeed, a group of people conducting a conversation also acquire the status of territory. This group is surrounded by a consensual and invisible border that others who are not members of that group will not violate without a clear need to do so (Lyman & Scott, 1967). A good illustration of this border is to be found in studies analyzing the behaviour of passers-by towards a group standing on the pavement near a shop window. If the members of the group were speaking among themselves (thus establishing a territory of interaction), passers-by avoided the entire group. However, if the members of the group were not communicating with one another, but rather examining the window display, passers-by were far more likely to walk between members of the group (Lindskold, Albert, Baer & Moore, 1976).

From the perspective of greatest interest to us here, research concerning the territory directly linked with the human body is particularly important. Individual cultures are characterized by clear preferences regarding what is referred to as personal space. If two Americans or Europeans engaged in conversation and standing up are not familiar with each other, they will assume a face-to-face position. How far apart do they stand? Setting aside particular situations such as a crowded bus, this distance will typically be the equivalent of an outstretched arm from the shoulder to the fingertips, measuring around 90 centimetres. In Latin American cultures this distance will be reduced by about a hand's length, measuring around 70 centimetres. Thus, if an American is engaged in conversation with a Haitian, the former will attempt to increase the distance between them while the latter will try to reduce it. As a result, the American may come to the conclusion that the Haitian is a boor without manners, while the Haitian may perceive the American as cold, distant or even calculating (Hall, 1969).

The need to maintain at least a minimal distance between one's own body and that of another person depends on a very large number of factors. The most obvious of them concerns the parts of the body one wishes to keep away from others. As a rule we have no problem shaking hands with a stranger. European and American politicians shake millions of potential voters' hands in the hope of getting their support, in spite of the absence of direct evidence that such activity really helps them. There is, however, evidence related to the acquisition of donations for charitable causes. Nicolas Gueguen (2013b) examined the reactions of people visited in their homes by volunteers who asked them for a donation of €1 for children from Madagascar. It occurred that when the greeting was accompanied by a handshake, the proportion of people supporting the charitable campaign rose dramatically (from 53.3% to 95.5%).

Mutual contact of the inside portions of hands is a gesture with a long tradition in our culture, both in situations involving two people familiar with each other and in conditions where they are not acquainted. What would happen, however, if someone touched a part of a stranger's body other than the inside of the hand? This would obviously contradict the rules in place in our culture, but would it influence that person's compliance with a request addressed to him/her?

A large number of studies have demonstrated that people are more disposed to fulfilling requests made by strangers when those requests are accompanied by a gentle touch on the arm or forearm. The first experiments exploring this area were conducted by Chris Kleinke (1977). In his research a scenario was set up in which a female experimenter exited a phone booth at the moment another person walked up to it. The individual approaching the phone booth thus automatically became a participant in the study. After a moment, the experimenter came back and asked for the return of 10 cents that she had left in the pay phone. When this request was accompanied by a light touch of the participant's arm, the chances of recovering the coin increased. Indeed, in these conditions 96% of participants gave the money back, compared to 63% who returned the 10-cent coin in the control conditions.

In a second study, a female experimenter attempted to borrow a 10-cent coin from a stranger, ostensibly needing it to make a phone call. She succeeded in receiving the coin with greater frequency when the request was accompanied by a gentle touch on the arm. When she did so, the experimenter received money in every second case (51% to be precise), while in control conditions she only received money in 29% of cases.

In another study dedicated to the role of touch (Smith, Gier & Willis, 1982) shoppers at a supermarket were offered a piece of pizza. In some instances this request was coupled with the shopper's arm being held for a brief moment. It turned out that this simple act increased not only the chances that shoppers would agree to test the quality of the product on offer, but also that they would buy it. Frank Willis and Hellen Hamm (1980) demonstrated that an individual asked to sign a petition would do so more readily when gently held by the arm while the request was being made. A personality test was also more likely to be completed by those who were asked to do so while their arm was gently held at the moment the request was submitted (Patterson, Powell & Lenihan, 1986). Other studies conducted in a department store showed that customers whose arm was grasped by those conducting a survey were more likely to accede to the request that they answer a series of questions (Hornik, 1987; Hornik & Ellis, 1988). Interestingly, those touched on the arm also expressed more favourable opinions about the structure of the survey itself, declared with greater frequency that they would participate in similar studies, and also were more likely to place their signatures on their survey.

Research has also shown that the effect on compliance that results from a touch on another person's arm can also appear following a certain period of time. Nicolas Gueguen and a group of collaborators (Gueguen, Meineri & Charles-Sire, 2010; Gueguen & Vion, 2009) demonstrated that if a doctor touches the arm of a patient leaving the surgery, that patient will be more likely to adhere to the medical advice given. This was determined by reviewing how many of the recommended pills had not been swallowed after a few days by those patients who were touched on the arm in comparison with those who were given a standard farewell (meaning without being touched).

Morton Goldman, Odette Kiyohara and Dorothy Pfannesteil (1985) made a rather simple request of study participants. Just in front of the entrance to a university library they asked people how to get to the education faculty building. In some conditions, they touched the forearm of the individual to whom their question was posed. Of course, those (unknowingly) participating in the study gave their assistance and explained the easiest way to get there. Inside the library another experimenter waited and invited these individuals to participate in a charitable campaign to help disabled children. This participation was to consist of a two-hour shift at a phone bank. Among those who had been touched on the arm, 40% gave their consent to participate while only 5% of those who were just asked about the way to the education faculty building agreed to man the phone.

Other interesting studies are those conducted by Jane Nannberg and Christie Hansen (1994), who examined whether touching another person on the arm would affect the quality of work done on a task that person had previously agreed to do. They approached students of both sexes with the request to fill in a questionnaire, which they did in a conventional manner, maintaining a certain physical distance. Individuals who agreed to complete the questionnaire were given a bundle of papers containing 150 questions, then were asked to sit down somewhere in the vicinity, familiarize themselves with the instructions and answer the questions in the survey. In half of the cases this information was given as the forearm of the participant was gently touched (for approximately 2 seconds). The questionnaire itself generally focused on controversial issues (e.g. assisted suicide, homosexuality, abortion, death penalty) or the private life of the respondent. The instructions given at the beginning stated that every response was valuable, but that it wasn't necessary to answer every single question. It turned out that those whose forearms had been grasped answered 25% more questions on average than those who were not touched. However, the subtle social influence technique being analyzed here was not helpful in distinguishing the manner in which participants responded to the questions they had answered.

What is the mechanism underlying the effectiveness of such a simple device as grasping someone by the arm while addressing a request, or even afterwards, as done in the last of the experiments described above? The relevant literature offers two competing explanations. First, attention is drawn to how touch is associated with not only the physical dimension of interpersonal closeness, but also its psychological aspect. This may also lead us to perceive an individual who delicately touches us as friendly and likable, enamouring that person to us and making us more likely to help (e.g. Patterson et al., 1986). This results primarily from the individual biographies of nearly every person. In the vast majority of cases people have positive experiences associated with being touched by someone. This assumption would also concur with the results of research demonstrating that hospital patients more favourably rated nurses that touched them frequently, and also were also more eager to engage them in conversation (Algulera, 1967), and that psychotherapists touching the hands and arms of their patients succeeded in motivating them to more quickly open up and discuss their pressing problems (Paulsell & Goldman, 1984).

The second interpretation refers to the social privilege motive (e.g. Henley, 1973). If someone grabs us by the arm, a signal is sent at the same time that this individual is authorized to address certain demands and expectations to us. Nancy Henley showed study participants photographs of pairs of people between whom there was a clear difference in status (e.g. master–slave, police officer–suspect). The participants' task consisted of indicating the person in the photograph who would initiate any sort of touching behaviour. The decisive majority of participants declared that it was the higher-status individual who would do so. The potential that the lower-status individual would engage in this behaviour was perceived as untactful (see Henley & LaFrance, 1984). In another study Brenda Major and Richard Heslin (1982) showed participants a series of slides containing pairs of individuals (some of the same sex, some of different sexes). Sometimes one of them was touching the other, sometimes there was no touch involved. The study participants were supposed to determine what kind of people were on display. It turned out that the estimation of individual figures' assertiveness and domination went up when they were shown touching others, and decreased when they were presented as being touched by others. Gueguen (2002) demonstrated in his study, during which men asked passers-by to participate in a brief research survey, that touch was particularly helpful for those men whose clothing suggested high status (suit and tie). If an experimenter who was dressed in this manner touched the hand of a passer-by, the chance that he would receive agreement for participation in the survey increased by more than twofold. When the experimenter was dressed in jeans and a t-shirt, the positive effect of touch on gaining compliance was clearly reduced.

Unfortunately, psychologists have demonstrated unusually deep reluctance to conduct research directly examining the question of which of the aforementioned factors (interpersonal closeness vs social privilege) is actually at the core of this simple social influence technique's efficacy. During one of our attempts at grappling with this problem (Dolinski, 2005) we assumed that certain verbal messages can be viewed as coherent or incoherent with these mechanisms. An unambiguous order would seem more consistent with the social privilege motive than with the interpersonal closeness motive, while the opposite would be true of a polite, sincere request. In our experiment we turned to participants with a request to help find a gold earring ostensibly lost on the sidewalk, either with an order ("Help me look for this!") or a polite request ("Would you be so kind as to help me look for this?");

regardless of the form of the message, we either simultaneously touched their arm/forearm or did not do so.

We assumed that if the efficacy of touch as a social influence technique rests in the social privilege motive, this technique should be more effective in conditions where an order is given rather than in conditions of a request, while if the mechanism responsible is interpersonal closeness then the pattern of results should be reversed. Results indicated that, while touching passers-by increased the possibility that they would help search for the lost object, there was no association demonstrated between touch and the manner in which the message was formulated. This experiment also failed to resolve the issue of which of the hypothesized mechanisms plays the fundamental role in the touch technique. Studies by Jack Powell and his collaborators proved equally inconclusive (Powell et al., 1994), as they confirmed neither the mechanism associated with affinity nor the one linked with signalling the authority to formulate expectations and requirements. Patterson et al. (1986) performed an experiment in which they examined whether people felt greater affinity towards an individual who touched their arm while addressing a request to them. If this were the case, the result would suggest that the social closeness motive came into play. However, there were no differences observed in judgements on the experimenter depending on whether he touched a study participant or not. The experiment's authors thus conclude that the social privilege motive is, in their view, a more likely mechanism for explaining the effectiveness of touch as a social influence technique. The problem is that such a conclusion would seem to be unjustified. Indeed, as of yet nobody has succeeded in demonstrating convincingly that this motive in fact plays a key role. There are, however, results indirectly indicating that an unobtrusive touch enhances affinity. During an experiment conducted in a university library, the library employees sometimes (ostensibly by accident) touched students' arms while returning their library cards. As they exited the building, students were asked to take a survey in which they were to assess the functioning of the library and its employees. It turned out that those students who had been touched on the arm by a librarian expressed more favourable opinions than those served in a standard manner (Fisher, Rytting & Heslin, 1976).

Perhaps the inconclusivity in the patterns of results discussed above derives from the co-occurrence of the two mechanisms. On the other hand, we also cannot exclude the conclusion that neither of them is involved. Indeed, it is possible that the essence of the technique consisting of touching the arm or forearm of an individual approached with a request is grounded in something else. A situation in which a stranger grabs us by the arm may shake us out of our routine, much as in the case of the pique and DTR, which have already been discussed earlier in this chapter. We should observe that this is a rather unusual situation, one which disrupts the course of a routine situation involving a request made of us by an unfamiliar individual. To a certain degree this interpretation would be in line with the pattern of results attained by one experiment in which it was examined whether touch would be an effective social influence technique when asking someone for help in tabulating the scores achieved by others in a questionnaire. The results proved less than clear-cut. Those individuals who were held by the arm during the addressing of the request then sacrificed more of their time counting scores on questionnaires than those who were not touched by the experimenter. However, the average number of questionnaires reviewed in both conditions was nearly the same (Patterson et al., 1986). It can therefore be said that those who were grabbed by the arm did work longer, but when converting their work into time units they were less efficient. Perhaps their functioning was disrupted by being knocked off balance. Participants who were held by the arm while having a request made of them may have been thinking (at least from time to time) about this odd situation while counting scores, which would have led to reduced intellectual efficiency. This assumption would also be consistent with the results of another experiment involving an examination of the efficiency of people who were touched during the course of performing tasks. Nan Sussman and Howard Rosenfeld (1978), the study's authors, came to the conclusion that the efficiency of an individual's functioning does not proceed from the mere fact of being touched by someone, but rather from the justification for such activity. A portion of participants were told that an individual keeping track of time would be seated next to them, and if that person felt that the task was being performed too slowly, an indication of this would be given by gently squeezing their arm and telling them how many seconds remained for completion of the task. The other participants were not given this information. In all cases, the woman whose purported task was to keep an eye on the time either held the study participant by the arm or did not. The task involved perception and its proper completion required the focus of one's concentration. As it turned out, male participants performed the task worse in conditions when they had not been told the reason for being touched by the experimenter than when they had been informed of why she was doing so. An analogous effect was noted in a second experiment conducted following a similar procedure.

Thus the question arises of whether holding someone by the arm while addressing a request is a separate social influence technique, or rather a variation of techniques based on strange or surprising situations (DTR, the pique). This question can only be answered through empirical research, and presently remains an entirely open one.

Chris Kleinke (1977, 1980) proposes an entirely different interpretation of the dependencies being discussed here. He suggests that touch functions in a similar manner to eye contact, and performs the role of a non-specific activator. If we are touched on the arm or forearm by a stranger, our state of physiological arousal is enhanced, our attention is directed towards the "here and now", and we adopt a more reflective approach to the matter of our behaviour and its compliance with our attitudes and value system. The conviction that touch and the maintenance of eye contact are based on the same mechanism of the non-specific activator would seem to be shared by a large number of researchers, as both of them are employed jointly in the course of some experiments. Presenting a request, the experimenter touches the arm or forearm of a participant while simultaneously looking that person in the eyes (e.g. Hornik, 1987; Hornik & Ellis, 1988; Kleinke, 1977). Unfortunately, while Chris Kleinke's theory – that touch operates as a non-specific activator – seems an interesting idea, in light of the lack of sufficient empirical evidence it remains merely an intriguing hypothesis.

Another issue concerns the sex of the people touching and being touched when the former is making a request of the latter. Experiments have typically accounted for the factor of sex. In a clear majority of published studies, a touch of the hand or arm of the addressee of a request increased the chances that the request would meet with acceptance in all possible configurations (and thus without regard to the sex of the person asking or the sex of the person being asked). Discrepancies across research results only concerned the strength of the effect in particular conditions. The most common results pattern observed was one indicating that touch is most effective if the participants in the interaction are of different sexes (e.g. Heslin, Nguyen & Nguyen, 1983; Stier & Hall, 1984) or when both are women (Patterson et al., 1986). However, in Poland we recorded a different pattern of results. The experiment (Dolinski, 2010) was conducted in the vicinity of a railway station. The experimenter (depending on the conditions this was either a young woman or a young man) asked a lone pedestrian – who appeared to be an adult – for a favour. Both women and men were addressed. The experimenter requested that the study participant send a letter for him/her, explaining that he/she was in a hurry to catch a train. In half of the cases the experimenter held the forearm of the individual with whom the interaction was taking place.

Every letter was appended with the same address, and a stamp was already stuck to the envelope. The envelope contained a piece of paper with a description of the experimental conditions (e.g. experimenter – woman; participant – man; condition – no touch). This facilitated the application of two indicators of compliance – verbal expression of consent to send the letter and actual sending of the letter (which was of course identified later). The results of this experiment are presented in Figure 5.2.

As we can see, the technique of touching a person to whom a request is addressed turned out to be effective in both the conditions in which a woman formulated the request, and when a man addressed the request to a woman. However, it was entirely ineffective when a man asked another man to send the letter. To be more precise, in these conclusions we observed a clear decline in the frequency of request fulfilment. We observed a similar pattern of results in a subsequent experiment involving the sale of incense sticks on the street to passers-by. Why is it that in Poland a man touching another man not only fails to increase the chance that he will fulfil his request, but in fact reduces it? Our conclusion was that the root may lie in this country's strong male homophobia. A typical (heterosexual) Polish man may react with aversion to the touch of another, unknown man and perceive the gesture in sexual terms. We confirmed the correctness of this interpretation in an additional study (Dolinski, 2010).

Concluding these deliberations over touch as a social influence technique, we should note that certain issues of a technical, or perhaps practical, nature are in need of clarification. First, an important parameter of touch is its strength. "Touch

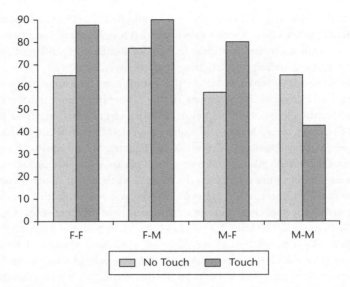

FIGURE 5.2 Percentage of compliance with the request to mail a letter in each of the experimental conditions. $N = 40$ in each condition. F-F: Female asking female; F-M: Female asking male; M-F: Male asking female; M-M: Male asking male

Source: Journal of Nonverbal Behavior, 2010, vol. 34, p. 183.
Copyright Springer Science + Business Media, LLC 2010.

someone on the arm or forearm" can signify a very delicate laying of the arm on that part of the body, a clear hold, or a squeeze of the hand with such force as to cause pain. Chris Segrin (1993), the author of a meta-analysis of studies addressing the link between touch and compliance, draws attention to this factor in stating that it may be of significance but that there is no clear criterion for determining what strength of touch is optimal in enhancing the compliance of study partici-pants. The authors of experimental studies generally do provide information in that regard, but they use vague terms such as "delicate" or "light" touch, which can mean something entirely different to two different researchers.

Second, we should observe that the experiments concerning the efficacy of touch as a social influence technique discussed above most frequently involve touching either the arm or forearm of the addressee. Which part of the body should we touch for the greatest effect? Or, to put it more precisely, which part of the arm should we touch for the greatest effect? Shari Paulsell and Morton Goldman (1984) posed just this question. Shoppers in a large mall were used as study participants, and they were asked to respond to four questions concerning literature. Depending on the experimental conditions, they were either not touched at all, or were touched while being asked to agree to a short interview; the touch was either on the arm above the elbow, between the elbow and the hand, or on the hand. Generally the mere fact of being touched was sufficient to spur compliance on the part of the addressee of the request, but this effect was clearly moderated by the sex of the person touching and the person being touched, as well as by the particular part of the body that was touched by the experimenter. A woman's touch raised to a much greater degree the chances that shoppers would agree to participate than did the touch of a man. A woman submitting the request was particularly effective when she touched the addressee of the request either above or below the shoulder, especially if she was touching a man.

It should be recalled, however, that this is the result of only one study, and in addition it involved only two experimenters (one man and one woman), which may have facilitated unwanted specific effects. For example, one may imagine that the different consequences of touching particular parts of the arm may result from the fact that the individual making the request was moving his/her hand up, down, or held it level. In this situation the experimenter's height could be the key factor. In studies concerning touch, the physical attractiveness of the experimenter may also play a significant role, and this factor may in turn interact with the portion of the arm being touched, etc. When several experimenters are performing a study, the absence of interaction effects with the variable of the experimenter him/her-self is an argument in support of the claim that we are dealing with a real rule. The studies being discussed here obviously do not fulfil this condition.

Summary

In many decision-making situations, we waver. It is no different in situations involving social influence, in which one person wants to induce another to engage in some defined behaviour. Certain arguments make the person being cajoled likely to give in, while other factors make this less likely. The two techniques described in this chapter are designed to break through this resistance. The first of them is rather simple, while the second is exceptionally sophisticated.

The origins of the "that's not all" technique are to be found in the classic idea of the sale. A normal discount is static in nature. The customer sees the old (higher) price and compares it with the new (lower) one. The "that's not all" social influence technique, in contrast to the previously described discounts, has a dynamic nature. Its essence consists of the initial offer being so interesting that the customer deliberates whether to take advantage or not. Then, an additional argument is supplied, offering something beneficial. This argument tips the scales, and the person targeted takes the decision. Research conducted by J. Burger, who was the first to describe this technique in the literature, demonstrated that when selling goods this technique is effective, both when a reduction in price is suddenly offered and when an additional product is proposed as a gift. Further studies on this technique generated results suggesting that it is only effective in the sale of less expensive goods, and a condition of its effectiveness is inducing a state of automaticity in people targeted with it.

The "disrupt-then-reframe" technique is based on the assumption that people who are asked for something experience an approach/avoid conflict. Approaching is associated with the desire to provide aid to a person in need and who asks for it, or with the desire to take advantage of an offer presented by someone. Avoidance, how-ever, is linked with the attendant effort and loss of time or money. People resist doing what someone else encourages them to do. Many social influence techniques are aimed at increasing others' desire to do something by highlighting the benefits that may result (the perfect example of which may by the "that's not all" trick discussed earlier) or by minimizing the losses resulting from it. The "disrupt-then-reframe" technique, however, is aimed simultaneously at reducing resistance and boosting incentive. This operation consists of finding a way to "jolt people out of their routine", making the course of the interaction a bit surprising and unusual (e.g. by giving a price in cents instead of dollars), and then supplying a new argument encouraging them to concede to a given request. In the light of what is now a very extensive body of research, this technique has proved itself effective not only in sales transactions, but also (perhaps first and foremost) in such areas as getting respondents to agree to participate in a telephone survey or encouraging people to sign a petition.

While the DTR technique requires a quite complex sequence of actions, the pique is far simpler. The idea is to present a request that people usually reject out of hand in an unusual manner (for example, asking for 37 cents instead of a quarter). While the experiments did demonstrate the effectiveness of this technique, its psychological mechanism remains unclear.

There is no codification of cultural norms determining the permissible (and optimal) physical distance that should exist between two people interacting directly with each other. The issue of physical distance is also important from the perspective of social influence. In this chapter we have considered two issues within this area in particular: eye contact and touch. A significant number of studies have demonstrated that people are more apt to fulfil requests directed to them when the person making the request looks straight into the eyes of the individual receiving it. Eye contact most likely performs the role of a so-called "non-specific activator". Awareness that someone is looking us in the eyes serves to increase our body's level of physiological stimulation, and our attention (at least initially) is drawn to the person looking at us. This leads us to engaging in a more careful analysis of the situation, and we begin to take care that our behaviour is consistent with our attitudes.

The second issue analyzed in this chapter concerns the role of touch. Many studies have demonstrated that people are more inclined to fulfil requests made by strangers if the request is accompanied by a delicate touch of the arm or shoulder. It has also been shown that touching someone on the shoulder or arm leads to that person improving the performance of a task taken up earlier.

What is the mechanism underlying the efficacy of such a simple device as grasping someone by the arm while addressing a request, or even after the request has been expressed? The subject literature generally presents two competing explanations. One of them draws attention to association between touch and interpersonal close-ness, not only in the physical sense but also the psychological aspect. This leads to us perceiving a person touching us as nice and affable, which leads to affinity, and in turn increases the likelihood that we will provide assistance to that individual. The alternative interpretation refers to the social privilege motive. While being held by the arm, we simultaneously receive the signal that the person doing so is authorized to address certain expectations and demands to us. Research done on the subject has yet to establish which of these interpretations is closer to the truth.

6

TECHNIQUES OF SOCIAL INFLUENCE USING MOOD AND EMOTION

On an almost daily basis, each of us experiences a myriad of affective states – some lasting longer, some shorter, some more intense, some less, with a colourful diversity of content. What, if any, is the impact of such states on our willingness to fulfil requests made of us? Does it increase, or perhaps reduce our compliance? Why are we inclined to react positively or negatively? This chapter is an attempt to answer these and other questions. First, I will address the role of the physiological stimulation experienced by individuals making a request or having a request addressed to them. Next, I will present studies that demonstrate the importance our mood has in affecting our susceptibility to social influence techniques; I will close the chapter with an analysis of the role played in social influence by specific (discrete) emotions.

Emotional arousal is a temporary state existing in the human body that is characterized by somatic energy and changes in consciousness, consisting of a narrowing of its field. This condition facilitates the body's engagement of adaptive behaviours under conditions of increased demands imposed either by the external environment or by the individual concerned. In this state of arousal the heart beats quickly, blood is directed to muscles as well as to the brain, whose bioelectric activity increases. It is assumed that arousal is a non-specific affective state in the sense that it may exhibit a sign (which may be perceived as pleasant or unpleasant), but it does not have the particular content possessed by emotions (Frijda, 1986). Insofar as emotional arousal is treated in psychology as a non-specific state, emotions are specific. For example, while sadness and fear are both negative emotions, we clearly perceive the differences between them. In turn, what links emotional arousal and emotions is the latter's intensity (high) and duration (short – usually seconds, rarely minutes). It is precisely these parameters that differentiate the two emotional states mentioned above from moods. A mood is low-intensity, but may last longer (hours, days, even weeks at a time). And while emotions are directed at an object ("I'm sad because", "I'm furious with"), moods are often objectless and undirected (Niedenthal, Krauth-Gruber & Ric, 2006).

We shall begin our analysis of the role played by affective states in social influence processes by examining some matters concerning physiological arousal.

Physiological arousal

Research conducted over half a century ago (Back, Bogdonoff, Shaw & Klein, 1963), during which the initial stage of the experiment involved measuring participants' levels of physiological arousal, demonstrated that this arousal is associated with the conformity later observed in their behaviour. Conformity in this study was tested using the Asch procedure, in which other experiment participants (de facto confederates of the experimenter) uniformly provide an erroneous answer in order to observe whether the "true" participant adopted their opinion. It turned out that the greater the real participant's physiological arousal at the very beginning of the experiment, the more likely he or she was to engage in conformist behaviour. Similarly enhanced conformist tendencies were observed by John Darley (1966) among study participants who were initially informed that they could expect to experience electric shocks. Information about the threat of experiencing a jolt of electricity naturally led to a significant increase in physiological arousal.

The role of arousal has also been examined in experiments on susceptibility to persuasion. In one of them, several of the participants were induced to engage in physical activity, which led to their physiological arousal (Sanbonmatsu & Kardes, 1988). It turned out that this state led them to attach less importance to the content of messages and the quality of the arguments contained in them, at the same time increasing their tendency to make use of peripheral cues (such as the authority of the individual issuing the communique).

Vera Corfield (1969) observed that the majority of situations involving social influence are accompanied by an increase in physiological arousal. The simple presence of other people (often strangers to us) evokes arousal. It may be further enhanced by the physical attractiveness of those people, or by the fact that they are famous. People attempting to exert influence over us often stand very close, touch us, look us in the eyes (see Chapter 5), additionally increasing the levels of arousal we experience. Another source of enhanced arousal may be the content of verbal messages that reach us. Someone collecting donations for a charitable cause may, for example, tell us graphic stories of people suffering pain or hunger. Various sensory experiences may also serve as stimulants of physiological arousal. Alternatively, it could be a black patch over the eye of a vagrant, or the perfume of a salesperson encouraging us to sample some cheese in the supermarket. Still another source of arousal may be the very object at the centre of our attention during a situation in which social influence is being applied to us. Thus, if we are expected to buy a new car, the very presence of that car and all accompanying information about its qualities will perform that role. If, however, we are in the process of selling our own used car, arousal may be generated by the sight or even the mere imagination of the pile of cash we may obtain.

Among people who have already experienced one source of arousal and then find themselves in another situation that gives rise to emotions, a synergistic effect from the accumulation of stimuli may occur. If the arousal is perceived as an unpleasant thing, this condition is obviously very disagreeable for such an individual, and in extreme cases may even be aversive. Acquiescence, the fulfilment of a request, consent to a proposal or performance of a task often become a means of reducing arousal. It thus comes as no surprise that, as a general proposition, high arousal levels are conducive to compliance. A good demonstration of this effect can be found in a study whose participants were students exiting a public toilet facility in a university building. An experimenter waited for prospective participants by the exit, and made an unexpected request of them. He said that he was in a hurry, and that a friend of his was waiting in another part of the building for some notes that he urgently needed. The request, obviously, concerned delivering the notes. An analogical request was made to students who were simply walking down the hallway. It was assumed that, because a public toilet and its surroundings are an area in which people experience a particularly salient need for privacy, contact with a stranger in such a place will generate unpleasant physiological arousal. This state of arousal should, however, be much weaker in a corridor, where contact with another person, even a stranger, is nothing out of the ordinary. Significantly, it turned out that while only 45% of people approached in the corridor agreed to pass the notes along to the other student, this figure rose sharply (to 80%) when the request was lodged in front of the door to the public toilet (Cann & Blackwelder, 1984). The question thus arises of why emotional arousal induced individuals to give their consent to the request of an experimenter whose very presence and behaviour served as the source of that arousal. In other words, could participants be unable to minimize this unpleasant emotional state by refusing to accede to the request and be quickly retreating from the place in which they were approached? It would seem that the key factor is that refusal to fulfil the simple, polite request may have served to additionally enhance the unpleasant arousal, as it could have led to unpleasant internal reflections by the participants as to their own person ("As it turns out, I'm disobliging and rude", "I behaved rudely for no good reason").

An alternative explanation for the compliance of individuals approached by the toilet may be based on the assumption that their capacity for processing information was at that moment slightly disrupted. A situation in which we are subjected to social influence often requires the engagement of our cognitive instrumentation in order to adequately assess the circumstances. For example, we must properly judge whether the fulfilment of a given request or agreement to some proposal is compliant with our system of values, or whether it runs contrary to our own interests. A significant body of empirical data (see e.g. Baron & Moore, 1987; Bodenhausen, 1993) allows us to assume that a high level of emotional arousal is not conducive to such rational analysis. Indeed, it is an exemplification of a general principle that assumes that while medium-intensity arousal optimizes the functioning of an individual, strong arousal leads to inhibited functioning (Lacey & Lacey, 1978; Pribram & McGuinness, 1975).

There is essentially universal agreement among psychologists that arousal evokes neurophysiological processes that induce disruption in the processing of information. However, there is no such agreement as to just which processes those are. Robert Baron (2000) offers three competing explanations for this phenomenon.

Supporters of what has assumed the mantle of the classic interpretation feel that physiological arousal leads to activation of certain areas of the cerebral cortex, but the consequence of stimulation of these areas is a reduction in the activity of neighbouring areas. It is the suppression of these areas of the brain that leads to reduced cognitive efficiency. Supporters of another interpretation make reference to data suggesting that strong physiological arousal reduces the volume of blood flowing into the brain. The presence of insufficient "power" leads to the brain behaving in the manner of a car on its last drop of petrol. Indeed, the car continues to move forward, but the engine splutters without a break. While these two approaches suggest that we are dealing with an automatic process that is completely independent of the individual concerned, those who subscribe to a third interpretation suggest that arousal, rather than impairing, actually induces thinking. The problem is, such thinking is not always directed towards the issue presented by the matter at hand. Thus a physiologically aroused customer in a shop may, for example, begin to wonder intensely about the sources of said arousal, but not about whether she really needs a pair of light-yellow trousers. Presently there is insufficient empirical evidence to definitively support any particular one of those three interpretations.

The role of positive and negative mood

In the early 1970s, Gordon Bower began studying the effect of mood on memory processes (e.g. Bower, Monteiro & Gilligan, 1971). In 1981 he published a widely-discussed article in which he described the numerous consequences of hypnotic induction on individuals experiencing joyful or gloomy moods. In one experiment, participants were requested to recall various episodes from their childhood. The following day, they categorized each of them as pleasant, unpleasant or neutral. The day after that, a positive or negative mood was induced among the participants, and they were then again asked to recall as many episodes as possible. Individuals experiencing a positive mood easily recalled pleasant episodes, but had difficulty in remembering unpleasant ones. The opposite was observed among participants experiencing a negative mood – they had an easier time recalling episodes that they had previously labelled as unpleasant. Attempting to explain this effect, the author formulated a rule known as "mood-state-dependent retention". According to this rule, one's mood (as well as – it may be assumed – other affective states) activates memories of those experiences that are affectively congruent with the mood. The obvious consequence of this is that it becomes easier to recall content that is consistent with a given affective state rather than inconsistent content. Symmetry in the relation between mood and cognitive processes does not apply only to memory. Bower observed that people attend to and learn more about events that correspond to their emotional state, and labels this as the mood-congruity effect (Bower, 1981).

As in the case of determinants of the course of cognitive processes, psychologists have devoted considerable attention to the role of mood in their work on the determinants of social behaviours. Results of exploratory research indicate that the mood-congruity effect concerns not only the relationship between emotional states and cognitive processes, but also with behaviours of a social character. A positive mood, evoked by various experimental procedures, led to increased readiness to help others. In one experiment it was demonstrated that individuals who have unexpectedly received a refund of 10 cents after a conversation in a phone booth were then more inclined to provide assistance to an individual who had dropped a pile of papers (Isen & Levin, 1972). Predisposition to altruism also rose during sunny days (Cunningham, 1979; Gueguen & Lamy, 2013), after listening to a pleasant piece of music (Wilson, 1981), and after receiving a cookie (Isen & Levin, 1972). A good mood also induced customers in shops to spend more money (Baker, Levy & Grewal, 1992; Sajjad & Tausif, 2012).

Other research, however, has demonstrated that people do not always react in a manner consistent with the emotional state they are experiencing. In one experiment, people in a good mood provided assistance to another person only sporadically. This help consisted of reading fragments of a book. When the participants were told that the contents to be read were cheerful in nature, and that reading and listening to them would improve one's mood, those who were in a positive mood were especially inclined to engage in such activity. However, when it was mentioned that the contents were sad, and that reading them would lead to a worse mood, it was precisely those people who were in a positive mood that very rarely agreed to perform the suggested actions (Isen & Simmonds, 1978). Similar effects were also observed in a number of other studies (e.g. Cunningham, Steiberg & Grev, 1980; Rosenhan, Salovey & Hargis, 1981). This led Alice Isen (1984; Clark & Isen, 1982) to formulate a rule according to which – since one of the motivations for human activity is the desire to maintain a good mood – people avoid behaviours that may lead to its worsening. This concerns not only engagement in emotionally costly forms of aiding others. People in a positive mood are, for example, unlikely to undertake serious financial risks (Isen & Geva, 1987). Obviously, financial loss may impair one from achieving the desired positive mood.

If the experience of positive emotional states is something that people fight to protect when it is happening to them, do people experiencing negative emotional states engage in activity that will help them feel better? Clark and Isen (1982) claim that this is often the case. Good examples of strategic improvements in mood are supplied by studies in which individuals experiencing depressive states eagerly engage in altruistic behaviour that has been presented as pleasant and attractive (Cunningham, Schaffer, Barbee, Wolff & Kelley, 1990). However, it is not always the case that negative emotional states lead to increased readiness to help others. Particularly, this is not the case when these states are intense, and people are focused on their own difficulties and problems (Berkowitz, 1993).

Research conducted by the Australian psychologist Joseph Forgas (1998) is important for understanding the role of mood in proclivity to accede to the requests of others. This researcher focused on the manner in which people react to a request for help and how they evaluate that request, as well as the manner in which they process the information that is reaching them. Forgas adopted the assumption that particular requests differ in their degree of complexity and peculiarity. At one extreme we may locate routine requests – generally polite requests concerning small favours; at the other – requests concerning unusual things, which are formulated in a highly atypical manner. It may be assumed that typical, conventional requests meet with automatic reactions, and that individuals don't "worry their heads too much", quickly forgetting about their content. The situation is different in the case of uncommon requests, and also those formulated in an unusual way (e.g. not very polite, or just the opposite: extraordinarily elaborate). In this event, the individual being approached with the request will process information more attentively, subject it to extensive analysis, and will, as a result, remember the content of the request and the circumstances in which it was lodged.

The application of an automatic or deliberative mode of processing information also facilitates distinct affective states. The experience of positive states is conducive to the application of intuitive formulae and "mental shortcuts". Experiencing negative emotional states, however, leads people to apply more systematic, and one may even say rational, cognitive strategies (Clark & Isen, 1982; Schwarz & Bless, 1991). The affective state one feels also exerts an influence on the perception of various events. The mood-congruity effect discussed above suggests that viewpoints of such events will be "filtered" through the affect an individual is going through at the time. Forgas therefore concluded that individuals in a positive mood will generally formulate more positive interpretations of requests directed at them in comparison to those experiencing a negative emotional state. People experiencing a good mood should, as a result, be more inclined to fulfil requests made of them than those in a negative mood. The eventual fulfilment of a request depends (often primarily) on the subjective interpretation of the entire event. What is more, he assumed that a request of a conventional nature (e.g. formed in a polite, standard way) should be accepted more or less automatically. Performance of a request should therefore not be directly dependent on the mood experienced by its addressee. However, things should be different in respect of untypical requests (e.g. formulated in a manner inconsistent with established tradition). In these cases the processing of information should be more systematic rather than automatic. Thus, in such a situation – according to Forgas – the affective state being experienced by the individual has a significant impact on the processing of information, even determining to a certain degree the assessments made and judgements reached. Assessment of a situation associated with being the addressee of another person's request will therefore be influenced by the affective state being experienced. Thus, concludes Forgas, the type of mood felt should exert a minimal impact on assessment of conventional requests and tendency to fulfil them, whereas the impact will be much stronger in respect of unconventional requests and decisions about their fulfilment.

In the first experiment dedicated to this issue, large envelopes were placed on desks in the reading room of a university library. Some of them contained sets of humorous cartoons, while the others contained pictures of automobile accidents. Library patrons were observed as they sat down at their desks and became unwitting participants in the experiment; they were given a few moments to familiarize themselves with the contents of the envelope. It was assumed that viewing a series of humorous cartoons would induce a good mood among the majority who saw them, while images of automobile accidents would result in experiencing a bad mood. After a few moments, an experimenter approached the subject and asked to borrow a piece of paper for the purpose of taking notes, or – in other conditions – ten pages of paper. Sometimes the request was formulated in a pleasant, conventional manner, while in others it took a direct and almost rude tone, contrary to convention ("Give me . . ."). Several minutes after that incident, another experimenter approached the participant and explained that the request for a piece of paper is part of a psychological experiment. Participants were then asked to evaluate the request that had been addressed using several different criteria (e.g. how unusual the request was, how polite, etc.), and also to evaluate their own mood. In line with expectations, it turned out that those who had seen the humorous drawings were in a better mood than those who were exposed to images of car accidents. The former were also more likely to fulfil the request for note-taking paper than were the latter. Participants also responded more positively to a request for one piece of paper than for ten pages. However, the most interesting data was that concerning the impact of mood in conditions differentiated by the politeness of the request as formulated. Consistent with Forgas's hypothesis, mood had practically no significance with respect to conditions in which the request was formulated in a pleasant, conventional manner. However, when the request was direct and inconsistent with custom, it was much more often met with acceptance by those in a positive mood than by participants experiencing negative emotions. Interestingly, an analogical pattern was observed regarding evaluation of the request itself. The conventional request was viewed as equally polite by both participants in a good mood and those in a bad mood. The unconventional request ("Give me . . ."), however, was clearly viewed with greater lenience by those in a good mood compared to those whose mood had been influenced negatively.

In the second experiment, these dependencies were successfully replicated while applying a different manner of mood induction. This time, the envelopes prepared for reading-room patrons contained either humorous short stories, or descriptions of the deaths of people ill with cancer (there was also a control group that read emotionally neutral texts with information about the library). The degree to which participants remembered the precise content of the request addressed to them was also examined. This last element facilitated the determination that polite, conventional requests are not remembered very accurately (which is entirely consistent with Forgas's assumptions that such situations are not analyzed with great attention to detail). Recollection of direct, unconventional requests, however, was significantly higher (which, obviously, is consistent with the assumption that people apply a more deliberate and systematic information processing strategy).

Generally, it can be said that the experiments conducted by Forgas allow us to understand the subtle differences in the reactions of people in different moods, but on the other hand their results concur with the theory that it is positive emotional states, rather than negative ones, that facilitate submission to requests. It should be added here that there are three points of view concerning research demonstrating an association between mood and tendency to fulfil various requests. The first of them holds that the mood an individual is experiencing has a direct influence on compliance. One supporter of this approach is Alice Isen, who assumes that people are motivated to attain and maintain a positive mood, and a decision about engaging or not engaging in a particular activity may be a means of achieving those objectives Clark & Isen, 1982; (Isen & Simmonds, 1978). A supporter of a second approach is Forgas, who suggests that mood may modify the very assessment of politeness and appropriateness of a request, and may alter the manner in which information concerning that request is processed. Under the third approach, however, mood induces associated cognitive states, such as thought, imagination and recollection (e.g. Niedenthal & Setterlund, 1994). In many cases, they may be consistent in content with the decision to provide assistance to a person asking for it. If we in fact are encountering the following sequence: positive mood – activation of positive cognitive elements – fulfilment of requests made by others, then the question arises of whether compliance can be induced by the mere activation of the aforementioned positive cognitive elements. Perhaps what comes into play here is not so much the content of such elements, but rather their positive or negative valence. The question of whether positive cognitive states alone are sufficient to induce compliance was asked by Bruce Rind (1997), who operated on the assumption that positive cognitive states are composed primarily of elements such as curiosity and interest, which in turn are mainly manifested in the response to a particular type of stimulus. Indeed, curiosity and interest are strongly intertwined, as it is generally the case that curiosity is the foundation of interest. Both of these states are rewarding for the individual, and in the subject literature they are contrasted with such states as boredom and monotony. This is particularly well put (albeit metaphorically) by Sudhir Kakar (1976), who says "what the libido is to sexuality, curiosity is to cognition" (p. 197).

In an experiment by Rind, the interest of participants selected from among students sitting alone in a university library was generated in such an original manner that I would like to describe it in detail here. Imagine, dear Reader, that you are participating in an experiment conducted by this researcher. Someone approaches you, apologizes for disturbing you, and shows you a white piece of paper containing the following message:

FINISHED FILES ARE THE RE-

SULT OF YEARS OF SCIENTIF-

IC STUDY COMBINED WITH THE

EXPERIENCE OF MANY YEARS.

Your task is to count the number of times the letter 'F' appears in the text. Have you done it already? I'm curious how many 'F's you've found . . . People generally declare that the letter 'F' appears in the text three times. However, the correct answer is six. In solving this exceptionally simple task, people generally do not take into consideration the letter 'F' that appears in the word "of", which appears in the text three times. If you, dear Reader, were a participant in Rind's study, you would certainly be surprised that you had made such a "serious" mistake, and you would be interested how this had occurred. That is precisely Rind's point. He then explained to his participants that the error results from the fact that 'F' in the word "of" sounds like 'V', and this is why the 'F' goes unnoticed when reading the text. These participants were treated as those exhibiting the element of interest. Another group was asked by the experimenter to review the same text, but rather than counting occurrences of the letter 'F', they were asked to find the letter 'R'. This task was also quite simple, and participants did not make any mistakes. However, there was no element that would induce interest among them.

Regardless of which letters participants had been asked to count, the experimenter then requested them for their participation in a survey. He informed them that the questionnaire was quite long, comprising 80 questions. It was not, however, necessary to respond to all of them. Participants were then asked how many of the questions they would agree to answer. The experimental design also included a control group, which was not asked at the beginning to perform any task. It turned out that the participants who had counted the letter 'F' declared that they would answer more questions than the remaining two groups.

The problem is, however, that the pattern of results recorded in this study may result from other factors than stimulation of cognitive interest. Above all, it is difficult to exclude the possibility that self-assessment of participants was impacted under the influence of information that they had performed poorly on such a seemingly simple task. Such a state is conducive to inducing compliance with regard to the requests of others. Doing something for them, insofar as it does not violate one's own moral principles, may aid in rebuilding one's self-image. Indeed, it supplies the conditions necessary for engaging in positive thinking about oneself in the form of "I'm an altruistic person" (e.g. Carlsmith & Gross, 1969; Cunningham et al., 1980). It can also not be excluded that participants experienced a feeling akin to guilt resulting from their poor execution of the task. A feeling of guilt – as many studies have shown, including those later on in this chapter – facilitates pliability in the face of requests. The mechanism that underlies this truth is, however, quite complex, and is discussed more broadly in a further section of this chapter.

Rind thus conducted another experiment based on a similar plan (this time, however, he eliminated the group that did not seek any letters in the text). Participants did have to complete a short questionnaire, in which they offered their views on how much their interest was sparked by the task involving a search for certain letters in the text, as well as the degree to which they felt performance of that task impacted their self-assessment, and of their feeling of guilt following the task. This experiment replicated the results indicating that after failing in their search for the letter 'F', participants were more inclined to provide answers to the questions in the survey, and regression analyses demonstrated that both interest and the experience of a feeling of guilt exerted an influence on compliance; the former element, however, was slightly more significant.

Unfortunately, Rind did not take account of two alternative explanations for the results he received. First, he failed to notice that the enhanced subservience of the participants who had been asked to find the letter 'F' may have resulted from the desire to show their gratitude to the experimenter for giving them the oppor- tunity to have a very interesting experience. Thus the mechanism of reciprocity, universally acknowledged as one of the primary forces governing social influence, would come into play (Cialdini, 2001). Second, there is an even simpler explana- tion, the truth of which may not be excluded: participants may have felt that if the experiment involving searching for the letter 'F' was so fascinating, then the survey questions may also be interesting and original. Obviously, those who were tasked with looking for the letter 'R', a boring job, had no reason to think that way (more precisely, they had reason to believe that the survey would be equally boring).

In order to exclude these two interpretations, it would be necessary to create an experimental situation in which the request to fulfil the key request would be advanced by an entirely different person than the one who aroused cognitive interest. Together with Tomasz Grzyb and Slawomir Spiewak I'm currently con- ducting such research, but there is still some time before the results come in. In any event, reliable evaluation of the theory that generalized positive cognitive states can generate compliance requires much more research.

Let us return to the issue of the relationship between the experience of affective states and submissiveness in the face of requests. We have already discussed the consequences of feeling physiological arousal and experiencing moods. Now it is time to proceed to analysis of the role of discrete emotions.

Among the various emotions familiar to all of us from personal experience, we may distinguish those whose occurrence (or even the potential that they might occur) provoke individuals to behaviours compliant with the norms and princi- ples which they or their social surroundings find acceptable. These emotions primarily include fear, guilt, shame and embarrassment. Of particular interest in the area of social influence is how the experience of such emotions (or at least the anticipation that they will occur) impacts people's compliance with requests, orders and commands.

Fear and anxiety

Most likely owing to the obviousness of the fact that people under the influence of fright or fear are often prepared to fulfil all sorts of threats and commands, researchers have engaged this issue extremely infrequently, focusing rather on the impact of the concentration of such emotions on the effectiveness of persuasive messages. In other words, psychologists have been interested in the way that fear induced by those messages influences changes in the attitudes of those to whom the messages are addressed. In these studies a range of interesting truths have been uncovered concerning the mechanisms of changes in attitudes (see e.g. Gass & Seiter, 2011; O'Keefe, 2002).

Because this book is focused on techniques that directly lead to changes in behaviour, it must be said that there are very few studies that have trained their fire at precisely the issue of the link between the degree of fear experienced by individuals and their tendency to submit to commands, requests and appeals addressed to them. Interestingly, the majority of research carried out in this area was done in the relatively distant past. In the 1950s, Irving Janis and Seymour Feshbach (1953) conducted an experiment in which the dependent variable was human behaviour. The experiment began by unsettling the participants with information that teeth infections might migrate to other parts of the body: the eyes, heart and joints. This information was accompanied by suggestive, revolting slides showing rotten teeth. By reducing the number of such slides as well as the volume of information about the negative consequences of dental illness, the researchers created two more versions of the same message. A portion of the participants was presented with a message inducing moderate fear, while another received a message evoking merely slight disquiet. It occurred that in the week following receipt of the message, those who had been frightened to a moderate degree had most frequently visited the dentist's office.

The curvilinear association between the saturation of a persuasive message with threatening elements and its effectiveness is described by Janis and Feshbach (1953) as being a result of a very weak fear being insufficient to pique an individual's interest, never mind to motivate people to change their beliefs. However, an excessively strong fear results in the occurrence of defensive reactions: information received by the individual is considered unreliable, or it is immediately subjected to interpretation and the assumption is made that, for example, while a particular threat does indeed concern the majority of people, the individual in question is not one of those at risk. In natural conditions such messages may, considering their aversiveness, prompt individuals to ignore them – for example, by turning off the TV or by putting down the newspaper mid-article (Wood, 2000).

The majority of psychological studies, however, have recorded a straight-line relationship between fear and effectiveness of a persuasive message (see Boster & Mongeau, 1984; O'Keefe, 2002). Lijiang Shen & James Dillard (2014) argue convincingly that this is exclusively due to their failure to account for the degree to which participants are scared. If this factor is taken into consideration, the analyzed dependency becomes curvilinear. It would seem that an analogical truth operates in respect of the link between fear and behavioural docility towards persuasive messages.

This is the precise effect observed in an experiment conducted by Clive Skilbeck, James Tulips and Philip Ley (1977), in which they examined the link between fear felt by obese people and their long-term actions aimed at reducing their body's fat content. Study participants were visibly overweight women aged 20–60. They were randomly allocated to various experimental conditions. Initially, all of the women listened to a 20-minute lecture on various dangers associated with obesity, but the content of the lecture was different for each group. In the condition of weak fear induction, the lecture focused on how obese people at older ages are more frequently at risk of various diseases, and that they have problems getting around. In the condition of moderate fear induction, the focus was on information about rather minor problems with the heart and arthritis. Strong fear induction conditions involved the lecturer discussing the very high risk of dangerous heart diseases and serious problems associated with arthritis. A special survey was used to assess how much the information had unsettled each participant. The participants were also weighed, and given special instructions concerning the diet they should follow in order to shed excess kilograms. The women participants were weighed four more times, at 2, 4, 8 and 16 weeks after the beginning of the experiment. What is of particular interest and importance to us here is the drop in weight among particular groups of participants. It turned out that the degree of saturation of the introductory lecture with fear-inducing information had no influence on the number of kilograms lost by the women undergoing therapy. However, a large role was played by the extent to which a given person was scared by the information contained in the lecture (after all, it is known that some people may be made more upset by the information that in 20 years they will have difficulty moving compared to others who have been told they may experience serious heart disease). This dependency is presented in Figure 6.1.

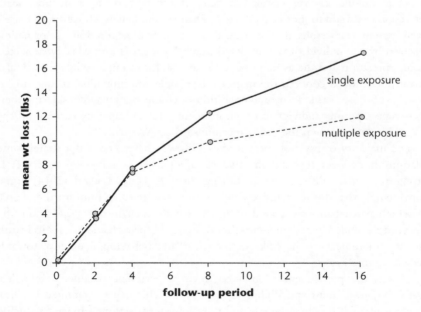

FIGURE 6.1 Fear exposure and weight loss

Source: European Journal of Social Psychology, 1977, vol. 7, p. 229.

The feeling of guilt and shame

The feeling of guilt is an averse experience. It is associated with the feeling of unpleasant tension and arousal, as well as the experience of regret and contrition (Baumeister, Reis & Delespaul, 1995). The feeling of guilt is frequently accompanied by the experience of shame (Izard, 1977; Tangney, 1995). The emotions of shame and of guilt are associated with an individual's feeling of violating a norm or a rule. The primary difference is that the first of these emotions is primarily of a public nature, while the second is private. In respect of the feeling of shame, the individual sends signals to those around informing them it is understood that a social norm has been violated, and that the very person responsible for the violation disapproves of it. This signal is a blush – men display it on their faces, while women show it along the neck and upper chest. Guilt, however, does not result in any obvious signal being sent to the external environment.

In the cases of both guilt and shame, it generally takes quite a long time for people to stop entertaining negative thoughts about themselves. These thoughts endanger one's feeling self-worth. The feeling of one's self-worth can be recovered by doing something considered socially acceptable. Fulfilment of the requests of others can therefore sometimes be a means of regaining the feeling that one is a positive and valuable individual (e.g. Konoske, Staple & Graf, 1979). If this requires sacrifice on the part of the individual – a significant engagement of time, effort or material resources – it can become a form of "penance". In many cultures (e.g. Catholic), people have internalized the belief that such a "penance" can cleanse a person, erasing a previous sin. People experiencing guilt or shame may also be inclined to punish themselves. This particular emotional state may induce individuals to think badly of themselves, which in turn may lead to inwardly-directed punitive behaviour (Freedman, Wallington & Bless, 1967). Fulfilling the requests of others when experiencing guilt or shame may also be a chance to engage in a cognitive escape from the unpleasant focus on oneself. Getting involved in any activity at all allows individuals to extricate themselves from negative reflections on themselves and their actions, and to focus on the new activity. We may assume that people generally aim to avoid experiencing negative emotions and seek opportunities to experience positive ones. Engaging in an activity that assists people in freeing themselves from the feeling of guilt or the experience of shame will thus be far more attractive (Cialdini, Darby & Vincent, 1973). The feelings of guilt and shame may also be associated with the conviction that one has lost control over the course of events. These emotions appear when we are subjected to conditions in our surrounding environment that we ourselves do not accept. Commencing an intentional behaviour aimed at achieving a specific, positive objective may be a means of recovering the desired feeling of control, on the condition that this activity proves successful (McMillen, 1971). In the past, the general consensus was that while the feeling of guilt led to increased compliance, shame did not do so; currently, a different position dominates the subject literature. Because the feeling of shame is a public emotion, submissiveness only becomes a consequence of it when it is witnessed by others. Only then can the feeling of shame be reduced (Whatley, Webster, Smith & Rhodes, 1999).

It is likely that the first researchers who conducted empirical research on the consequences of experiencing shame and guilt were John Wallace and Edward Sadalla (1966). In their experiment, participants worked on completing a Thematic Apperception Test (TAT test). In the meantime, an experimenter examined – in a quite ostentatious manner – the condition of various laboratory instruments, and then left the laboratory under the pretext of needing to transport some questionnaires. In his absence, the participants either waited passively for him to return, or they were egged on by another participant (in fact a confederate of the experimenter) to play around with one of the laboratory instruments. Inevitably, this led to damage to the device. The participant saw a flash of light and smoke rising up over the machine, and could clearly smell the odour of burning electrical cables. Upon the experimenter's return, his confederate either confessed that he and another participant wanted to test the device out but unfortunately damaged it, or said that something strange had happened to the device while he and the other participant were working on completing the TAT test. The experimenter then examined the equipment, and depending on the experimental conditions either said that the participants had damaged the unit, or that he completely accepted their explanation that the device had failed on its own. In the control conditions (i.e. those in which the participant was not induced to play with the equipment), the experimenter examined the device after his return, and declared that it was malfunctioning. In all three conditions this led to the cancellation of the next portion of the experiment for the same reason: damage to the instrument. After that, the experimenter thanked participants for taking part, at the same time requesting that they agree to participate in another study during which they would, at times, be given an electric shock (the study was supposed to concern physiological determinants of reactions to stress). As it turned out, participants who had previously broken the device were more often willing to participate in the new experiment than those in the control group. The variable of informing the experimenter about who the real culprits of the device's failure were did not have a statistically significant impact on the tendency to accept the proposal to engage in the unpleasant experiment.

Similar effects, indicating an association between pliancy and the experience of shame and guilt, were also reported in later experiments. In one of them (Carlsmith & Gross, 1969), participants were encouraged to submit other people to suffering. In half of the cases, this suffering consisted of giving them jolts of electricity of increasing strength. In the others, the suffering was far less serious – the electrical current was replaced with sounds of increasing loudness. After this experiment was completed, the individuals who were the purported recipients of the unpleasant stimuli approached the participants with a request for help in a campaign to save Californian sequoia trees. As it turned out, participants who had administered electric shocks agreed to participate in the campaign more frequently than those who had administered the loud sounds. In addition, the study demonstrated that this effect did not result from increased sympathy towards the people who had suffered as the result of experiencing the shocks. Other participants who merely observed the experiences of people being shocked were not eager to join in the campaign to save the sequoia. Thus, the most likely factor contributing to the fulfilment of the request to take part in a social campaign was the experience of guilt or shame on the part of participants.

In other experiments (Freedman et al., 1967), the emotions being discussed here were evoked in a different manner. Participants were provoked into lying to the person conducting the study, or they were induced to make a mistake that was difficult to repair and rendered the work of another person pointless. It turned out that in both cases, participants in the experimental conditions more frequently agreed to fulfil requests addressed to them than in control conditions. The study's authors demonstrated that, at least in some cases, an increase in submissiveness only occurred when fulfilling the request was not associated with the necessity of meeting the person who had been harmed. It may be said that contact with a wronged individual serves as a constant reminder to people of their earlier inappropriate behaviour. The prospect of this manner of spending time is thus subjectively very unpleasant. Helping someone else, however, is very attractive: it both facilitates "erasing the guilt" and eliminating negative thoughts about oneself. This "someone else" can even be an entirely anonymous person. For example, Richard Darlington and Clifford Macker (1966) demonstrated that people among whom a feeling of guilt had been induced were more likely to donate blood for their local hospital.

Another interesting experiment is one conducted by Nicolas Gueguen (2001), in which participants were approached by a female experimenter who asked them to assist her by keeping watch over a heavy bag. She explained that she wanted to purchase a magazine in a bookstore around the corner. If the participant agreed, the experimenter then walked away. On the surface of the bag, there was a package with the phrase "horse meat" visibly written on it. After a short while another female experimenter appeared, who looked disapprovingly at the woman guarding the bag and said that consumption of horse meat was vile, and that people who eat it should be ashamed. Without waiting for a response, she walked away. After 20 seconds the owner of the bag reappeared, thanked the participant, then left. The participant, left alone, was shortly thereafter asked by yet a third female experimenter to sign a petition. Depending on the experimental conditions the petition either concerned protection of animal rights, or reducing air pollution in large cities. Of course, participants in control conditions were also asked to sign petitions. While in the situation where the petition was associated with greater care for the fate of animals, the tendency to sign it was clearly greater among those from the experimental group (70%) than the control group (40%); in the case of the petition regarding pollution there was practically no difference (35% in the experimental group, 37.5% in the control group). It could be said that signing a petition on the matter of protection for animals was a better means of erasing guilt than was signing a petition concerning something entirely unrelated to the relationship between man and horse.

In another experiment, Paul Konoske, Sandra Staple and Richard Graf (1979) engaged in a more direct examination of the psychological mechanism that leads people burdened by guilt to accede to the requests and suggestions of others. These

authors took as their starting point the assumption that if such a request or suggestion involved participation in a laudable goal to the benefit of society, people
affected by the emotion of interest to us here would consent to it both in order to
punish themselves, and to recover their feeling of self-worth or to create the
opportunity to feel positive emotions. If, however, such a request exhibits a clearly
different and non-altruistic character, the increased compliance of individuals
experiencing the feeling of guilt could not be explained in terms of maintaining
self-worth or seeking positive emotions. If compliance actually occurred in such a
situation, it could be explained only by the tendency to inflict punishment on
oneself. Conditions for the experiment were created in which a portion of participants accidentally knocked over a pile of perforated computer cards, which led
to their being scattered about and to the inability to restore the order in which
they had been sorted. Participants were then asked to place a call to potential successive participants. Some of them were told that this was to remind them of the
time and place in which the experiment would be held. The others were informed
that they were assisting in recruiting for research concerning reactions to fear-
inducing stimuli. Because it was difficult to acquire participants for this particular
experiment, the researchers requested those making the phone calls to mislead the
people they would be speaking to. The participants were to inform their interlocutors that they themselves had taken part in the very same experiment, and that
it was not at all unpleasant. Similar requests (i.e. to remind others of the time and
place of an experiment, or to lie to them by saying that the planned experiment is
not unpleasant) were also made of participants from the control group. The number
of people whom each participant agreed to call was recorded. It turned out that
the feeling of guilt only enhanced the tendency to fulfil requests made by others
when they were of a purely pro-social nature, and thus served as an opportunity to
experience positive emotions and recover their positive self-image. If an attempt
was made to induce experiment participants to lie to others, their experiences of
the feeling of guilt did not have any influence on their behaviour. By the same
token, we may reject the hypothesis that people experiencing the emotions being
analyzed here fulfil the requests of others so as to punish themselves by engaging
in activity that is a source of discomfort and unpleasantness.

Discovering the psychological mechanism underlying the susceptibility to social
influence of people experiencing the emotions discussed here was the objective of
research by Brad Kelln and John Ellard (1999). Participants in the experiment
conducted by these authors worked on a task associated with memory. They used
a special device in the course of the experiment that – allegedly – was damaged.
The cause of the damage, which had of course been planned as a part of the
experimental design, was supposedly due to a mistake committed by the participant. In some cases, the experimenter only stated that the experiment had to be
stopped owing to the failure. In other conditions, the experimenter declared that
he had forgiven the participant for the error. He said not to be worried about what
had happened. In further conditions, participants were told that since the failure
required the involvement of more people in the experiment, they would not

receive the compensation they had been promised for taking part in the experiment ($4). The experiment plan also included conditions in which the experimenter both forgave participants and cheered them up, and informed them that they would not receive any money. All of the participants were asked to do the experimenter a favour. He said that he needed to deliver 50 envelopes to various individuals working at the university campus, and asked participants to help him in that task: every quantity of envelopes that a given participant agreed to deliver to the addresses on them would be of invaluable assistance. An analogous request was made of participants from the control group, who had not experienced the situation with the supposed failure of research instrumentation. It turned out that in "pure" conditions of experiencing the feeling of guilt and shame (i.e. when the experimenter did not comment on the causes of the device's failure), participants on average delivered more envelopes than in control conditions. An even higher degree of compliance was recorded in the group of participants whom the experimenter forgave and cheered up. When participants were informed that they would not receive the promised sum of $4, the level of compliance was the same as in the "pure" conditions of experiencing guilt and shame. The mere withdrawal of payment of the $4, however, led to participants taking fewer envelopes than those from the control group.

How should these results be interpreted? Kelln and Ellard refer to the concept of striving for equity in interpersonal relationships (see e.g. Walster, Walster & Berscheid, 1978). The assumptions of this concept state that the majority of people prefer situations in which their relations with others are equitable. Thus, people do not want to be in debt to anyone, nor have anyone in their debt. This rule is not limited to money, but rather has a far broader reach. From the perspective that is of interest to us here, we may say that participants who believe that it was their mistake that led to the device's failure and resultant problems felt that they were in debt to the experimenter. This is why they were eager to accede to his request to deliver envelopes. This assistance served as an opportunity to do something for him and to restore equity in the interpersonal relationship that had been disrupted by the participants' own mistake. If the experimenter reacted with empathy, assuring the participant that it was no big deal, then the equity of the relationship became even more imbalanced. The experimenter's pleasant behaviour is a sort of undeserved "present" received by the participants. From this perspective it is not surprising that these were the conditions in which participants took the largest number of envelopes. However, if the experimenter did not behave empathetically, but rather took a participant's money away, equity was by the same token restored to the relationship between the experimenter and the participant. The arrangement became equitable: while the participant had indeed damaged the instrument, this was balanced by the loss of the remuneration. The balance present in the exchange results in participants being not particularly inclined to assist the experimenter. If the retention of the money is accompanied by cheering up of the participant, the arrangement becomes inequitable, but only to a limited degree. The participant's loss of $4 is balanced out by the problems that the experimenter experiences.

The pleasant behaviour of the experimenter towards the participant requires reciprocity, but it need not be particularly elaborate. In this case, the submissiveness of participants is thus higher than in the control conditions, but it does not exceed the level recorded in conditions of a "pure" feeling of guilt.

It would seem that the theory of equity under discussion here may, in some conditions, be a good predictor of behaviour by people experiencing the feeling of guilt or shame. However, its utility is limited to one particular class of situations. Above all, it does not facilitate an explanation of the readiness of people experiencing the emotions analyzed here to execute the requests and orders of people whom they had not previously harmed in any way.

Embarrassment

Embarrassment is an emotion that we experience relatively infrequently, but also one which practically every adult person has undoubtedly experienced. The majority of psychological experiments concerning the consequences of experiencing this state have been oriented towards demonstrating that it gives rise to a tendency to avoid others and to isolate oneself (e.g. Jankowski & Takahashi, 2014). The issue of whether the state of embarrassment enhances submission to requests, suggestions or orders of others has been relatively rarely examined in empirical studies. Among the few exceptions are two experiments conducted by Robert Apsler (1975). In the first of them, two students came to a laboratory, of which only one was an actual study participant; the other was a confederate of the female experimenter, which was, of course, a secret to the participant. The experimenter explained that the study was focused on the process of forming impressions about other people, and that one of the invited participants would perform certain tasks, while the other would observe through a one-way mirror. Next, the experimenter tossed a coin and asked the "real" participant to choose a side. Whether the choice was heads or tails, it "turned out" that the real participant would remain in the laboratory and perform some tasks. The experimenter's confederate went into the neighbouring room to engage in observation. Depending on the experimental conditions the participant performed either four relatively neutral tasks (turning on a radio and listening to a song; walking around the room for 1.5 minutes; counting out loud to 50; reading a fragment of a book out loud), or tasks which, if performed in public, would result in embarrassment (turning on a radio and dancing alone; laughing for 30 seconds as though a very funny joke had been told; singing a particular song; and imitating the hysterical reaction of a child who desperately refuses to go to preschool). After performing the last task, the participant again met with the experimenter's confederate, who then asked for help in performing a certain task. The confederate explained that he had to conduct research on the mood of a large group of people as a class assignment. Participants in this research undertaking had to complete a survey taking around 30 minutes. It would be best if they completed the questionnaire for the next 20 days, but even a shorter period would also supply valuable information. The experimenter's assistant asked participants to agree to participate in the experiment, and to declare in how many days they would be willing to complete the questionnaire. This request was also addressed to participants from a control group in which the students did not work on any specific tasks, but rather just completed a standard psychological survey. It turned out that in conditions in which the participants were embarrassed by the tasks they were asked to perform, the average number of days for which they declared their readiness to complete the mood survey was greater than in the remaining conditions.

Of course, the question arises of why the state of embarrassment facilitates compliance. Apsler looks primarily at two possibilities. First, it may be thought that the motivation to "recover one's lost face" may be present. Participants are aware that another student observing them through the one-way mirror was a witness to their idiotic activity. Consent to engage in beneficial and desirable behaviour may be a way of making a good impression on that witness, a means of proving that we are far more valuable as people than would result from the activity we engaged in during the experiment. An alternative possibility refers to an intrapsychic mechanism. Involvement in helping another person who not only needs but asks for that help may be a vehicle for achieving a positive mood or for recovering positive self-image. Both mood and self-image suffered while "making an idiot of ourselves" during the experiment. Apsler arrived at the conclusion that a situation in which the request for assistance in psychological experiments was formed by person other than the witness to the performance of "stupid" tasks by the participants would settle the matter. If increased compliance were to also appear in those conditions, it would mean that intrapsychic mechanisms were at the heart of the matter (i.e. the desire to improve mood or self-image). If, however, no such jump in compliance were recorded, this would serve as support for the motivation to "recover face".

In Apsler's second experiment, study participants were female students and the experiment was conducted by a male experimenter. The experiment was based on the same plan, with three exceptions. The first of them concerned the dependent variable. This time it was determined that the maximum time for completing the mood survey was the following 30 days. The second difference concerned the person who asked for help in conducting the study. The person requesting participation in the experiment was either a person about whom participants knew had witnessed their behaviour during part of the experiment, or an entirely different person who, as the participants were aware, had no idea about their previous behaviour. The third difference was associated with the elimination of the control group.

The results of this experiment are presented in Table 6.1.

As we can see, in conditions under which the students were experiencing embarrassment, their compliance with the request was greater than in conditions in which they performed neutral tasks. Importantly, it was of no significance who (witness to their behaviour vs an individual with no knowledge of it) requested help in their research. In Apsler's opinion, this reflected the presence of an intrapsychic

TABLE 6.1 Means of the transformed compliance measure as a function of embarrassment and person making the request in Apsler (1975) experiment

Embarrassment	Requester	
	Observer	Nonobserver
High	53.8	52.2
Low	47.7	46.3

Source: *Journal of Personality and Social Psychology*, 1975, vol. 32, p. 151.
Copyright 1975 by the American Psychological Association, Inc.

mechanism. Without excluding the foregoing in any way, I am rather inclined to think that the motivation to recover face can also not be excluded. The point, however, is not about making a good impression on precisely the very same person who had cause to think poorly about the individual, but rather about "people in general". Put differently, what may come into play is a general motivation to make a good impression on others. Of course, the mechanisms being analyzed here need not necessarily be considered alternatives. It is not excluded (in fact, it is even rather likely) that all of them lie at the foundation of the relationship between the experience of embarrassment and submissiveness. Whether, in fact, this is the case, can only be determined by future experiments.

Emotional see-saw

Ryszard Nawrat and I (Dolinski & Nawrat, 1998) examined the functioning of an individual who experiences strong fear, then encounters a situation in which the stimulus evoking that emotion suddenly and unexpectedly disappears. One example of this kind of situation is an interrogation conducted according to the "good cop/bad cop" script. As we know from books and action films, the interrogee first experiences exceptionally brutal treatment – he is threatened with death, yelled at and humiliated. However, everything suddenly and unexpectedly changes. The phone rings, and the bad cop leaves the interrogation room. He is replaced by another – kind, polite, calm. He offers the interrogee a cup of coffee and a cigarette, and conducts a normal conversation. In films and books it is often the case that the person being questioned, previously refusing to cooperate, begins to testify and incriminates himself and his associates. It would seem that books and films do a good job of presenting the situation. This was in fact the way that statements from political prisoners were obtained in the Soviet Union (Herling-Grudzinski, 1965).

Of course, the sudden withdrawal of a source of fear does not necessarily apply to a situation as specific as a police interrogation, and compliance need not be associated with making statements and admitting one's guilt. Let us imagine a situation in which we are jaywalking, and when we are in the middle of the street we hear the sound of a police whistle. We would naturally be frightened. We also feel a similar emotion when we leave our car in a forbidden place, then upon returning we see a small piece of paper placed under the wiper blade. What, however, happens when we turn around on the street and discover that the whistler is not a police officer, but rather a smiling jokester, and after we pick up the paper underneath our wiper, it turns out to be not a fine but rather an advert for a hair formula or an appeal to donate blood? At this moment we experience a sudden feeling of relief. The dynamics of emotions experienced in such situations are similar to those that occur in the case of a person being interrogated by a bad cop followed by a good cop.

These are precisely the situations that we created in our experiments. In one of them, the participants were drivers parking their cars in a forbidden spot. We placed pieces of paper behind their windscreen wipers that had the appearance of a fine issued by the police. At the moment when a driver returned to his car and picked up the paper, it turned out to be an advert for Vitapan – an incredible (supposedly, for it did not actually exist) substance for stimulating hair growth, or an appeal to donate blood. In other situations, the same pieces of paper were stuck on doors using adhesive tape. Because the police never issue fines to drivers by sticking them to car doors, participants treated in this manner had no reason to experience fear. The experiment plan also included an additional control group in which the car owners were not given any papers.

At the moment when the driver/participant was preparing to leave, an experimenter approached him, presented himself as a student conducting an experiment for his MA thesis, then asked for the completion of a survey concerning possibilities for improving vehicle traffic in the city. We treated consent to the request as an indicator of compliance. As can be seen in Table 6.2, individuals who had occasion to experience the condition of "fear-relief" more frequently agreed to participate in that study than did people from the remaining groups.

In later experiments we succeeded in demonstrating that compliance to such requests does not result from the simple fact of experiencing fear (we introduced a group in which participants did in fact receive a police fine for parking in an unauthorized place), nor from the experiencing of positive emotions resulting from the state of relief (we measured the level at which positive emotions were experienced in particular experimental conditions). Thus, it is a specific situation involving the experience of fear-then-relief that leads to people

TABLE 6.2 Percentage of subjects who complied with a request in Dolinski and Nawrat (1998) experiment

Behind a wiper/Advert for Vitapan	56	28/50
Behind a wiper/Appeal for blood donation	68	34/50
Car door/Advert for Vitapan	34	17/50
Car door/Appeal for blood donation	40	20/50
Control (no card)	36	18/50

Source: Journal of Experimental Social Psychology, 1998, vol. 34, p. 31
Copyright 1998 Academic Press. Reproduced by permission of Elsevier.

subjected to such an influence demonstrating pliancy towards requests and commands addressed to them.

Why is this the case? Every emotion experienced by an individual sets into motion a unique plan of action characteristic to that individual (e.g. Frijda, 1986; Niedenthal et al., 2006). For example, a feeling of happiness emerges under the influence of achievement of a milestone in some activity, which in turn activates a programme directed at continuing the action plan and introducing any necessary modifications. Sadness appears as a consequence of failure in achieving an important goal, or missing a milestone, and leads to the inception of a programme consisting of passivity, the creation of another plan, or perhaps a search for assistance. Anger is the result of frustration resulting from the inability to carry out one's intentions, and leads to a redoubling of efforts to achieve that goal, or to aggression. Contempt, in turn, appears when one individual meets with another who hails from a social milieu that the former does not accept and considers to be worthless. The programme initiated by this emotion involves treating the other person with a total lack of respect.

The emotion of fear that interests us here initiates a reaction consisting of suspending our current activity coupled with a simultaneous increase of wariness towards the surrounding environment, immobility or flight (e.g. Denny, 1991; Tomkins, 1991; Tuma & Maser, 1985). Because fear, in the majority of cases, appears in conditions of threat to an individual or conflict between an individual's chosen objectives, such a reaction is usually sufficient. However, if the sources of fear suddenly disappear, the programme of action activated by that emotion becomes inadequate in relation to the transformed circumstances. A new programme, appropriate for the new situation, still remains to be initiated. Thus we find ourselves in a specific (and surely short-term) state of being "between programmes". The execution of one of them has been suspended by the sudden absence of the stimulus giving rise to the experience of fear, while a new programme in response to the evolving situation has not yet been activated. It would also seem very likely that when the source of an emotion suddenly disappears, an individual may engage in retrospective reflections concerning the events that have taken place, or which could have taken place. Both concentration on the past and engaging in hypothetical thinking may lead to insufficient cognitive resources for dealing effectively with the task at hand. The absence of free cognitive resources that could be devoted to analysis of the current situation in turn leads to automatic and mindless reactions to external stimuli. These automatic and mindless behaviours are unusually frequent in our everyday lives. People undertake a number of everyday decisions without reflection, they communicate mindlessly, and they learn and teach mindlessly (Langer, 1989, 1992). However, while it is generally assumed that the state of mindlessness is induced by a routine situation that has occurred frequently in the past, and thus one which is accompanied by a low level of physiological arousal (Langer & Moldoveanu, 2000), we feel that a similar state may also be evoked by a sudden and unexpected source of arousal and the equally sudden and unexpected withdrawal of the stimulus evoking this condition; in other words, the fear-than-relief sequence.

In one of our studies (Dolinski & Nawrat, 1998) we applied the aforementioned paradigm of using a whistle on people crossing the street in an unauthorized place. The experimenter then held out a collections box and asked for a donation. Similarly to the original 1978 study by Langer et al. (see also Chapter 5 of this book), the experimenter either formulated a simple request ("Madam/Sir, would you please give us some money?"), a request accompanied by a superficial (placebo) justification ("Madam/Sir, we are collecting money. Would you please give us some money because we have to collect as much money as possible?"), or a request accompanied with a real justification ("Madam/Sir, we are members of the 'Students for the Handicapped' organization. Would you please join our charity campaign, because we have to collect as much money as possible to cover the cost of a holiday camp for mentally handicapped children?"). It turned out that in emotionally neutral conditions (e.g. those in which participants crossed the street without being disturbed by the whistle), people behaved in a rational, mindful manner. Only very infrequently did they place money in the donation can when the request had no justification or when it had a superficial justification, but they did so with far greater frequency when the request was accompanied by an explanation of who was gathering the money and for what purpose. People experiencing an emotional see-saw, however, reacted in an entirely different manner. In this case it was enough to have any kind of justification at all for participants to be more likely to reach into their wallets when compared to conditions in which the request was made without any accompanying justification (see Table 6.3).

It also transpired that in conditions of fear-then-relief, people to whom an unusual message was addressed (i.e. a request accompanied by an entirely superficial justification) extremely rarely decided to ask any questions at all concerning the

TABLE 6.3 Percentage of people who offered money, mean amounts of money given, and a tendency to seek additional information under each condition in Dolinski and Nawrat (1998) experiment

	Jaywalkers with whistle			Jaywalkers		
	Request only	Placebo info	Real info	Request only	Placebo info	Real info
Percentage of participants offering money spontaneously (without asking any questions)	38.7	76.0	71.9	11.3	15.1	58.5
Mean amount of money given (in Polish zl)	.80	1.65	1.48	.31	.55	1.53
Percentage of participants asking for additional information	20	8	–	49	57	–

Source: Journal of Experimental Social Psychology, 1998, vol. 34, p. 44

purpose and the organizers of the campaign. Such a reaction was nearly universal among people in a neutral emotional state.

This pattern of results concerning both the frequency of request fulfilment and the verbal expression of doubts is therefore entirely consistent with the assumption that conditions of relief occurring after the experience of fear induce a condition of mindlessness, which in turn facilitates compliance. We have also demonstrated in other studies that a sudden feeling of relief puts people into a condition of compromised intellectual functioning, such as a study in which participants were required to solve simple mathematical tasks, or point as quickly as possible to a face in a picture that displayed a different emotion from all the others presented in it (Dolinski, Ciszek, Godlewski & Zawadzki, 2002). Results of a study on drivers were also consistent with this assumption. In experiments conducted using driving simulators (Dolinski & Odachowska, 2015), we demonstrated that drivers who had avoided a collision (and thus were in a state of relief) very frequently committed a simple mistake in the period immediately following the first incident, leading to an accident.

If compliance with requests and propositions is undergirded by a sudden withdrawal of the source of emotions, one should expect that we will encounter such a truth not only in the event of withdrawal of a source of fear, but also when the causes of other emotions are suddenly removed as well. Is this, in fact, the case? In one of the experiments I conducted jointly with Ryszard Nawrat (Nawrat & Dolinski, 2007), a female experimenter called randomly selected people and presented herself as an employee of a telecommunications company. In one condition she informed her interlocutor that the computer indicated a large overpayment, and that he would soon be refunded a significant sum of money (evoking a positive emotion); in another, she said that the computer indicated a significant underpayment, and that the interlocutor would soon have to make up the difference (evoking a negative emotion). In half of the cases, participants were left in the induced emotional state, while in the remaining cases the experimenter "in order to make sure there was no mistake" asked participants for their address, and after a moment explained that the matter in fact concerned another customer with the same surname. Regardless of the type of manipulation, the experimenter then said "Polish Telecom is testing the sound quality of the telephone transmission using the new TELPOCOL system. Would you put the receiver to your other ear, please?" After 3 seconds she asked "Have you done so already?"

In the control group where no emotional states were induced among participants, this message was communicated by the experimenter immediately after introducing herself as an employee of the phone company. Confirmation by participants of shifting the receiver to their other ear was treated as mindless compliance with a senseless request. While such a reaction occurred sporadically in both the control group and in groups where only negative or positive emotions were induced, it was recorded with far greater frequency (a statistically significant difference) in conditions involving the unexpected withdrawal of information justifying the experience of both negative and positive emotions.

Other research we have conducted (Nawrat & Dolinski, 2007) also indicates that compliance may be induced not only by the sudden withdrawal of sources of the emotion of fear, but also of entirely different ones – positive emotional states. It should, however, be emphasized that these effects were generally weaker than in conditions involving the application of the fear-then-relief sequence, while in the case of withdrawal of sources of some emotions (e.g. disgust), we were entirely unsuccessful in achieving increased compliance.

Summary

The majority of social influence situations are associated with increased physiological arousal. Just the simple presence of other people is a source of arousal. It may be additionally enhanced by the physical attractiveness of such people, by the fact that they are famous people or otherwise authorities, and by many other factors. A synergetic effect involving the accumulation of stimuli may occur among individuals who are emotionally aroused for some reason and then find themselves in another situation giving rise to emotions. If such a state is perceived as unpleasant, the individual aims to reduce the level of arousal. Compliance, acceding to a request, proposal or demand is often the most readily-available means of achieving that desired state. It is thus no surprise that the majority of studies devoted to this question generated results indicating that increased arousal was conducive to compliance.

Because one of the natural human motivations is the desire to attain and maintain a positive mood, people avoid behaviours that may lead to a worsening of mood, and strive to engage in those which lead to that very state. It is often the case that improving and maintaining a good mood may be achieved by agreeing to the requests of others. This is particularly true when fulfilling the request is not associated with actions that themselves would cause discomfort. On the other hand, in some situations fulfilling the request of another person may lead to a worsening of one's positive mood. This happens, for example, when the activity involved in fulfilment of the request is time-consuming or boring. In such cases the positive mood being experienced by the individual reduces (rather than increases) the chances that the request will be fulfilled.

In many cases, the potential for fulfilment of a request depends not so much on its level of difficulty, but rather a subjective interpretation of the entire event. This, in turn, may remain under the influence of the affective state being experienced. Studies have shown that the type of mood one experiences has a minimal impact on evaluation of conventional requests and the tendency to fulfil them, but has a relatively large influence on the assessment of unconventional requests and on the decision to carry them out.

Among the emotions well known to all of us, we may distinguish those whose occurrence motivates us to behave in a manner consistent with the norms and rules accepted internally and by our social surroundings. These emotions include fear, guilt and shame, and also embarrassment. It has been demonstrated that the experience of these emotions (or even the mere anticipation of their emergence) often influences people's submissiveness towards requests, recommendations and commands.

Psychologists have rarely studied situations in which an individual experiencing some emotion is faced with the sudden and unexpected withdrawal of the stimulus that evoked it and was responsible for its continuation. In the meantime, this type of situation occurs quite frequently in the daily life of every person. The studies presented in this chapter demonstrate that in these situations, given the label "emotional see-saw", individuals' tendency to comply with requests, orders and suggestions addressed to us is increased.

The most likely mechanism at the heart of pliancy in such conditions is associated with the manner in which every emotion generates a specific programme of action. When one is in a situation where this programme suddenly becomes utterly inadequate in the face of altered external circumstances, individuals begin functioning mindlessly. This gives rise to automatic reactions that do not take into account the particulars of the situation at hand. This assumption was confirmed by an experiment that applied the classic paradigm of studies on the mindless fulfilment of requests. The results of other research, presented in this chapter, are also consistent with this assumption. They demonstrate that the emotional see-saw leads to the individual experiencing disruptions in cognitive functioning.

7

A FEW MORE ISSUES AND FINAL REMARKS

Academic researchers vs practitioners of social influence

While those who research techniques of social influence are interested in their effectiveness and the psychological mechanisms underlying their success, practitioners of social influence are, for obvious reasons, interested (exclusively, or at least primarily) in only the former of these two issues. This does not, however, mean that practitioners take into account fewer factors than researchers do. A beggar may be very interested in knowing the part of the city and the time of the day when people toss the most change into a hat, as well as when and where they do it the least. His thinking can also take on an interactive character: entirely different techniques and tricks may prove effective in neighbourhoods inhabited by people of average wealth compared to those populated by richer individuals. An employee of a real estate agency might, in turn, apply completely different techniques of persuasion on a student looking to rent a small apartment for nine months compared to a businessman looking to purchase a large house with a pool. Arnie Cann and Jill Blackwelder (1984) correctly observe that in order to fully grasp the mechanisms leading to effectiveness of a social influence technique in real social life, we must consider who is addressing whom, at what time, in what place, and with what objective. At times it may be the case that seemingly insignificant details are of key significance. For example, it is known that women pick up hitchhikers far less often than men. However, if a male hitchhiker is holding a bouquet of flowers in his hand, there is an eight-fold greater chance that a female driver will pick him up (Gueguen, Meineri & Stefan, 2012).

Also of importance is that a practitioner of social influence must frequently select the people he will approach with a request or a proposition. Let us imagine, for example, that we are collecting donations in the city centre for some charitable cause. There are so many people that we have no chance of approaching all of them with our donation boxes; we have to decide who will be asked for a gift, and who will not. In such situations it seems unlikely that people simply leave things to chance; rather they assess the subjective likelihood that a given passer-by will agree to their request. Jaroslaw Kulbat (2003) asked his study participants to imagine that they worked for a charitable organization, then showed them films presenting adults walking along the sidewalk. The participants were asked to assess the probability that the person being shown to them would toss money into a donation can. It turned out that, regardless of the sex of the person making the judgement, higher estimations of the likelihood of making a donation were made when a woman appeared on the screen than when a man was shown.

Practitioners may also be very interested in the results of studies concerning long-term campaigns, as is the case with the majority of collections taken up for charitable purposes, or for marketing campaigns. The effectiveness of particular efforts to exert influence may depend on whether the campaign is just getting underway, in progress, or approaching its conclusion. One example of this can be found in the experiments of Jakob Jensen, Andy King and Nick Carcioppolo (2013). These researchers observed that behaviourists conducting studies on rats had previously recorded increased motivation in individual rats when they were close to achieving a goal (laboratory rats ran faster as they got closer to food). The organizers of various collection drives could provide not only information about the objective (e.g. "We're trying to raise $20,000 for a wheelchair for our paralyzed friend"), but also about the progress of the campaign (e.g. "We've already got $2,000" or "We've already got $18,000"). The first piece of information indicates that there is a long way to the goal, while the second shows how close it is. In accordance with the goal-gradient hypothesis, people approached for a donation and hearing the latter piece of information should be more motivated to give money than in the first case. While the experiments conducted by the aforementioned researchers did not provide entirely definitive results, it would seem that this dynamic approach to social influence techniques is worthy of close attention. Publicizing information about sums collected can at times benefit a charity drive, while at times it can be detrimental.

Also of potential importance for the practitioner of social influence is the amount of time and the level of effort necessary to apply particular techniques. Adding the phrase "even a penny will help" (see Chapter 4) is, from this perspective, far more tempting than using the time-and energy-consuming "foot-in-the-door" technique (see Chapter 2). This does not mean, however, that those practising social influence always seek to expend the minimum amount of effort. Quite the opposite, if they see there is a real chance of achieving their objectives, they may not stop at applying time- and resource-intensive influence techniques, but may even go so far as to combine them in chains of complex techniques (Howard, 1995). Are such "chains of techniques" more effective than applying individual techniques? The issue is far more complicated than it might appear at first glance and, interestingly, has already been studied quite extensively by social psychologists. Morton Goldman (1986) posed questions about the effectiveness of the combined application of the classic foot-in-the-door and door-in-the-face sequential techniques. His starting point was the assumption that the main limitation in the former technique's effectiveness is associated with the difficulty of the introductory request. If it is too easy then nearly everyone will agree, but the fact that it is so easy means that the addressee does not analyze the reasons why he carried it out. As a result, self-perception does not occur, and the technique is ineffective. On the other hand, if the request is overly difficult, a large percentage of people will refuse to accede (and thus they will – even more so – refuse to carry out the second, target request). Thus, the technique also fails in this case. What can be done? There are two potential remedies. One is to ensure that people think about why they have fulfilled the easier request and that they do not find simple explanations that refer to external factors, or another is to make them more inclined to fulfil a relatively difficult request. Goldman focuses on the second of those possibilities. He suggests using three requests rather than two. The third request should be the most difficult one, and it should serve as the initial request in the interaction with the person whom we wish to influence. It will most likely be rejected but, as with the door-in-the-face technique, it is now time to submit the easiest request of the three. When this request is fulfilled (which is quite probable in light of what we know about this technique), we should then, in accordance with the foot-in-the-door technique, submit the target request. Goldman therefore proposes applying a chain of techniques consisting of door-in-the-face + foot-in-the-door.

His experimental design included conditions designed to measure the effectiveness of the foot-in-the-door technique, door-in-the-face, and a sequence consisting of door-in-the-face + foot-in-the-door, as well as control conditions in which the target request was directly formulated. The experimenter called study participants and introduced himself as a member of an organization supporting the local zoo. The individual requests concerned various activities benefiting the zoological gardens (such as an easy request consisting of answering survey questions, or conducting individual surveys with 150 people in the case of the very difficult request). The target request concerned the study participant addressing 75 envelopes to various people and institutions containing letters with a request to provide financial support to the zoo. Both foot-in-the-door (first the request for a response to the survey, then the request to address the envelope) and door-in-the-face (first the request for conducting 150 interviews, then – after hearing a refusal – the request to address the envelopes) techniques proved successful. In both conditions more people agreed to carry out the target request than in the control conditions. However, the most effective technique was one based on the sequence of door-in-the-face + foot-in-the-door, in which the very difficult request was first issued (conducting an interview with 150 people), then after the refusal the easy request was lodged (giving answers to survey questions), and then after the easy request was fulfilled, the target request was made (addressing the envelopes). In these conditions the target request was agreed to by 57% of participants compared to 46% in door-in-the-face conditions, and

42% in foot-in-the-door conditions. In the control conditions 22% of participants agreed to address the envelopes.

Jacob Hornik, Tamar Zaig and Dori Shadmon (1991) linked the foot-in-the-door technique with low ball, also described in Chapter 2. People who work professionally conducting public opinion surveys by telephone are aware that the high percentage of people who refuse to answer questions is a frequent source of difficulty. This percentage goes even higher when the questions are of a personal nature and touch on private issues. The high proportion of people who refuse to speak to those conducting surveys renders the sample far from representative, which can frequently undermine the entire sense of such studies. Hornik et al. examined whether using the foot-in-the-door technique, low ball, or a sequence containing those techniques would increase people's readiness to respond to interview questions. In the foot-in-the-door conditions a respondent was called and then asked three questions concerning personal matters; these did not, however, involve sensitive issues the respondent would be unlikely to discuss with a stranger. Next, an appointment to conduct a longer interview at a convenient time for the respondent was made. In the case of the low-ball technique, an appointment for an interview on various personal issues was first made, then the respondent was called and told that the subject matter would be slightly broader as the organization designing the survey had added some questions about intimate matters to the survey. Further conditions involved combining the two techniques while changing their order. It turned out that all of the techniques proved effective. In every case, the percentage of people responding to questions in the primary interview was greater than in the control group, to which the request to answer intimate questions was made directly. The most effective technique, however, was one based on the sequence of low ball + foot-in-the-door (in these conditions 83% of study participants consented to give the interview). When the order of the aforementioned techniques was reversed, their effectiveness was slightly reduced (77.4% compliance). It also turned out that, similarly to many other studies (e.g. Burger & Petty, 1981; Joule, 1987), the low-ball technique was more effective than foot-in-the-door. The former technique achieved 70.1% compliance, while the latter only 59.7% (in the control group 46.7% of respondents agreed to the interview).

A similar pattern of results was recorded by those authors in their other studies, which concerned obtaining agreement to a 20-minute interview concerning behaviours associated with a healthy lifestyle (Hornik & Zaig, 1991). The sequence of low ball + foot-in-the-door again proved the most effective in these studies.

A range of other studies have demonstrated the effectiveness of such techniques as touch and gaze (Hornik, 1987), touch and vocal intensity (Rembland & Jones, 2001), labelling and foot-in-the-door (Goldman et al., 1982), and dialogue involvement and even a penny will help (Dolinski et al., 2005). It is worth devoting a bit more attention to the combined effects of dialogue involvement with other social influence techniques.

Catalysts of social influence

Chemists use the term "catalyst" to define a substance that speeds up a chemical reaction. One may posit the theory that the establishment of dialogue by an individual with a person whom he is seeking to influence is a sort of psychological catalyst. As I have already discussed in Chapter 4, dialogue is a typical element of our conversations with acquaintances, and social norms demand that we help those we know, particularly when such assistance is of little cost to us. Taken by surprise by a stranger who involves us in a dialogue, we automatically activate the "dealing with an acquaintance script". It could be assumed that a social influence technique being applied after engaging someone in dialogue finds fertile ground, and by the same token should prove exceptionally effective. To put it differently, the dialogue serves as a catalyst for the workings of that technique. One example of this can be found in studies we conducted involving a charity drive held for victims of leukaemia (Dolinski et al., 2005). In these studies we tested the effectiveness of the legitimizing a paltry contribution technique, which you are familiar with from Chapter 4. In asking for a donation, we placed a collection box in front of a passer-by and in half of the cases we said "even a penny will help". Before the request to make a donation was formulated, however, we informed participants about the purpose of the charity drive. In half of the cases we did this in the form of a monologue, describing how leukaemia is a serious problem and how important it is to support institutions that work to treat it. A dialogue was used in relation to the other participants. We asked if they felt leukaemia was a serious social problem, and what they thought about institutions engaged in the fight against it. We recorded both the number of people in each condition who placed money in the box, as well as the average sum of money donated. The technique of legitimizing a paltry contribution was particularly effective when participants had previously been engaged in dialogue. A similar pattern of results was noted in our other studies, including one where the request was not to donate money, but rather to distribute flyers.

Much would seem to indicate that connecting dialogue with various social influence techniques is often a natural thing to do, and at times even difficult to avoid. Let us observe that the initial phase of interaction with a person applying some technique to exert social influence (in psychological research this person is the experimenter) usually involves posing a question to the person being influenced, then listening to his answer. However, in the control conditions of studies on influence techniques we are dealing with a situation in which the experimenter addresses the participant directly (without engaging him in dialogue). For example, the door-in-the-face technique assumes that a difficult request should first be made, then rejected by the participant, after which the easier target request should be immediately presented. It is impossible to even conceive of a situation in which the interaction between the researcher and participant would not take on the form of a dialogue. In the control conditions, the experimenter begins at once with the target request, and the monologue format is not only possible, but simply natural. I am not making the suggestion that the techniques described in this book are simply variations of the dialogue engagement technique – this is most certainly not the case! For example, the door-in-the-face technique requires that the second request be easier than the first. If the rejection of the initial request is followed by another one which is very similar and equally difficult, the technique ceases to be effective (Cialdini et al., 1975). Dialogue engagement can thus be both a stand-alone social influence technique (as you have read about in Chapter 4) and a catalyst for the workings of other techniques.

Phenomena that can serve as such catalysts are explored in even greater detail by Jerry Burger together with his collaborators (Burger et al., 2001; Burger et al., 2004; for review see Burger, 2007). They treat dialogue engagement as one of the means of evoking fleeting attraction towards a stranger. Engaging in dialogue with another person leads us to begin liking that individual. This, in turn, provides an obvious boost to the chances that we will agree to requests he makes of us. Another means of increasing one's own attractiveness in the eyes of our partner may be simply being present in the same space. Here we are taking advantage of the phenomenon of mere exposure, which consists of being more favourably disposed to stimuli (including social stimuli, and thus people) we are familiar with than ones that are unknown to us. Thus if a request is addressed to a study participant by someone he already knows in some way (he has seen or heard him), the chances are greater that the request will be carried out. Yet another way of boosting one's own attractiveness in the eyes of a partner in an interaction is to discreetly draw his attention to the fact that we share some similarities (as I have already discussed in Chapter 3, these need not necessarily be real similarities, they can be made up by the individual seeking to exert social influence). Interestingly, the similarity may even relate to matters that are trivial and of no consequence from the perspective of the request, such as a supposedly exceptional fingerprint. In such conditions people are more inclined to fulfil the request of a student to take part in a research project he needs to get a grade (Burger et al., 2004), as well as to purchase various products presented to them (Jiang et al., 2010) .

Another particular catalyst of social influence techniques is the condition of cognitive exhaustion that can be experienced by an individual to whom we are addressing a request. Bob Fennis, Loes Janssen and Kathleen Vohs (2009) present results of research that indicate the depletion of cognitive resources leads to less attentive and less critical acceptance of information, which in turn makes the individual more susceptible to social influence (see also Fennis & Aarts, 2012). That said, the issue of the link between ego-depletion and susceptibility to social influence techniques seems to be a complex one. Slawomir Spiewak (2002) demonstrated that some techniques (door-in-the-face and fear-then-relief) become ineffective in conditions of cognitive resource depletion. This is an area which undoubtedly requires further exploration.

Unethical social influence

Readers of this book have most certainly noticed that I have primarily addressed how to convince people to make a donation to a charitable cause, to complete psychological questionnaires, to attend a laboratory experiment, give blood or sign a petition to improve road traffic safety. It would be difficult to find something immoral in any of these activities. In essence, psychologists examine social influence primarily as it relates to the possibility of convincing people to behave in ethically positive or neutral ways.

This does not, however, mean that the psychological literature is totally devoid of research concerning the effectiveness of social influence techniques involving an attempt to convince people to do things that are clearly unethical. Examples are delivered by experiments on the "Imagine that . . ." technique described in Chapter 4. Let us recall that many studies have shown how successfully inducing people to imagine certain events with their participation (e.g. leaving for a holiday to another continent), we increase the chances that they will behave in that manner (in this case, they go on holiday). What happens if we convince someone to imagine engaging in an unethical manner? In two of her experiments Barbara Weigl (1990) demonstrated that if one suggests to children that they imagine cheating, and then they are exposed to the temptation to do so, they will engage in this moral transgression with far greater frequency and intensity than children exposed to an analogical temptation but without being previously induced to imagine themselves behaving unethically. However (thankfully!), we can use social influence techniques to achieve the opposite effect, meaning a reduction in the likelihood of cheating. Eric Spangenberg and Carl Obermiller (1996) asked their study participants if they could resist the temptation to cheat. As we remember from Chapter 4, people asked to state the probability of their engaging in a particular behaviour demonstrate a tendency to overestimate the likelihood of acting in a moral and socially desirable manner, while underestimating the frequency of immoral and undesirable actions. It thus comes as no surprise that in this case they estimated the likelihood of their own dishonesty as very low. The subjective certainty of overcoming temptation then led to participants less frequently taking advantage of the chance to cheat on a quiz compared to those in the control group. Very interesting studies exploring means of influencing the likelihood of unethical behaviours, described in Chapter 2 of this book, have also been conducted by Magdalena Paska (2002).

How to study social influence techniques. A short guide for students and novice researchers

A key element in all psychological experiments is randomization – the chance assignment of study participants to particular experimental conditions. Of course, this is equally crucial in research on social influence techniques. In studies that involve addressing people with a request (which is the case with social influence techniques) it is very important to eliminate the influence of the researcher's expectations regarding the reaction of the participant. If someone operates under the theory that people will be more inclined to agree to requests addressed to them than in other circumstances, at times the researcher can – entirely unintentionally – behave either more or less pleasantly, look straight into the eyes of participants in certain situations while avoiding their gaze in others, etc. In professional experiments the standard procedure is to engage people who are blind to the hypotheses tested, and to practise the course of the interaction with study participants beforehand so as to make their behaviours as similar as possible in comparable conditions.

What if an experiment of this nature is to be conducted by students of social psychology as part of their course work? And what if everyone knows the hypothesis that is being tested in that experiment? There is a way around this as well. Let us use a certain example. We may assume that the experiment concerns certain aspects of the sequential techniques you have read about in Chapter 2. We wish to explore a situation in which the first (initial) and second (target) requests are formulated by different people. In order to exclude the undesired effects described above, we should organize the experiment so that the individual formulating the target request does not know if he is addressing someone from the control group (i.e. people who did not hear the initial request) or from the experimental group (people who have already been exposed to a request). Of course, if the experiment plan is more complicated, such a person should not know which condition he is involved in. How to do this? The simplest way is to find the right place. Let us imagine that we are in the hallway of a building shaped like the letter 'L', or on a path of a similar shape. The experiment can be conducted by three people. Let us assume that they are occupying the positions shown in Figure 7.1

This allows person X to maintain eye contact with person A and person B, but persons A and B do not see each other. Let us assume that there is relatively little foot traffic along the hallway or the path, and we have decided to engage every fifth person passing by who appears to be an adult and is walking in such a way that he first passes person A, and then person B (but not B then A). Only experimenter X possesses a piece of paper with the results of the randomization determining which conditions a given participant will be assigned to; when experimenter X sees that a participant is approaching experimenter A, he gives him the appropriate signal. This signal could be something like removing his glasses, taking off his hat, or touching his hair using either his left or right arm. Every gesture is a different command issued to experimenter A. X can also communicate with A by mobile phone, giving him the necessary instructions. When a participant completes his interaction with person A, he heads towards person B (passing X along the way). X now communicates with B, telling him to approach the study participant. B does not know if this person is from the control conditions (thus already approached by A) or from one of the experimental conditions.

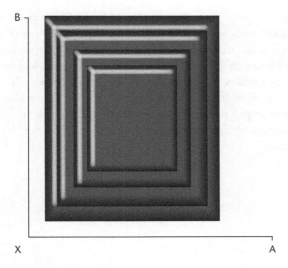

FIGURE 7.1   A, X, B – experimenters

Source: Image by author

Let us consider for a moment what experimenter B will ask the participant for. If it is money for a charitable purpose, then we may interrupt the experiment in the moment when the participant reaches for his wallet and explain that he is in a psychological experiment designed to examine if people in such conditions are inclined to help those in need. However, it seems to me that it would be better to make contact with some charity and really collect money for it. We can enrich our knowledge of psychology while directly helping people who can benefit from it. And what if the target request involves completing a long survey? From our perspective, the only important thing is whether participants agree to complete it and how many questions they respond to. But perhaps one of our colleagues is in the process of a survey-based study? Maybe we could help him gather some important data? And maybe – in exchange – he will agree to help us with our experiment? He says that he has no idea what we're exploring? He's not familiar with such studies? He's never done it before? That's even better!

★

Just a moment ago I received a phone call from a radio journalist. He wanted to discuss social influence techniques. He began by asking how many such techniques have been discovered by social psychologists. When I told him that I didn't know, he was surprised. After all, I should know. In reality, there is no way to answer this question. Human ingenuity is virtually unlimited. Practitioners of social influence are constantly inventing new tricks; psychologists are constantly engaging in experiments and presenting their results in scientific journals. Unfortunately, there is not a large amount of empirical studies dedicated to social influence, nor articles and books on the subject. Research by psychologists on people's real behaviour – as I wrote in the Introduction – is becoming less and less common. In writing this book I wished to acknowledge those psychologists who go against the grain conducting incredibly time-consuming and unfashionable experiments (computer and neuropsychological experiments are all the rage now). It is my hope that you will agree with me: what is unfashionable can, however, be interesting.

REFERENCES

Abrahams, M.F. & Bell, R.A. (1994). Encouraging charitable contributions: An examination of three models of door-in-the-face compliance. *Communication Research, 21*, 131–153.

Algulera, D.C. (1967). Relationships between physical contact and verbal interaction between nurses and patients. *Journal of Psychiatric Nursing, 5*, 5–21.

Apsler, R. (1975). Effects of embarrassment on behaviour toward others. *Journal of Personality and Social Psychology, 32*, 145–153.

Argyle, M. & Henderson, M. (1984). The rules of friendship. *Journal of Social and Personal Relationships, 1*, 211–237.

Aronson, E. (1969). A theory of cognitive dissonance: A current perspective. In L. Berkowitz (Ed.), *Advances in experimental social psychology* (vol. 4, pp. 1–34). New York: Academic Press.

Aronson, E. (1997). The theory of cognitive dissonance: The evolution and vicissitudes of an idea. In C. McGarty & S.A. Haslam (Eds), *The message of social psychology* (pp. 20–36). Oxford: Blackwell Publishers.

Aronson, E., Fried, C. & Stone, J. (1991). Overcoming denial and increasing the use of condoms through the induction of hypocrisy. *American Journal of Public Health, 81*, 1636–1638.

Aune, R.K. & Basil, M.D. (1994). A relational obligations approach to the foot-in-the-mouth effect. *Journal of Applied Social Psychology, 24*, 546–556.

Back, K.W., Bogdonoff, M.D., Shaw, D.M. & Klein, R.F. (1963). An interpretation of experimental conformity through physiological measures. *Behavioral Science, 8*, 34–40.

Baek, T.H. & Reid, L.N. (2013). The interplay of mood and regulatory focus in influencing altruistic behavior. *Psychology and Marketing, 30*, 635–646.

Baker, J., Levy, M. & Grewal, D. (1992). An experimental approach to making retail store environmental decisions. *Journal of Retailing, 68*, 445–460.

Baron, R.S. (2000). Arousal, capacity, and intense indoctrination. *Personality and Social Psychology Review, 4*, 238–255.

Baron, R.S. & Moore, D.L. (1987). The impact of exercise induced arousal on social cognition. *Social Cognition, 5*, 166–177.

Bateson, M., Nettle, D. & Roberts, G. (2006). Cues of being watched enhance cooperation in a real-world setting. *Biology Letters, 2*, 412–414.

Baumeister, R.F., Reis, H.T. & Delespaul, P.A.E.G. (1995). Subjective and experiential correlates of guilt in daily life. *Personality and Social Psychology Bulletin, 21,* 1256–1268.

Baumeister, R.F. & Tice, D.M. (1990). Anxiety and social exclusion. *Journal of Social and Clinical Psychology, 9,* 165–195.

Baumeister, R.F., Vohs, K.D. & Funder, D.C. (2007). Psychology as the science of self-reports and finger movements: Whatever happened to actual behavior? *Perspectives on Psychological Science, 2,* 396–403.

Beaman, A.L., Cole, C.M., Preston, M., Klentz, B. & Steblay, N.M. (1983). Fifteen years of foot-in-the-door research: A meta-analysis. *Personality and Social Psychology Bulletin, 9,* 181–196.

Bell, R.A. & Cholerton, M. (1994). Encouraging donations to charity: A field study of competing and complementary factors in tactic sequencing. *Western Journal of Communication, 58,* 98–115.

Bem, D.J. (1967). Self-perception: An alternative interpretation of cognitive dissonance phenomena. *Psychological Review, 74,* 183–200.

Bem, D.J. (1972). Self-perception theory. In L. Berkowitz (Ed.), *Advances in Experimental Social Psychology* (vol. 6, pp. 1–62). New York: Academic Press.

Berkowitz, L. (1993). *Aggression: Its causes, consequences, and control.* New York: McGraw-Hill.

Bodenhausen, G.V. (1993). Emotions, arousal, and stereotypic judgments: A heuristic model of affect and stereotyping. In D.M. Mackie & D.L. Hamilton (Eds), *Affect, cognition, and stereotyping: Interactive processes in group perception* (pp. 13–37). San Diego, CA: Academic Press.

Bolkan, S. & Andersen, P.A. (2009). Image induction and social influence: Explication and initial tests. *Basic and Applied Social Psychology, 31,* 317–324.

Boster, F.J. & Mongeau, P. (1984). Fear-arousing persuasive messages. *Communication Yearbook, 8,* 330–375.

Boster, F.J., Shaw, A.S., Hughes, M., Kotowski, M.R., Strom, R.E. & Deatrick, L.M. (2009). Dump-and-chase: The effectiveness of persistence as a sequential request compliance-gaining strategy. *Communication Studies, 60,* 219–234.

Bower, G. H. (1981). Mood and memory. *American Psychologist, 36,* 129–148.

Bower, G.H., Monteiro, K.P. & Gilligan, S.G. (1971). Emotional mood as context for learning and recall. *Journal of Verbal Learning and Verbal Behavior, 17,* 573–585.

Bowerman, W.R. (1978). Subjective competence: The structure, process and function of self-relevant causal attributions. *Journal of the Theory of Social Behavior, 8,* 45–57.

Bradley, G.W. (1978). Self-serving biases in the attribution process: A reexamination of the fact or fiction question. *Journal of Personality and Social Psychology, 36,* 56–71.

Brehm, J.W. (1966). *A theory of psychological reactance.* New York: Academic Press.

Brennan, I. & Bahn, K.D. (1991). Door-in-the-face, that's-not all, and legitimizing a paltry contribution: Reciprocity, contrast effect and social judgment theory explanations. *Advances in Consumer Research, 18,* 586–590.

Brockner, J., Pressman, B., Cabitt, J. & Moran, P. (1982). Nonverbal intimacy, sex, and compliance: A field study. *Journal of Nonverbal Behavior, 6,* 253–258.

Brooks, C., Church, M. & Fraser, L. (1986). Effects of duration of eye contact on judgments of personality characteristics. *Journal of Social Psychology, 126,* 71–78.

Bull, R. & Gibson-Robinson, E. (1981). The influence of eye-gaze, style of dress, and locality on the amounts of money donated to charity. *Human Relations, 34,* 895–905.

Burger, J.M. (1986). Increasing compliance by improving the deal: The that's-not-all technique. *Journal of Personality and Social Psychology, 51,* 277–283.

Burger, J.M. (1999). The foot-in-the-door compliance procedure: A multiple-process analysis and review. *Personality and Social Psychology Review, 3,* 303–325.

Burger, J.M. (2007). Fleeting attraction and compliance with request. In A.R. Pratkanis (Ed.), *The science of social influence: Advances and future progress.* (pp. 155–166). New York and Hove: Psychology Press.

Burger, J.M., Hornisher, J., Martin, V., Newman, G. & Pringle, S. (2007). The pique technique: Overcoming mindlessness or shifting heuristics? *Journal of Applied Social Psychology, 37*, 2086–2096.

Burger, J.M., Messian, N., Patel, S., del Prado, A. & Anderson, C. (2004). What a coincidence! The effects of incidental similarity on compliance. *Personality and Social Psychology, 30*, 35–43.

Burger, J.M. & Petty, R.E. (1981). The low-ball compliance technique: Task or person commitment? *Journal of Personality and Social Psychology, 40*, 492–500

Burger, J.M., Soroka, S., Gonzago, K., Murphy, E. & Somervell, E. (2001). The effect of fleeting attraction on compliance to requests. *Personality and Social Psychology Bulletin, 27*, 1578–1586.

Campbell, J.D. (1990). Self-esteem and clarity of the self-concept. *Journal of Personality and Social Psychology, 59*, 538–549.

Cann, A. & Blackwelder, J.G. (1984). Compliance and mood: A field investigation of the impact of embarrassment. *Journal of Psychology, 117*, 221–226.

Cann, A., Sherman, S.J. & Elkes, R. (1975). Effects of initial request size and timing of a second request on compliance: The foot in the door and the door in the face. *Journal of Personality and Social Psychology, 32*, 774–782.

Cantrill, J.G. & Seibold, D.R. (1986). The perceptual contrast explanation of sequential request strategy effectiveness. *Human Communication Research, 13*, 253–267.

Carli, L. (1990). Gender, language, and influence. *Journal of Personality and Social Psychology, 59*, 941–951.

Carlsmith, J.M. & Gross, A.E. (1969). Some effects of guilt on compliance. *Journal of Personality and Social Psychology, 11*, 232–239.

Carpenter, C.J. & Boster, F.J. (2009a). *A cognitive processing explanation of the disrupt-then-reframe compliance gaining technique.* Paper presented at the International Communication Association Convention, Chicago, IL.

Carpenter, C.J. & Boster, F.J. (2009b). A meta-analysis of the effectiveness of the disrupt-then-reframe compliance gaining technique. *Communication Reports, 22*, 55–62.

Carroll, J.S. (1978). The effect of imagining an event on expectations for the event: An interpretation in terms of availability heuristic. *Journal of Experimental Social Psychology, 14*, 88–96.

Chaiken, S., Liberman, A. & Eagly, A.H. (1989). Heuristic and systematic processing within and beyond the persuasion context. In J.S. Uleman & J.A. Bargh (Eds), *Unintended thought* (pp. 212–252). New York: Guilford Press.

Chaiken, S. & Stangor, C. (1987). Attitudes and attitude change. *Annual Review of Psychology 38*, 573–630.

Chartrand, T. & Bargh, J.A. (1999). The Chameleon effect: The perception-behavior link and social interaction. *Journal of Personality and Social Psychology, 76*, 893–910.

Cialdini, R.B. (1980). Full-cycle social psychology. *Applied Social Psychology Annual, 1*, 21–45.

Cialdini, R.B. (2001). *Influence. Science and practice* (4th edn). Needham Heights, MA: Allyn & Bacon.

Cialdini, R.B. (2009). We have to break up. *Perspectives on Psychological Science, 4*, 5–6.

Cialdini, R.B., Borden, R.J., Thorne, A., Walker, M.R., Freeman, S. & Sloan, L.R. (1976). Basking in reflected glory: Three (football) field studies. *Journal of Personality and Social Psychology, 34*, 366–375.

Cialdini, R.B., Cacioppo, J.T., Bassett, R. & Miller, J.A. (1978). Low-ball procedure for producing compliance: Commitment then cost. *Journal of Personality and Social Psychology, 36*, 463–476.

Cialdini, R.B., Darby, B.L. & Vincent, J.E. (1973). Transgression and altruism: A case for hedonism. *Journal of Experimental Social Psychology, 9*, 502–516.

Cialdini, R.B. & Sagarin, B.J. (2005). Interpersonal influence. In T. Brock & M. Green (Eds), *Persuasion: Psychological insights and perspectives* (pp. 143–169). Newbury Park, CA: Sage Press.

Cialdini, R.B. & Schroeder, D. (1976). Increasing compliance by legitimizing paltry contributions: When even a penny helps. *Journal of Personality and Social Psychology, 34*, 599–604.

Cialdini, R.B., Trost, M.R. & Newsom, J.T. (1995). Preference for consistency: The development of a valid measure and the discovery of surprising behavioral implications. *Journal of Personality and Social Psychology, 69*, 318–328.

Cialdini, R.B., Vincent, J.E., Lewis, S.K., Catalan, J., Wheeler, D. & Darby, B.L. (1975). Reciprocal concessions procedure for inducing compliance: The door-in-the-face technique. *Journal of Personality and Social Psychology, 31*, 206–215.

Clark, H.H. (1985). Language use and language users. In G. Lindzey & E. Aronson (Eds) *Handbook of social psychology* (vol. 2, pp. 179–231). New York: Random House.

Clark, H.H. & Schunk, D. (1980). Polite responses to polite requests. *Cognition, 8*, 111–143.

Clark, M.S. & Isen, M. A. (1982). Toward understanding the relationship between feeling states and social behavior. In A. H. Hastorf & A. M. Isen (Eds), *Cognitive social psychology* (pp. 73–108). New York: Elsevier.

Cook, M. & Smith, M.C. (1975). The role of gaze in impression formation. *British Journal of Social and Clinical Psychology, 14*, 19–25.

Corfield, V.K. (1969). The role of arousal and cognitive complexity in susceptibility to social influence. *Journal of Personality, 37*, 554–566.

Cornelissen, G., Dewitte, S. & Warlop, L. (2007). Whatever people say I am that's what I am: Social labeling as a social marketing tool. *International Journal of Research in Marketing, 24*, 278–288.

Crano, W.D. & Sivacek, J. (1982). Social reinforcement, self-attribution, and the foot-in-the-door phenomenon. *Social Cognition, 1*, 110–125.

Cunningham, M.R. (1979). Weather, mood and helping behavior: Quasi experiments with sunshine Samaritan. *Journal of Personality and Social Psychology, 37*, 1947–1956.

Cunningham, M.R., Schaffer, D.R., Barbee, A.P., Wolff, P.L. & Kelley, D.J. (1990). Separate processes in the elation and depression to helping: Social versus personal concerns. *Journal of Experimental Social Psychology, 26*, 13–33.

Cunningham, M.R., Steinberg, J. & Grev, R. (1980). Wanting to and having to help: Separate motivations for positive mood and guilt-induced helping. *Journal of Personality and Social Psychology, 38*, 181–192.

Czapinski, J. (1993). *Polski Generalny Sondaz Dobrostanu Psychicznego.* [*Polish General Survey of Well-Being*] Warszawa -Olsztyn: Pracownia Wydawnicza Polskiego Towarzystwa Psychologicznego.

Darley, J. (1966). Fear and social comparison as determinants of conformity behavior. *Journal of Personality and Social Psychology, 4*, 73–78.

Darlington, R.B. & Macker, C.E. (1966). Displacement of guilt-produced altruistic behavior. *Journal of Personality and Social Psychology, 4*, 442–443.

Davis, B.P. & Knowles, E.S. (1999). A disrupt-then-reframe technique of social influence. *Journal of Personality and Social Psychology, 76*, 192–199.

deCharms, R. (1968). *Personal causation: The internal affective determinants of behavior.* New York: Academic Press.

DeJong, W. (1979). An examination of self-perception mediation of the foot-in-the-door effect. *Journal of Personality and Social Psychology, 37*, 2221–2239.

DeJong, W. & Musilli, L. (1982). External pressure to comply. Handicapped vs. nonhandicapped requesters and the foot-in-the-door phenomenon. *Personality and Social Psychology Bulletin, 8,* 522–527.

DeJong, W. & Oopik, A.J. (1992). Effect of legitimizing small contributions and labeling potential donors as 'helpers' on responses to a direct mail solicitation for charity. *Psychological Reports, 71,* 923–928.

Denny, M.R. (Ed.). (1991). *Fear, avoidance, and phobias: A fundamental analysis.* Hillsdale, NJ: Erlbaum.

Dickerson, C.A., Thibodeau, R., Aronson, E. & Miller, D. (1992). Using cognitive dissonance to encourage water conservation. *Journal of Applied Social Psychology, 22,* 841–854.

Dillard, J.P. (1990). Self-inference and the foot-in-the-door technique: Quantity of behavior and attitudinal mediation. *Human Communication Research, 16,* 442–447.

Dillard, J.P., Hunter, J.E. & Burgoon, M. (1984). Sequential request persuasive strategies: Meta-analysis of foot-in-the-door and door-in-the-face. *Human Communication Research, 10,* 461–488.

Dolinska, B. & Dolinski, D. (2006). To command or to ask? Gender and effectiveness of "thought" vs "soft" compliance-gaining strategies. *Social Influence, 1,* 48–57.

Dolinski, D. (1996). The mystery of the Polish soul. B.W. Johnson's effect a rebours. *European Journal of Social Psychology, 26,* 1001–1005.

Dolinski, D. (2000). On inferring one's beliefs from one's attempts and consequences for subsequent compliance. *Journal of Personality and Social Psychology, 78,* 260–272.

Dolinski, D. (2005). *Techniki wpływu społecznego* [*Techniques of social influence*] Warszawa: Scholar.

Dolinski, D. (2009). People in a freezer: Self-perception as an explanatory mechanism for the effectiveness of the foot-in-the-door technique. *Polish Psychological Bulletin, 40,* 113–116.

Dolinski, D. (2010). Touch, compliance, and homophobia. *Journal of Nonverbal Behavior, 34,* 179–192.

Dolinski, D. (2011). A rock or a hard place: The foot-in-the-face technique for inducing compliance without pressure. *Journal of Applied Social Psychology, 41,* 1514–1537.

Dolinski, D. (2012). The nature of the first small request as a decisive factor in the effectiveness of the foot-in-the-door technique. *Applied Psychology: An International Review, 61,* 437–453.

Dolinski, D., Ciszek, M., Godlewski, K. & Zawadzki, M. (2002). Fear-then-relief, mindlessness, and cognitive deficits. *European Journal of Social Psychology, 32,* 435–447.

Dolinski, D., Gromski, W. & Szmajke, A. (1988). Perpetrator's freedom of choice as a determinant of responsibility attribution. *Journal of Social Psychology, 128,* 697–710.

Dolinski, D., Grzyb, T., Olejnik, J., Prusakowski, S. & Urban, K. (2005). Let's dialogue about penny. *Journal of Applied Social Psychology, 35,* 1150–1170.

Dolinski, D. & Nawrat, R. (1998). Fear-then-relief procedure for producing compliance. Beware when the danger is over. *Journal of Experimental Social Psychology, 34,* 27–50.

Dolinski, D., Nawrat, M. & Rudak, I. (2001). Dialogue involvement as a social influence technique. *Personality and Social Psychology Bulletin, 27,* 1395–1406.

Dolinski, D. & Odachowska, E. (2015). *Beware when danger on the road has passed: The state of relief impairs a driver's ability to avoid accidents.* Manuscript submitted for publication.

Droney, J. & Brooks, C. (1993). Attributions of self-esteem as a function of duration of eye contact. *Journal of Social Psychology, 133,* 715–722.

Duval, S. & Wicklund, R.A. (1972). *A theory of objective self-awareness.* New York: Academic Press.

Ebster, C. & Neumayr, B. (2008). Applying the door-in-the-face compliance technique to retailing. *Review of Retail, Distribution and Consumer Research, 18,* 121–128.

Eisenberg, N., Cialdini, R.B., McCreath, H. & Shell, R. (1987). Consistency based compliance: When and why children become vulnerable. *Journal of Personality and Social Psychology, 52*, 1174–1181.

Ellsworth, P.C. & Langer, E. (1976). Staring and approach: An interpretation of the stare as a nonspecific activator. *Journal of Personality and Social Psychology, 33*, 117–122.

Erickson, M.H. (1964). The confusion technique in hypnosis. *American Journal of Clinical Hypnosis, 6*, 183–207.

Ernest, R.C. & Cooper, R.E. (1974). "Hey mister, do you have any change?" Two real world studies of proxemic effects on compliance with a mundane request. *Personality and Social Psychology Bulletin, 1*, 158–159.

Escalas, J.E. & Luce, M.F. (2003). Process versus outcome thought-focus and advertising. *Journal of Consumer Psychology, 13*, 246–254.

Escalas, J.E. & Luce, M.F. (2004). Understanding the effects of process-focused versus outcome focused thought in response to advertising. *Journal of Consumer Research, 31*, 274–285.

Feeley, T. H., Anker, A. E. & Aloe, A. (2012). The Door-in-the-Face Persuasive Message Strategy: A Meta-Analysis of the first 35 Years. *Communication Monographs, 79*, 316–343.

Fennis, B.M. & Aarts, H. (2012). Revisiting the agentic shift: Weakening personal control increases susceptibility to social influence. *European Journal of Social Psychology, 42*, 824–831.

Fennis, B.M., Das, E.H.H.J. & Pruyn, A. Th. H. (2004). "If you can't dazzle them with brilliance, baffle them with nonsense": Extending the impact of the disrupt-then-reframe technique of social influence. *Journal of Consumer Psychology, 14*, 280–290.

Fennis, B.M., Janssen, L. & Vohs, K. (2009). Acts of benevolence: A limited-resource account of compliance with charitable requests. *Journal of Consumer Research, 35*, 906–924.

Fern, E.F., Monroe, K.B. & Avila, R.A. (1986). Effectiveness of multiple request strategies: A synthesis of research results. *Journal of Marketing Research, 23*, 144–152.

Festinger, L. (1957). *A theory of cognitive dissonance.* Evanston, IL: Row, Peterson.

Finkiel, E.J. & Baumeister, R.F. (2010). *Advanced social psychology: The state of the science.* Oxford: Oxford University Press.

Firmin, M.W., Helmick, J.M., Iezzi, B.A. & Vaughn, A. (2004). Say please: The effect of the word "please" in compliance-seeking request. *Social Behavior and Personality, 32*, 67–72.

Fisher, J., Rytting, M. & Heslin, R. (1976). Hands touching hands: Affective and evaluative effects on interpersonal touch. *Sociometry, 39*, 416–421.

Fointiat, V. (2000). 'Foot-in-the-mouth' versus 'door-in-the-face' requests. *Journal of Social Psychology, 140*, 264–266.

Fointiat, V. (2004). "I know what I have to do, but . . ." When hypocrisy leads to behavioural change. *Social Behavior and Personality, 32*, 741–746.

Fointiat, V. (2008). Being together in a situation of induced hypocrisy. *Current Research in Social Psychology, 13*, 443–451.

Fointiat, V., Somat, A. & Grosbras, J-M. (2011). Saying, but not doing: Induced hypocrisy, trivialization and misattribution. *Social Behavior and Personality, 39*, 465–476.

Forgas, J.P. (1998). Asking nicely? The effects of mood on responding to more or less polite requests. *Personality and Social Psychology Bulletin, 24*, 173–185.

Freedman, J.L. & Fraser, S. (1966). Compliance without pressure: The foot in the door technique. *Journal of Personality and Social Psychology, 4*, 195–202.

Freedman, J.L., Wallington, S.A. & Bless, E. (1967). Compliance without pressure: The effects of guilt. *Journal of Personality and Social Psychology, 7*, 117–124.

Fried, C. (1998). Hypocrisy and identification with transgressions: A case of undetected dissonance. *Basic and Applied Social Psychology, 20*, 145–154.

Frijda, N.H. (1986). *The emotions: Studies in emotion and social interaction.* Paris: Maison de Sciences de l'Homme and Cambridge University Press.

Gamian-Wilk, M. & Dolinski, D. (2015). *Compliance without pressure: The role of self-perception in the mechanism of the foot-in-the-door strategy.* Manuscript submitted for publication.

Garner, R. (2005). What's in a name? Persuasion perhaps. *Journal of Consumer Psychology, 15*, 108–116.

Gass, R.H. & Seiter, J.S. (2011). *Persuasion, social influence, and compliance gaining* (4th edn). Boston, MA: Allyn & Bacon.

Gilbert, D.T. (1991). How mental systems believe. *American Psychologist, 46*, 107–119.

Gilbert, D.T. (1995). Attribution and interpersonal perception. In A. Tesser (Ed.), *Advanced social psychology* (pp. 99–147). Boston, MA: McGraw-Hill.

Gilbert, S.J. (1981). Another look at the Milgram obedience studies: The role of gradated series of shocks. *Personality and Social Psychology Bulletin, 7*, 690–695.

Goffman, E. (1959). *The presentation of self in everyday life.* Garden City and New York: Doubleday.

Goldman, B.M. (2006). Making diamonds out of coal: The role of authenticity of healthy (optimal) self-esteem and psychological functioning. In M.H. Kernis (Ed.), *Self-esteem issues and answers. A sourcebook of current perspectives.* (pp. 132–139). New York: Psychology Press.

Goldman, M. (1986). Compliance employing a combined foot-in-the-door and door-in-the-face procedure. *Journal of Applied Social Psychology, 126*, 11–116.

Goldman, M. & Fordyce, J. (1983). Prosocial behavior as affected by eye contact, touch, and voice expression. *Journal of Social Psychology, 121*, 125–129.

Goldman, M., Kiyohara, O. & Pfannensteil, D.A. (1985). Interpersonal touch, social labeling, and the foot-in-the-door effect. *Journal of Social Psychology, 152*, 143–147.

Goldman, M., Seever, M. & Seever, M. (1982). Social labeling and the foot-in-the-door effect. *Journal of Social Psychology, 117*, 19–23.

Gorassini, D.R. & Olson, J.M. (1995). Does self-perception change explain the foot-in-the-door effect? *Journal of Personality and Social Psychology, 69*, 91–105.

Gottlieb, J. & Carver, C.S. (1980). Anticipation of future interaction and the bystander effect. *Journal of Experimental Social Psychology, 16*, 253–260.

Gouldner, A.W. (1960). The norm of reciprocity: A preliminary statement. *American Sociological Review, 25*, 161–178.

Greenwald, A.G. & Banaji, M.R. (1995). Implicit social cognition: Attitudes, self-esteem, and stereotypes. *Psychological Review, 102*, 4–27.

Greenwald, A.G., Carnot, C.G., Beach, R. & Young, B. (1987). Increasing voting behavior by asking people if they expect to vote. *Journal of Applied Psychology, 72*, 315–318.

Gregory, W.L., Cialdini, R.B. & Carpenter, K.M. (1982). Self-relevant scenarios as mediators of likelihood estimates and compliance: Does imagining make it so? *Journal of Personality and Social Psychology, 43*, 89–99.

Gueguen, N. (2001). Social labelling and compliance: An evaluation of the link between the label and the request. *Social Behaviour and Personality, 29*, 743–748.

Gueguen, N. (2002). Status, apparel and touch: Their joint effects on compliance to a request. *North American Journal of Psychology, 4*, 279–286.

Gueguen, N. (2003). Fund-raising on the web: The effect of an electronic door-in-the-face technique on compliance to a request. *CyberPsychology and Behavior, 6*, 189–193.

Gueguen, N. (2013a). "Even a donation one time in your life will help . . .": The effect of the legitimization paltry contribution technique on blood donation. *Transfusion and Apheresis Science, 49*, 489–493.

Gueguen, N. (2013b). Handshaking and compliance with a request: A door-to-door setting. *Social Behavior and Personality, 41*, 1585–1588.

Gueguen, N. & Jacob, C. (2002). Direct look versus evasive glance and compliance with a request. *Journal of Social Psychology, 142*, 393–396.

Gueguen, N., Joule, R-V., Courbet, D., Halimi-Falkowicz, S. & Marchand, M. (2013). Repeating "yes" in a first request and compliance with a later request: The fourth walls technique. *Social Behavior and Personality, 41*, 199–202.

Gueguen, N., Joule, R-V., Halmi-Falkowicz, S., Pascual, A., Fisher-Lokou, J. & Dufcorcq-Brana, M. (2013). I'm free but I'll comply with your request: generalization and multidimensional effects of the "evoking freedom" technique. *Journal of Applied Social Psychology, 43*, 116–137.

Gueguen, N. & Lamy, L. (2013). Whether and helping: Additional evidence of the effect of sunshine Samaritan. *Journal of Social Psychology, 153*, 123–126.

Gueguen, N., Martin, A. & Meineri, S. (2013). "Even a single marble will make him/her happy . . .": Further evidence and extension of the legitimizing paltry contribution technique on helping. *Social Influence, 8*, 18–26.

Gueguen, N., Meineri, S. & Charles-Sire, V. (2010). Improving medication adherence by using practitioner nonverbal techniques: A field experiment on the effect of touch. *Journal of Behavioral Medicine, 33*, 466–473.

Gueguen, N., Meineri, S. & Stefan, J. (2012). "Say it with flowers" . . . to female drivers: Hitchhikers holding flowers and driver behavior. *North American Journal of Psychology, 14*, 623–628.

Gueguen, N. & Pascual, A. (2000). Evocation of freedom and compliance: The "But you are free of . . ." technique. *Current Research in Social Psychology, 5*, 264–270.

Gueguen, N. & Pascual, A. (2005). Improving the response rate to street survey: An evaluation of the "But you are free to accept or to refuse" technique. *Psychological Record, 55*, 297–303.

Gueguen, N., Pichot, N. & Le Dreff, G. (2005). Similarity and helping behavior on the web: The impact of convergence of surnames between a solicitor and a subject in a request made by e-mail. *Journal of Applied Social Psychology, 35*, 423–429.

Gueguen, N. & Vion, M. (2009). The effect of practitioner's touch on a patient's medication compliance. *Psychology, Health and Medicine, 14*, 689–694.

Hall, E.T. (1969). *The hidden dimension*. New York: Doubleday.

Harris, M.B. (1972). The effects of performing one altruistic act on the likelihood of performing another. *Journal of Social Psychology, 88*, 65–73.

Henley, N. & LaFrance, M. (1984). Gender and culture: Difference and dominance in nonverbal behavior. In A. Wolfgang (Ed.), *Nonverbal behavior: Perspectives, applications, intercultural insights* (pp. 351–357). Ashland, AL: Hogrefe & Huber Publishers.

Henley, N.M. (1973). Status and sex: Some touching observations. *Bulletin of the Psychonomic Society, 2*, 91–93.

Herling-Grudzinski, G. (1965). *Inny swiat. [A different world]*. Paris: Institut Literaire S.A.R.I.

Heslin, R., Nguyen, T.D. & Nguyen, M.L. (1983). Meaning of touch: The case of touch from a stranger or same sex person. *Journal of Nonverbal Behavior, 7*, 145–157.

Higgins, E.T. (1996). Knowledge activation: Accessibility, applicability, and salience. In E.T. Higgins & A.W. Kruglanski (Eds), *Social psychology: Handbook of basic principles* (pp. 133–168). New York: Guilford.

Hornik, J. (1987). The effect of touch and gaze upon compliance and interest of interviewers. *Journal of Social Psychology, 127*, 681–683.

Hornik, J. & Ellis, S. (1988). Strategies to secure compliance for a mall intercept interview. *Public Opinion Quarterly, 52*, 539–551.

Hornik, J. & Zaig, T. (1991). Reducing refusals in telephone surveys on sensitive topics. *Journal of Advertising Research, 31*, 49–56.

Hornik, J., Zaig, T. & Shadmon, D. (1991). Comparison of three inducement techniques to improve compliance in a health survey conducted by telephone. *Public Health Reports, 105*, 524–529.

Howard, D.J. (1990). The influence of verbal responses to common greetings on compliance behavior: The foot-in-the-mouth effect. *Journal of Applied Social Psychology, 20*, 1185–1196.

Howard, D.J. (1995). 'Chaining' the use of influence strategies for producing compliance behavior. *Journal of Social Behavior and Personality, 10*, 169–185.

Howard, D.J. & Gengler, C. (1995). Motivating compliance with a request by remembering someone's name. *Psychological Reports, 77*, 123–129.

Howard, D.J., Gengler, C. & Jain, A. (1995). What's in a name? A complimentary means of persuasion. *Journal of Consumer Research, 22*, 200–211.

Howard, D.J., Gengler, C. & Jain, A. (1997). The name remembrance effect: A test of alternative explanations. *Journal of Social Behavior and Personality, 12*, 801–810.

Isen, A.M. (1984). Toward understanding role of affect on cognition. In R. Wyer, T. Srull & A.M. Isen (Eds), *Handbook of social cognition* (vol. 3, pp. 179–236). Hillsdale, NJ: Erlbaum.

Isen, A.M. & Levin, P.F. (1972). The effect of feeling good on helping: cookies and kindness. *Journal of Personality and Social Psychology, 21*, 384–388.

Isen, A.M. & Geva, N. (1987). The influence of positive affect on acceptable level of risk and thoughts about losing: The person with a large canoe has a large worry. *Organizational Behavior and Human Decision Processes, 39*, 145–154.

Isen, A.M. & Simmonds, S.F. (1978). The effect of feeling good on a helping task that is incompatible with good mood. *Social Psychology, 41*, 345–349.

Izard, C.E. (1977). *Human emotions.* New York and London: Plenum Press.

Jacob, C., Charles-Sire, V. & Gueguen, N. (2013). "Even a single package of pastas will help . . .": The effect of the legitimization paltry contribution technique on altruism. *Nonprofit and Voluntary Sector Quarterly, 4*, 828–836.

Jacob, C., Gueguen, N., Martin, A. & Boulbry, G. (2011). Retail salespeople's mimicry of customers: Effects on consumer behavior. *Journal of Retailing and Consumer Services, 18*, 381–388.

Janis, I.L. & Feshbach, S. (1953). Effects of fear-arousing communications. *Journal of Abnormal and Social Psychology, 48*, 78–92.

Jankowski, K.F. & Takahashi, H. (2014). Cognitive neuroscience of social emotions and implications for psychopathology: Examining embarrassment, guilt, envy, and schadenfreude. *Psychiatry and Clinical Neurosciences, 68*, 319–336.

Jensen, J. D., King, A. J. & Carcioppolo, N. (2013). Driving toward a goal and the goal-gradient hypothesis: the impact of goal proximity on compliance rate, donation size, and fatigue. *Journal of Applied Social Psychology, 43*, 1881–1895.

Jiang, L., Hoegg, J., Dahl, D.W. & Chattopadhyay, A. (2010). The persuasive role of incidental similarity on attitudes and purchase intentions in a sales context. *Journal of Consumer Research, 36*, 778–791.

Johnson, W.B. (1937). Euphoric and depressed mood in normal subjects. *Character and Personality, 6*, 79–98.

Joule, R.V. (1987). Tobacco deprivation: The foot-in-the-door technique versus the low-ball technique. *European Journal of Social Psychology, 17*, 361–365.

Joule, R.V., Gouilloux, F. & Weber, F. (1989). The lure: A new compliance procedure. *Journal of Social Psychology, 129*, 741–749.

Kakar, S. (1976). Curiosity in children and adults: A review essay. *Indian Journal of Psychology*, 51, 181–201.

Kardes, F.R., Fennis, B.M., Hirt, E.R., Tormala, Z.L. & Bullington, B. (2007). The role of need for cognitive closure in the effectiveness of the disrupt-then-reframe influence technique. *Journal of Consumer Research, 36*, 1033–1049.

Kelln, B.R.C. & Ellard, J.H. (1999). An equity theory analysis of the impact of forgiveness and retribution on transgressor compliance. *Personality and Social Psychology Bulletin, 25*, 864–873.

Kenrick, D.T. & Gutierres, S.E. (1980). Contrast effect and judgments of physical attractiveness. When beauty becomes a social problem. *Journal of Personality and Social Psychology, 38*, 131–140.

Kiesler, C.A. (1971). *The psychology of commitment*. Academic Press: New York.

Kitayama, S. & Karasawa, M. (1997). Implicit self-esteem in Japan: Name letters and birthday numbers. *Personality and Social Psychology Bulletin, 23*, 736–742.

Kleinke, C.L. (1977). Compliance to request made by gazing and touching experiments in field settings. *Journal of Experimental Social Psychology, 13*, 218–223.

Kleinke, C.L. (1980). Interaction between gaze and legitimacy of request on compliance in a field setting. *Journal of Nonverbal Behavior, 5*, 3–12.

Kleinke, C.L. & Singer, D.A. (1979). Influence of gaze on compliance with demanding and conciliatory request in field setting. *Personality and Social Psychology Bulletin, 5*, 386–390.

Knowles, E. S., Butler, S. & Linn, J. A. (2001). Increasing compliance by reducing resistance. In J. P. Forgas & K. D. Williams (Eds), *Social influence: Direct and indirect processes* (pp. 41–60). New York: Psychology Press.

Kojima, S. (1994). Psychological approach to consumer buying decisions: Analysis of the psychological purse and psychology of price. *Japanese Psychological Research, 36*, 10–19.

Konoske, P., Staple, S. & Graf, R.G. (1979). Compliant reactions to guilt: Self-esteem or self-punishment. *Journal of Social Psychology, 108*, 207–211.

Koole, S.L., Dijksterhuis, A. & van Knippenberg, A. (2001). What's in a name: Implicit self-esteem and automatic self. *Journal of Personality and Social Psychology, 80*, 669–685.

Koole, S.L. & Pelham, B.W. (2003). On the nature of implicit self-esteem: The case of the name letter effect. In S.J. Spencer, S. Fein, M.P. Zanna & J.M. Olson (Eds), *Motivated social perception: The Ontario Symposium* (vol. 9, pp. 93–116). Mahwah, NJ: Erlbaum.

Koscielniak, R. (1998). *Wpływ autoprezentacji na uległość. [The influence of self-presentational motives on compliance]* Unpublished master thesis. Wroclaw University.

Kraut, R.E. (1973). Effects of social labelling on giving to charity. *Journal of Experimental Social Psychology, 9*, 551–562.

Kruglanski, A.W. (1989). *Lay epistemic and human knowledge: Cognitive and motivational bases*. New York: Plenum Press.

Kruglanski, A. W. & Webster, D. M. (1996). Motivated closing of the mind: "Seizing" and` "freezing". *Psychological Review, 103*, 263–283.

Kubala, I. (2002). 420 sekund to mniej niż 7 minut. Eksploracja zakresu efektywności techniki, Dobrze To Rozegraj". [420 seconds is less than 7 minutes. Empirical exploration into disrupt-then-reframe technique]. *Studia Psychologiczne, 40*, 111–125.

Kulbat, J. (2003). *Strategie selekcji obiektow wpływu spolecznego [Strategies of selections of social influence targets]*. Unpublished doctoral thesis., University of Opole, Poland.

Kulesza, W., Dolinski, D., Huisman, A. & Majewski, R. (2014). The echo effect: The power of verbal mimicry to influence pro-social behavior. *Journal of Language and Social Psychology, 33*, 185–203.

Kulesza, W., Szypowska, Z., Jarman, M & Dolinski, D. (2014). Attractive chameleons sell: The mimicry-attractiveness link. *Psychology and Marketing, 31*, 549–561.

Lacey, B.C. & Lacey, J.I. (1978). Two-way communication between the heart and the brain: Significance of time within cardiac cycle. *American Psychologist, 33,* 99–113.

Langer, E.J. (1978). Rethinking the role of thought in social interaction. In J.H. Harvey, W.I. Ickes & R.F. Kidd (Eds), *New directions in attribution research* (vol. 2, pp. 35–58). Hillsdale, NJ: Erlbaum.

Langer, E.J. (1989). Minding matters: The consequences of mindlessness–mindfulness. In L. Berkowitz (Ed.), *Advances in experimental social psychology* (vol. 22, s. 137–173). San Diego, CA: Academic Press.

Langer, E.J. (1992). Matters of mind: Mindfulness/mindlessness in perspective. *Consciousness and Cognition, 1,* 289–305.

Langer, E.J., Blank, A. & Chanowitz, B. (1978). The mindlessness of ostensibly thoughtful action: The role of 'placebic' information in interpersonal interaction. *Journal of Personality and Social Psychology, 36,* 635–642.

Langer, E.J. & Moldoveanu, M. (Eds) (2000). Mindfulness theory and social issues. *Journal of Social Issues, 56.*

Leary, M.R. & Allen, A.B. (2011). Personality and persona: Personality processes in self-presentation. *Journal of Personality, 79,* 889–916.

Lindskold, S., Albert, K.P., Baer, R. & Moore, W.C. (1976). Territorial boundaries of interacting groups and passive audiences. *Sociometry, 39,* 71–76.

Lindskold, S., Forte, R., Haake, C. & Schmidt, E. (1977). The effects of directness of face-to-face request and sex of solicitor on street corner donations. *Journal of Social Psychology, 101,* 45–51.

Lyman, S.M. & Scott, M.B. (1967). Territoriality: A neglected sociological dimension. *Social Problems, 15,* 236–249.

Maio, G.R. & Olson, J.M. (1995). Involvement and persuasion: Evidence for different types of involvement. *Canadian Journal of Behavioural Science, 27,* 64–78.

Maj, K. (2002). Zachowanie uprzejme jako czynnik warunkujacy skutecznocc techniki wplywu spolecznego 'niska pilka' [Polite behaviour as a condition determining the effectiveness of low-ball social influence technique]. *Studia Psychologiczne, 40,* 93–109.

Major, B. & Heslin, R. (1982). Perceptions of cross-sex and same-sex nonreciprocal touch: It is better to give than to receive. *Journal of Nonverbal Behavior, 6,* 148–162.

Martin, A. & Gueguen, N. (2013). The influence of incidental similarity on self-revelation in response to an intimate survey. *Social Behavior and Personality, 41,* 353–356.

McMillen, D.L., (1971). Transgression, self-image, and compliant behavior. *Journal of Personality and Social Psychology, 20,* 176–179.

Meineri, S. & Gueguen, N. (2011). "I hope I'm not disturbing you, am I?" Another operationalization of the foot-in-the-mouth paradigm. *Journal of Applied Social Psychology, 41,* 965–975.

Meineri, S. & Gueguen, N. (2014). Foot-in-the-door and action identification. Binding communication applied to environmental conservation. *European Review of Applied Psychology, 64,* 3–11.

Milberg, S. & Clark, M.S. (1988). Moods and compliance. *British Journal of Social Psychology, 27,* 79–90.

Milgram, S. (1974). *Obedience to authority: An experimental view.* New York: Harper and Row.

Miller, R.L., Brickman, P. & Bolen, D. (1975). Attribution versus persuasion as a means for modifying behavior. *Journal of Personality and Social Psychology, 31,* 430–441.

Miller, R.L., Seligman, C., Clark, N.T. & Bush, M. (1976). Perceptual contrast versus reciprocal concession as mediators of induce compliance. *Canadian Journal of Behavioral Science, 8,* 401–409.

Morgan, C., Lockard, J., Fahrenbruch, C. & Smith, J. (1975). Hitchhiking: Social signals at a distance. *Bulletin of the Psychonomic Society, 5,* 459–461.

Morin, A. (2011). Self-awareness. Part 1: Definition, measures, effects, function, and antecedents. *Social and Personality Psychology Compass, 10*, 807–823.

Mowen, J.C. & Cialdini, R.B. (1980). On implementing the door-in-the-face compliance technique in a business context. *Journal of Marketing Research, 17*, 253–258.

Nannberg, J.C. & Hansen, C.H. (1994). Post-compliance touch: An incentive for task performance. *Journal of Social Psychology, 134*, 301–307.

Navon, D. (1984). Resources: A theoretical soup stone? *Psychological Review, 91*, 216–234.

Nawrat, M. (1997). Empiryczne rozstrzygniecie miedzy alternatywnymi wyjasnieniami skutecznosci techniki "stopa w ustach" [Empirical test of alternative explanations of the "foot-in-the-mouth" effect]. *Przeglad Psychologiczny, 40*, 157–167.

Nawrat, R. & Dolinski, D. (2007). 'See-saw of emotions' and compliance: Beyond the fear-then-relief rule. *Journal of Social Psychology, 147*, 556–571.

Neisser, U. (1976). *Cognition and reality*. San Francisco, CA: Freeman.

Niedenthal, P.M., Krauth-Gruber, S. & Ric, F. (2006). *Psychology of emotion. Interpersonal, experiential, and cognitive approaches*. New York and Hove: Psychology Press.

Niedenthal, P.M. & Setterlund, M.B. (1994). Emotion congruence in perception. *Personality and Social Psychology Bulletin, 20*, 401–411.

Nuttin, J.M.N. Jr. (1984). *'What's in a name?'* Opening lecture of the General Meeting of the European Association of Experimental Social Psychology, Tilburg.

O'Keefe, D.J. (2002). *Persuasion: Theory and research* (2nd edn). Thousand Oaks, CA: Sage.

O'Keefe, D.J. & Figge, M. (1997). A guilt-based explanation of the door-in-the-face influence strategy. *Human Communication Research, 24*, 64–81.

O'Keefe, D. J. & Hale, S. L. (1998). The door-in-the-face influence strategy: A random-effects meta-analytic review. *Communication Yearbook, 21*, 1–33.

Pallak, M.S., Cook, D.A. & Sullivan, J.J. (1980). Commitment and energy conservation. *Applied Social Psychology Annual, 1*, 235–253.

Pandelaere, M.B., Briers, B., Dewitte, S. & Warlop, L. (2010). Better think before agreeing twice. Mere agreement: A similarity-based persuasion mechanism. *International Journal of Research in Marketing, 27*, 133–141.

Pascual, A., Oteme, Ch., Samson, L., Wang, Q., Halmi-Falkowicz, S., Souchet, L., Girandola, F., Gueguen, N. & Joule, R-V. (2012). Cross-cultural investigation of compliance without pressure: The "you are free to . . ." technique in France, Ivory Coast, Romania, Russia, and China. *Cross-Cultural Research, 20*, 1–23.

Paska, M. (2002). "Ja nie chciałem . . ." Sekwencyjne techniki wplywu spolecznego a zachowania nieetyczne. ["I didn't mean it . . ." The sequential techniques of social influence and unethical behaviour]. *Studia Psychologiczne, 40*, 69–91.

Patch, M.E., Hoang, V.R. & Stahelski, A.J. (1997). The use of metacommunication in compliance: Door-in-the-face and single-request strategies. *Journal of Social Psychology, 137*, 88–94.

Patterson, M.L., Powell, J.L. & Lenihan, M.G. (1986). Touch, compliance, and interpersonal affect. *Journal of Nonverbal Behavior, 10*, 41–50.

Paulsell, S. & Goldman, M. (1984). The effect of touching different body areas on prosocial behavior. *Journal of Social Psychology, 122*, 269–273.

Pelham, B.W., Mirenberg, M.C. & Jones, J.T. (2002). Why Susie sells seashells by the seashore: Implicit egotism and major life decisions. *Journal of Personality and Social Psychology, 82*, 469–487.

Pendleton, M.G. & Batson, C.D. (1979). Self-presentation and the door-in-the-face technique for inducing compliance. *Personality and Social Psychology Bulletin, 5*, 77–81.

Petrova, P. & Cialdini, R.B. (2008). Evoking the imagination as a strategy for influence. In C. Haugtvedt, P. Herr & F. Kardes (Eds) *Handbook of Consumer Psychology*. (pp. 505–523). Mahwah, NJ: Erlbaum.

Petty, R.E. & Cacioppo, J.T. (1990). Involvement and persuasion: Tradition versus integration. *Psychological Bulletin, 107*, 367–374.

Pliner, P., Hart, H., Kohl, J. & Saari, D. (1974). Compliance without pressure: Some further data on the foot-in-the-door technique. *Journal of Experimental Social Psychology, 10*, 17–22.

Pollock, C.L., Smith, S.D., Knowles, E.S. & Bruce, H.J. (1998). Mindfulness limits compliance with the that's-not-all technique. *Personality and Social Psychology Bulletin, 24*, 1153–1157.

Posner, M.I. & Snyder, C.R.R. (1975). Attention and cognitive control. In R.L. Solso (Ed.), *Information processing and cognition. The Loyola symposium.* (pp. 55–85). Hillsdale, NJ: Erlbaum.

Powell, J.L., Meil, W., Patterson, M.L., Chouinard, E.F., Collins, B., Kobus, T.J., Habermeier, W. & Arnone, W.L. (1994). Effects of timing of touch on compliance to a request. *Journal of Social Behavior and Personality, 9*, 153–162.

Powell, K.L., Roberts, G. & Nettle, D. (2012). Eye images increase charitable donations: Evidence from an opportunistic field experiment in a supermarket. *Ethnology, 118*, 1096–1101.

Pratkanis, A.R. & Uriel, Y. (2011). The expert snare as an influence tactic: Surf, turf, and ballroom demonstrations of some compliance consequences of being altercast as an expert. *Current Psychology, 30*, 335–344.

Pribram, K.H. & McGuiness, D. (1975). Arousal, activation, and effort in the control of attention. *Psychological Review, 82*, 116–149.

Reeves, R.A., Baker, G.A., Boyd, J.G. & Cialdini, R.B. (1991). The door-in-the-face technique: Reciprocal concessions vs. self-presentational explanations. *Journal of Social Behavior and Personality, 6*, 545–558.

Reingen, P.H. (1978). On inducing compliance with requests. *Journal of Consumer Research, 5*, 96–102.

Rembland, M.S. & Jones, T.S. (2001). The influence of vocal intensity and touch on compliance gaining. *Journal of Social Psychology, 134*, 89–97.

Rind, B. (1997). Effects of interest arousal on compliance with a request for help. *Basic and Applied Social Psychology, 19*, 49–59.

Rind, B. & Benjamin, D. (1994). Effects of public image concerns and self-image on compliance. *Journal of Social Psychology, 134*, 19–25.

Rittle, R.H. (1981). Changes in helping behavior: Self vs. situational perceptions as mediators of the foot-in-the-door effect. *Personality and Social Psychology Bulletin, 7*, 431–437.

Rodafinos, A., Vucevic, A. & Sideridis, G.D. (2005). The effectiveness of compliance techniques: Foot in the door versus door in the face. *Journal of Social Psychology, 145*, 237–239.

Roloff, M.E. (1987). Communication and reciprocity within intimate relationships. In M.E. Roloff, G.R. Miller (Eds), *Interpersonal processes: New directions in communication research* (pp. 11–38). Newbury Park, CA: Sage.

Rosenhan, D. L., Salovey, P. & Hargis, K. (1981). The joys of helping: Focus of attention mediates the impact of positive affect on altruism. *Journal of Personality and Social Psychology, 40*, 899–905.

Sajjad, H. & Tausif, M. (2012). Consumer behavior knocked intense by mood, communication and product value. *International Journal of Information, Business and Management, 4*, 111–120.

Sanbonmatsu, D.M. & Kardes, F.R. (1988). The effects of physiological arousal on information processing and persuasion. *Journal of Consumer Research, 15*, 379–385.

Santos, M.D., Leve, C. & Pratkanis, A.R. (1994). Hey buddy, can you spare seventeen cents? Mindful persuasion and the pique technique. *Journal of Applied Social Psychology, 24*, 755–764.

Scherer, S.E. (1974). Influence of proximity and eye contact on impression formation. *Perceptual and Motor Skills, 38,* 538.

Schlosser, A. E., (2003). Experiencing products in the virtual world: The role of goal and imagery in influencing attitudes versus purchase intentions. *Journal of Consumer Research, 30,* 184–198.

Schur, E.M. (1971). *Labeling deviant behavior: Its sociological implications.* New York: Harper and Row.

Schwarz, N. & Bless, H. (1991). Happy and mindless, but sad and smart? The impact of affective states on analytic reasoning. In J.P. Forgas (Ed.), *Emotion and social judgments* (pp. 55–71). Oxford, UK: Pergamon Press.

Schwarzwald, J., Bizman, A. & Raz, M. (1983). The foot-in-the-door paradigm: Effects of second request size on donation probability and donor generosity. *Personality and Social Psychology Bulletin, 9,* 443–450.

Segrin, C. (1993). The effects of nonverbal behavior on outcomes of compliance gaining attempts. *Communication Studies, 44,* 169–187.

Shen, L. & Dillard, J. P. (2014). Threat, fear, and persuasion: Review and critique of questions about functional forms. *Review of Communication Research, 2,* 94–114.

Sherman, S.J. (1980). On the self-erasing nature of errors in prediction. *Journal of Personality and Social Psychology, 39,* 211–221.

Sherman, S.J., Cialdini, R.B., Schwartzman, D.F. & Reynolds, K.D. (2002). Imaging can heighten or lower the perceived likelihood of contracting a disease: The mediating effect of ease of imagery. In T. Gilovich & D. Griffin (Eds) *Heuristic and biases: The psychology of intuitive judgment* (pp. 98–102). New York: Cambridge University Press.

Shotland, R.L. & Johnson, M.P. (1978). Bystander behavior and kinesics: The interaction between helper and victim. *Environmental Psychology and Nonverbal Behavior, 2,* 181–190.

Skilbeck, C., Tulips, J. & Ley, P. (1977). The effects of fear arousal, fear position, fear exposure, and sidedness on compliance with dietary instructions. *European Journal of Social Psychology, 7,* 221–239.

Smith, D.E., Gier, J.A. & Willis, F.N. (1982). Interpersonal touch and compliance with a marketing request. *Basic and Applied Social Psychology, 3,* 35–38.

Snyder, M., Grether, J. & Keller, K. (1974). Staring and compliance: A field experiment on hitchhiking. *Journal of Applied Social Psychology, 4,* 165–170.

Solomon, S., Greenberg, J. & Pyszczynski, T. (1991). A terror management theory of social behavior: The psychological function of self-esteem and cultural worldviews. In M. Zanna (Ed.), *Advances in experimental social psychology* (vol. 24, pp. 93–159). San Diego, CA: Academic Press.

Spangenberg, E.R. (1997). Increasing health club attendance through self-prophecy. *Marketing Letters, 8,* 23–32.

Spangenberg, E.R. & Obermiller, C. (1996). To cheat or not to cheat: Reducing cheating by requesting self-prophecy. *Marketing Education Review, 6,* 95–103.

Spangenberg, E.R., Sprott, D.E., Grohmann, B. & Smith, R.J. (2003). Mass-communicated prediction request: Practical application and a cognitive dissonance explanation for self-prophecy. *Journal of Marketing, 67,* 47–62.

Spiewak, S. (2002). Miedzy drzwiami a hustawka: drenaz poznawczy a skutecznosc wybranych technik wplywu spolecznego [Cognitive depletion and the effectiveness of the door-in-the-face and fear-then-relief compliance techniques] *Studia Psychologiczne, 40,* 23–47.

Sprott, D.E., Spangenberg, E.R. & Perkins, A.W. (1999). Two more self-prophecy experiments. In E. Arnould, L. Price (Eds) *Advances in consumer research* (vol. 25, pp. 621–626). Provo, UT: Association for Consumer Research.

Stier, D.S. & Hall, J.A. (1984). Gender differences in touch: An empirical and theoretical review. *Journal of Personality and Social Psychology, 47*, 440–459.

Stone, J. & Fernandez, N.C. (2011). When thinking about less failure causes more dissonance: The effect of elaboration and recall on behavior change following hypocrisy. *Social Influence, 6*, 199–211.

Stone, J., Wiegand, A.W., Cooper, J. & Aronson, E. (1997). When, exemplification fails: Hypocrisy and the motive for self-integrity. *Journal of Personality and Social Psychology, 72*, 54–65.

Strack, F., Martin, L.L. & Stepper, S. (1988). Inhibiting and facilitating conditions of facial expressions: A non-obtrusive test of facial feedback hypothesis. *Journal of Personality and Social Psychology, 54*, 768–776.

Strenta, A. & DeJong, W. (1981). The effect of a prosocial label on helping behavior. *Social Psychology Quarterly, 44*, 142–147.

Sussman, N.M. & Rosenfeld, H.M. (1978). Touch, justification, and sex: Influences on the aversiveness of spatial violations. *Journal of Social Psychology, 106*, 215–225.

Takada, J. & Levine, T.R. (2007). The effects of the even-a-few-minutes-would-help strategy, perspective taking, and empathy concern on the successful recruiting volunteers on campus. *Communication Research Reports, 24*, 177–184.

Tangney, J.P. (1995). Shame and guilt in interpersonal relationships. In J.P. Tangney & K.W. Fisher (Eds), *Self-conscious emotions: The psychology of shame, guilt, embarrassment, and pride* (pp. 114–142). New York: Guilford.

Tanner, R. J., Ferraro, R., Chartrand, T. L., Bettman, J. R. & van Baaren, R. (2008). Of chameleons and consumption: The impact of mimicry on choice and preferences. *Journal of Consumer Research, 34*, 754–766.

Taylor, S.E. (1981). The interface of cognitive and social psychology. In J. Harvey (Ed.), *Cognition, social behavior, and the environment.* (pp. 189–211). Hillsdale, NJ: Erlbaum.

Taylor, S.E. & Brown, J.D. (1988). Illusion and well-being: A social psychological perspective on mental health. *Psychological Bulletin, 103*, 67–85.

Taylor, S.E., Pham, L.B., Rivkin, I.D. & Armor, D.A. (1998). Harnessing the imagination: Mental simulation, self-regulation, and coping. *American Psychologist, 53*, 429–439.

Terrier, L. & Joule, R. V. (2008). La procédure de porte-au-nez : Vers une interprétation motivationnelle [The door-in-the-face procedure: Toward a motivational interpretation]. *Cahiers Internationaux de Psychologie Sociale, 77*, 5–14.

Tomkins, S.S. (1991). *Affect, imagery, consciousness. Vol. III. The negative affects: Anger and fear.* New York: Springer.

Tourangeau, R. & Yan, T. (2007). Sensitive questions in surveys. *Psychological Bulletin, 133*, 859–883.

Tuma, A.H. & Maser, J.D. (1985). (Eds), *Anxiety and anxiety disorder.* Hillsdale, NJ: Erlbaum.

Tusing, K.J. & Dillard, J.P. (2000). The psychological reality of the Door-in-the-face: It's helping, not bargaining. *Journal of Language and Social Psychology, 19*, 5–25.

Tversky, A. & Kahneman, D. (1982). Judgment under uncertainty: Heuristics and biases. In: D. Kahneman, P. Slovic & A. Tversky (Eds), *Judgment under uncertainty* (pp. 3–20). New York: Cambridge University Press.

Tybout, A.M., Sternthal, B. & Calder, B.J. (1983). Information-availability as a determinant of multiple request effectiveness. *Journal of Marketing Research, 20*, 280–290.

Uehara, E.S. (1995). Reciprocity reconsidered: Gouldner's 'moral norm of reciprocity' and social support. *Journal of Social and Personal Relationship, 12*, 483–502.

Uranowitz, S. (1975). Helping as self-attributions: A field experiment. *Journal of Personality and Social Psychology, 31*, 852–854.

Valentine, M.E. (1980). The attenuating influence of gaze upon the bystander intervention effect. *Journal of Social Psychology, 111*, 197–203.

Vallacher, R.R. & Wegner, D.M. (1985). *A theory of action identification.* Hillsdale, NJ: Erlbaum.

Vallacher, R.R. & Wegner, D.M. (1987). What do people think they're doing? Action identification and human behavior. *Psychological Review, 94,* 2–15.

van Baaren, R. B., Holland, R. W., Kawakami, K. & van Knippenberg, A. (2004). Mimicry and prosocial behavior. *Psychological Science, 15,* 71–74.

van Baaren, R. B., Holland, R. W., Steenaert, B. & van Knippenberg, A. (2003). Mimicry for money: Behavioral consequences of imitation. *Journal of Experimental Social Psychology, 39,* 393–398.

Vaughn, A.J., Firmin, M.W. & Hwang, C-E. (2009). Efficacy of request presentation on compliance. *Social Behavior and Personality, 37,* 441–450.

Wagener, J.J. & Laird, J.D. (1980). The experimenter's foot-in-the-door: Self-perception, body weight, and volunteering. *Personality and Social Psychology Bulletin, 6,* 441–446.

Wallace, J. & Sadalla, E. (1966). Behavioral consequences of transgression: I. The effects of social recognition. *Journal of Experimental Research in Personality, 1,* 187–194.

Walster, E., Walster, G.W. & Berscheid, E. (1978). *Equity theory and research.* Boston, MA: Allyn & Bacon.

Wegner, D.M., Vallacher, R.R., Macomber, G., Wood, R. & Arps, K. (1984). The emergence of action. *Journal of Personality and Social Psychology, 46,* 269–279.

Weigl, B. (1990). *Fantazjowanie na temat własnego zachowania jako przesłanka nieuczciwości w sytuacji pokusy. [Dreaming about one's own behaviour as a predictor of honesty in temptation situation]* Unpublished Research Report. Opole.

Weyant, J.M. & Smith, S.L. (1987). Getting more by asking for less: The effects of request size on donations of charity. *Journal of Applied Social Psychology, 17,* 392–400.

Whang, Y-O. (2012). When and why does the that's-not-all compliance technique work? *Journal of Business and Economic Research, 10,* 171–178.

Whatley, M.A., Webster, M.J., Smith, R.H. & Rhodes, A. (1999). The effect of a favour on public and private compliance: How internalized is the norm of reciprocity? *Basic and Applied Social Psychology, 21,* 251–259.

Wicklund, R.A. & Gollwitzer, P.M. (1987). The fallacy of the private-public self-focus distinction. *Journal of Personality, 55,* 491–523.

Willis, F.N. & Hamm, H.K. (1980). The use of interpersonal touch in securing compliance. *Journal of Nonverbal Behavior, 6,* 49–55.

Wills, T.A. (1981). Downward comparison principles in social psychology. *Psychological Bulletin, 90,* 245–271.

Wilson, D.W. (1981). Is helping a laughing matter? *Psychology, 18,* 6–9.

Wojciszke, B. & Baryla, W. (2005). Kultura narzekania, czyli o psychicznych pułapkach ekspresji niezadowolenia. In M. Drogosz (Ed.), *Jak Polacy przegrywaja. Jak Polacy wygrywaja [How Poles lose, how Poles win]* (pp. 35–51). Gdansk: GWP.

Wood, W. (2000). Attitude change: Persuasion and social influence. *Annual Review of Psychology, 51,* 539–570.

Zuckerman, M., Lazzaro, M.M. & Waldgeir, D. (1979). Undermining effects of the foot-in-the-door technique with extrinsic rewards. *Journal of Applied Social Psychology, 9,* 292–296.

INDEX